VORWORT

Mit FAST TRACK ENGLISH, PART TWO setzen wir unseren Auffrischungskurs der englischen Sprache fort. Analog zu PART ONE nimmt das Begleitbuch die Untergliederung der Fernsehsendungen in Module auf und bringt für jede der 13 *units* die folgenden fünf Abschnitte:

● Die Module A und B geben die Dialoge und *statements* im Wortlaut, in Ausschnitten oder in Zusammenfassungen wieder. Da sie in besonderer Weise auf die Prüfung vorbereiten sollen, empfiehlt es sich, die Texte und die daran anschließenden Fragen gründlich zu bearbeiten. Wörter und Wendungen, die nicht zum Grundwortschatz gehören, haben wir wieder aufgelistet und – bezogen auf den Kontext – ins Deutsche übersetzt. Dennoch möchten wir in diesem Zusammenhang noch einmal ausdrücklich darauf hinweisen, wie wichtig der regelmäßige Gebrauch eines guten einsprachigen Wörterbuchs für das Erlernen einer Fremdsprache ist. Die Grammatik von PART TWO, die auf den bereits in PART ONE vermittelten Kenntnissen aufbaut, wird in den *Helping Hands (HH)* wieder auf Deutsch erläutert und durch einen vielfältigen Übungsteil ergänzt. Aber auch hier gilt, wie zuvor beim Wortschatz: Grundwissen wird vorausgesetzt. Zudem kann bzw. soll nicht jedes Phänomen mit allen Besonderheiten berücksichtigt werden.

● Modul C ist, wie in PART ONE, eine ausgesprochene Hörverständnisübung. Es wäre günstig, wenn Sie sich insbesondere diesen Teil der Fernsehsendung, in dem *native speakers* – mit ihren unterschiedlichen Dialektfärbungen und mit unterschiedlichen Sprechtempos – aus ihrem Alltag erzählen, mehrmals ansehen bzw. anhören könnten. Auch sollten Sie sich die Fragen im Begleitbuch nach Möglichkeit bereits vor der Sendung aufmerksam durchlesen. Und für all diejenigen, die die Aussagen der einzelnen *native speakers* lieber noch einmal nachlesen möchten, gibt es wieder den Abschnitt *"Module C Tapescripts"*.

● Im Modul D kehrt Meterman zurück. Genießen Sie den humorvollen Umgang mit dem jeweiligen Thema und die spielerisch konzipierten Übungen.

● Damit jede *unit* etwas „ruhiger" ausklingt, bietet Modul E, analog zur Fernsehsendung, überwiegend etwas fürs Auge: Bilder, Cartoons, kleine „Originaldokumente".

Have fun with – and continue to enjoy – FAST TRACK ENGLISH.

Robert Parr, Günther Albrecht und Keith Jones

CONTENTS

UNIT 18 THE WEATHER IS CHANGING 76

Communicative functions:	Talking about gradual change ● Commenting on the weather ● Expressing your point of view
Helping Hands:	to lie/to lay – to rise/to raise ● The present perfect continuous ● The question words "what" and "how"

UNIT 19 GETTING AROUND 91

Communicative functions:	Talking about locations ● Talking about names of places ● Talking about movement and direction
Helping Hands:	Prepositions of place and direction ● Quantifiers

UNIT 20 THE BRITISH PASSION 107

Communicative functions:	Talking about right and wrong ● Talking about possibilities and probabilities
Helping Hands:	Stative verbs ● Preposition + gerund ● Revision of helping verbs ● Zero if-sentences

UNIT 25 THE OFFICE AT HOME 184

Communicative functions: Talking on the telephone ● Using short forms ●
Explaining information technology
Helping Hands: The small word "will" ● Multi-word verbs (III)

UNIT 26 A SECOND CHANCE 201

Communicative functions: Giving reasons ● Talking about purposes ●
Describing qualifications
Helping Hands: Overview of tenses ● Connecting words

Southern England and Wales

THE DRINKS BUSINESS

14A

Meeting people

In a pub

William and Debbie have gone to "The Flying Horse", a pub near to where they
live. The landlord, Howard, greets them. *begrüßen*

5 Howard: Morning, William. Hello, Debbie.
   William: Morning, Howard. *How are you?*
   Howard: Not so bad. And yourselves?
   Debbie: We're fine.
   Howard: *What's it to be?* Was darf es sein
10 William: (to Debbie:) *What are you having?* Was trinks du
   Debbie: A half of shandy for me.
   William: A pint of bitter and a half of shandy, please.
   Howard: A pint of bitter and a half of shandy.

(William and Debbie notice some friends.) wie kaum/B

15 William: Hi, Kevin. *How are you doing?*
   Kevin: Hi, William. Pretty good. Join the crowd. – Menge
   William: (raising his glass:) Cheers.
   Everybody: Cheers.

Viviane:	Well, look, who's here! I haven't seen you *for ages*.
20 Debbie:	Hello, Viviane. It's nice to see you again. *What have you been up to?*
Viviane:	Oh, this and that. Keeping busy.
Debbie:	(to William:) William, we must go. Look at the time.
William:	Our time is up, I'm afraid. *We must be off.*
William:	(to Kevin:) Good to see you. *Mind how you go.*
25 Debbie:	Viviane, lovely to see you again. Take care and don't work too hard.
Viviane:	*Bye, see you soon.*
William:	Bye, Kevin.

(As William and Debbie leave the pub they say goodbye to the landlord.)

William:	Cheerio, Howard. See you soon.
30 Debbie:	Cheers, Howard. See you.
Howard:	Bye now. Thank you.

At a brewery ●●

Tony and Jackie Richards, who run a pub, have gone to Shepherd Neame brewery in Faversham.

35 Mr Dixon:	Good morning.
Mr Richards:	Good morning.
Mr Dixon:	I'm Ian Dixon. I'm Production Director here at Shepherd Neame. Welcome to the brewery.
Mr Richards:	Thank you very much. I'm Tony Richards. This is my wife, Jackie.
40 Mr Dixon:	*How do you do*, Jackie.
Mrs Richards:	How do you do.
Mr Dixon:	I do hope you'll be buying some of our beers.
Mr Richards:	I'm certainly looking forward to *sampling* them.
Mr Dixon:	Good. Would you like to have a look round the brewery?
45 Mr Richards:	Certainly. It's very kind of you to show us around.

(At the end of the tour)

Mr Dixon:	I think that's everything you need. If there's any other information you'd like, please give us a ring.
Mr Richards:	Well, thanks very much for a most interesting visit.
50 Mrs Richards:	I really enjoyed it. I learnt a lot. It was fascinating.
Mr Richards:	And thanks for the tasting. I'm sure my customers will be very happy.
Mr Dixon:	So we look forward to hearing from you.

Sampling the beers

Mr Richards:	That's right. *I'll be in touch soon.* In a day or two. Thank you very
Mr Dixon:	much. *Ich melde mich bald*
Mr Richards:	Goodbye.
	Goodbye.

55 (line number)

How are you?	Wie geht es dir (Ihnen)?	Mind how you go.	Pass auf dich auf. (Passen Sie ...)
What's it to be?	Was darf es sein?	Bye, see you soon.	Auf Wiedersehen,
What are you having?	Was trinkst du (trinken Sie)?	brewery	bis bald. Brauerei
How are you doing? (*coll*)	Wie läuft's?	How do you do.	Guten Tag. (*beim ersten Kennen-*
... for ages	... eine Ewigkeit	sample	*lernen*) (aus)probieren,
What have you been up to? (*coll*)	Was hast du so „getrieben"?		testen
We must be off.	Wir müssen jetzt gehen.	I'll be in touch soon.	Ich melde mich bald.

Understanding the text.

Which ending (a-c) finishes sentences 1-5 best? Tick it.

1. William and Debbie ...
   a) have never been to "The Flying Horse" before.
   b) have often been to "The Flying Horse".
   c) have sometimes been to "The Flying Horse" before.

2. William and Kevin ...
    a) have never met before.
    b) seem to know each other well.
    c) don't want to talk to each other.

3. Debbie ...
    a) knows Viviane very well.
    b) knows Viviane quite well.
    c) hardly knows Viviane.

4. The Richards have gone to Shepherd Neame brewery to ...
    a) meet Ian Dixon and his colleagues.
    b) find out how beer and lager is made.
    c) decide if they want to sell Shepherd Neame beer in their pub.

5. It seems as if the Richards found the brewery tour ...
    a) informative.   b) boring.   c) amusing.

Further question. Answer it in your own words as far as possible.

6. Do you think Mr Dixon was pleased with the visit Mr and Mrs Richards paid
    to the brewery? Say why/why not.

Underline the appropriate reply to these remarks.

7. How are you?
    a) Hello.   c) Pleased to meet you.
    b) Not too bad.   d) A pint, please.

8. How do you do.
    a) Fine, thanks.   c) How do you do.
    b) I run a pub.   d) Not too much, please.

9. Which three expressions do British people use when they say goodbye?
    a) Goodbye.   c) The same again.
    b) Cheerio.   d) Bye.

10. Which three expressions can you use when you ask somebody what they would
    like to drink?
    a) What's it to be?   c) What are you having?
    b) What is it?   d) What do you want?

And what about you?

11. What differences are there in your opinion between pubs in England and *Gaststätten* in Germany?

12. In what ways do you think English people use names differently from German people when they are doing business?

Revision of tenses

Wiederholung der Zeiten

In *Fast Track English, Part One* wurden die wichtigsten Zeiten der englischen Grammatik behandelt:

◆ die **einfache Form der Gegenwart**
   (für gewohnheitsmäßige und zeitlich unbegrenzte Handlungen)
◆ die **Verlaufsform der Gegenwart**
   (für eine zum Zeitpunkt des Sprechens ablaufende oder zeitlich begrenzte Handlung)
◆ die **einfache Form der Vergangenheit**
   (für ein in der Vergangenheit abgeschlossenes Ereignis)
◆ die **Verlaufsform der Vergangenheit**
   (für einen in der Vergangenheit längere Zeit andauernden Vorgang)
◆ die **einfache Form des *Present Perfect***
   (für eine Handlung, die in der Vergangenheit stattgefunden bzw. begonnen hat, jedoch unmittelbare Auswirkungen auf die Gegenwart besitzt)
◆ die **Verlaufsform des *Present Perfect***
   (für einen Vorgang, der in der Vergangenheit begonnen hat und bis – oder fast bis – in die Gegenwart andauert)

	simple	continuous
present	I live	I am living
past	I lived	I was living
present perfect	I have lived	I have been living

(Das **Passiv** wird im Modul 14B (vgl. S. 18), die **Hilfsverben** im Modul 20B (vgl. S. 116) behandelt. Die **Vergangenheitsformen** und das *Present Perfect* werden in den Modulen 16B bzw. 18B (vgl. S. 49 und 51 bzw. 84) nochmals geübt.)

Exercises

I. Read the pairs of sentences and answer the question below.

1a. Mr Smith lives in England.
1b. Mr Jones is living in England.   *Lahrscheinlich*

Which of the men – Mr Smith or Mr Jones – is probably not going to live in England in the future?

2a. Mr Smith worked in London for five years.
2b. Mr Jones has worked in London for five years.

Which of the men – Mr Smith or Mr Jones – works in London?

3a. Mr Smith went to work while it was snowing.
3b. Mr Jones arrived at work when it snowed.

Which of the men – Mr Smith or Mr Jones – saw more snow on the way to work?

4a. Mr Smith has been writing letters all morning.
4b. Mr Jones has written letters all morning.

Which of the men - Mr Smith or Mr Jones - has not finished his correspondence?

5a. Mr Smith came to the meeting after it had started.
5b. Mr Jones came to the meeting when it started.

Which of the men – Mr Smith or Mr Jones – missed the first part of the meeting?

II. Complete the following paragraph using the correct form of the words in brackets. ●●

William and Debbie ... (live) in the village of Kemsing for the last five years. They ... (move) there after they ... (sell) their old house in Derby. "When we ... (drive) past the cottage," Debbie explains, "it ... (be) love at first sight. Since then we ... (never, regret) our decision to come down here." "It's perfect for us," William continues. "We ... (make) lots of friends in the village. Now we ... (can, not, imagine, live) anywhere else."

III. Complete these sentences by adding one word only.

1. You say "How do you do" to somebody when you meet them for the ... time. This expression is often written without a question mark because it is not really a question.

2. You say "How are you?" to somebody who you have met before. This expression is a real question so you need to ... it by saying "Fine, thanks", "Not too bad" or "Very well".

IV. Use the phrases from the box to make one formal and one informal dialogue. ●●

> Fine, thank you. ● Great, thanks. ● How do you do. ● It was OK. ●
> Oh, that would be lovely. ● Yeah, lovely.

1. – How do you do, Ms Wheeler.
    – ...
    – How was your journey?
    – ...
    – Would you like a cup of coffee?
    – ...

2. – Hi, Jenny. How're things?
    – ...
    – How was the journey?
    – ...
    – Cup of coffee?
    – ...

V. Make two four-line dialogues out of the eight lines below. As in exercise IV,
one dialogue is formal, one is informal. ●●

a. Fine. See you then. Bye.
b. I'll ring you at the weekend. —
c. It was a pleasure.
d. Thank you very much for helping us. —
e. Thanks for your help. —
f. That's OK. —
g. That's very kind of you. Goodbye. —
h. We will be contacting you in the next few days. —

VI. Test your knowledge of English pubs.
Are the following statements true or false?

1. English pubs open at midday and close at midnight.
2. In English pubs you pay for your drinks when you order them.
3. English pubs serve drinks but no food.
4. In English pubs you can play games like darts, billiards and cards.
5. In England beer is drunk in pints and half pints.
6. The word "pint" is difficult to pronounce. It does not rhyme with "hint".
7. A "soft drink" does not contain alcohol.

8. In English the words "crisps" and "chips" have the same meaning.
9. Draught / drɑːft / beer (*Fassbier*) is stored in barrels, not bottles.
10. Your "local" is any pub within 20 miles from your home.

14B

A tour of a brewery ●●

As Mr Dixon is showing Mr and Mrs Richards around the Shepherd Neame brewery
he explains to them how beer is made.

"The *malted barley* is *crushed* to produce a *meal* called *grist*. In these *mash tuns* the
5 water is heated and added to the grist. After about an hour and a half the *liquid* is
drained off. This sweet liquid is known as *wort*. It's the main ingredient of beers and
lagers."

Mr Dixon then shows the Richards the *coppers*. "It is here that the *hops* are added
to the wort to give it that special *flavour*. The wort *is* boiled for about an hour and
10 then *run off into* the *fermenting vessels*. Here *yeast* is added. The wort is then left to
ferment in these vessels. *Ales* ferment for a week and lagers ferment for ten days.
Traditional ales are *stored* for another seven days and then pumped into *casks* or *barrels* ready to deliver to our pubs."

At the end of their tour the Richards see the *bottling and canning hall* where bottles
15 are *processed* automatically at the rate of 15,000 per hour.

barley	Gerste	be run off into	abgeleitet werden
malted barley	Brau-, Darrmalz		in ... (hinein)
crush	zerkleinern,	fermenting vessel	Gärbottich
	zermahlen	yeast	Hefe
meal	Schrot (*grob gemah-*	ferment	gären
	lene Getreidekörner)	ales	*hier: alle eng-*
grist	*hier:* Malzschrot		*lischen Biersorten*
mash	Maische		*außer "lager"*
mash tun	Maischbottich	store	lagern
liquid	Flüssigkeit	cask	hölzernes Fass
drain off	ableiten, ablassen	barrel	Fass (*meist aus*
wort	Bierwürze		*Holz*)
lager	Lagerbier (*engl.*	bottling and	*Fabrikhalle, in der*
	helle Biersorte mit	canning hall	*Flaschen und*
	Kohlensäure; wird		*Büchsen abgefüllt*
	kalt getrunken)		*werden*
copper	Kupferkessel	process	*hier:* abfüllen und
hops	Hopfen		weiterverarbeiten
flavour	Geschmack, Aroma		

Understanding the text.

Complete this table using words from the text. There is one word missing in each line.

1.	Barley is crushed to make ... .
2.	... is added.
3.	The liquid is drained off to make ... .
4.	... are added to the wort.
5.	The wort is ... .
6.	The wort is put into ... vessels.
7.	... is added.
8.	After fermentation the beer is ... into barrels or bottled.

And what about you?

9. What is your opinion of English beer?   *Anlaß*
10. Do you drink alcohol? How often and on what occasions? If you don't drink alcohol, say why you don't.   *klassche*

H The passive

Das Passiv

Water **is heated**.	Wasser wird erhitzt.
Yeast **is added**.	Hefe wird hinzugefügt.
Traditional ales **are stored**	Traditionelle Biersorten werden weitere
for another seven days.	sieben Tage gelagert.

◆ Das **Passiv** wurde bereits in *Part One*, Modul 8B (S. 129) vorgestellt und geübt. Diese Form wird oft verwendet, wenn betont werden soll, dass mit einer **Person** oder **Sache etwas geschieht** (wie z.B. in technischen Beschreibungen). Die **handelnde Person** wird **häufig nicht erwähnt**, weil sie für den Sprecher nicht wichtig oder ihm nicht bekannt ist oder gar verschwiegen werden soll. So geht es z.B. in dem Satz *"Beer was brewed here 300 years ago."* nicht um diejenigen, die vor 300 Jahren das Bier gebraut haben, sondern um das vor 300 Jahren gebraute Bier.

◆ Es gibt allerdings auch Fälle, in denen die **handelnde Person** für das **Verständnis eines Sachverhalts erforderlich** ist. Sie wird dann mit der **Präposition** *by* ergänzt, z.B.: *In former times beer was mainly brewed by monks (Mönchen).*

◆ Da Passivformen mit dem **Hilfsverb** *to be* und dem *past participle* des jeweiligen **Hauptverbs gebildet** werden, können sie sowohl einen **Vorgang** als auch einen **Zustand** beschreiben. Der Satz *"The bottle was broken."* kann z.B. zweierlei bedeuten: erstens, dass die Flasche zerbrochen wurde (= Vorgang), oder zweitens, dass sie zerbrochen war (= Zustand). Dies ist insbesondere dann wichtig, wenn es darum geht, einen englischen Text ins Deutsche zu übertragen.

Exercises

I. Turn the verbs into passive forms and change the focus of attention in these sentences. Begin with the words in brackets. ●●

1. Somebody built this house before the war broke out. (This house ... .)
2. Someone wants you on the telephone. (You ... .)
3. A friend of mine is picking me up at nine o'clock. (I ... .)
4. Nobody must take books out of the reading library. (Books ... .)
5. People made these computers in Taiwan. (These ... .)
6. They will tell you what to do when you get there. (You ... .)

Zustand

II. *State or process? Tick the appropriate column.*

Vergang

	S	P
1. The shop was closed when they arrived.		
2. Are your bags unpacked every time you go through customs?		
3. The countryside is ruined by people dropping their litter.		
4. The suitcases are packed. Shall we go?		
5. The shop was closed after the last customer had left.		
6. Look at my jacket! It's ruined!		

Now translate the six sentences into German.

III. *Newspaper headlines. Write the headlines out in complete sentences using a passive form of the verb.*

drinjend brauchen

1. **Twenty badly injured in car crash** → *beschädigen schaden*

2. £10 MILLION STOLEN FROM LONDON BANK

3. Dog, three cats and parrot rescued from burning house *retten, befreien*

4. Rock star caught drinking and driving *ertappt*

IV. *Explain what these signs mean. Use the words in brackets to form your sentences.*

1. PLEASE DO NOT FEED THE BEARS

   (visitors/allow/not/feed/bears)

2. LUNCH 12.00 – 2.00

   (lunch/serve/12–2)

3. DO NOT TOUCH THE FURNITURE

   (customers/ask/not/touch/furniture)

4. TICKETS FOR MODEL RAILWAY HERE

   (tickets/can/buy/here)

V. Describing a process. Complete the text using passive forms of the verbs in brackets. ● ●

How instant coffee is made

First the coffee beans ... (roast). Then they ... (grind). Afterwards water ... (pass) slowly through the coffee. The resulting liquid ... (pump) through tubes at a high temperature and high pressure. What ... (leave) is a kind of coffee "liquor". This ... (pour) through large driers at a very high temperature. The resulting coffee powder ... (collect) and ... (put) into jars.

14C

Howard and Christine Smith – landlord and landlady

Listen carefully to what Howard and Christine Smith say about running a pub. Then answer the questions below.

I. Choose the most suitable ending (a-c) to the sentence.

1. Howard and Christine's pub, "The Flying Horse", offers ...
   a) drinks.
   b) food and drinks.
   c) food, drinks and accommodation for the night.
2. Howard and Christine seem to lead ...
   a) a busy life.   b) an easy life.   c) an expensive life.

The Flying Horse Inn

3. Howard and Christine appear to ...
   a) enjoy their work.
   b) be frustrated with their job.
   c) be interested in a quiet life.

II. Which word from the interview completes the sentences? (The first letter is given.)

1. A man who runs a pub – or rents out a room – is called a l... in English. If it
   ·is a woman, she is called a l... .
2. People who go to the same pub all the time are called l... or regulars.
3. If you have an a... with somebody, you have arranged a time and place to meet
   them.
4. Traditional beer is often called r... a... in Britain. This means that it comes
   straight from the barrel and is drunk at room temperature.
5. Bottled beer is in bottles but draught beer is in b... .
6. The t... and the c... of beer must be checked before it can be sold in a pub.
7. In a restaurant the m... lists all the food that are served.
8. A product is something which has been made in a factory. P..., on the other
   hand, is something which has grown in a field.

III. Match the definition (a-c) to the corresponding sentence (1-3).

a. when something is superficial (*oberflächlich*)   *ärmlich*
b. when you do something without using anything similar or the same which
    has been done before   *gleich*
c. when something is not of a high standard

1. Nobody has built anything like this before so we've got to <u>start from scratch</u>.
2. His English is good but his Maths doesn't really <u>come up to scratch</u>.
3. The article you wrote was interesting but it only really <u>scratched the surface</u>.

Now translate the sentences (1-3) into German.

14D

Meterman at the pub

I. Read the text and decide which ending (a-c) below is the most appropriate.
If possible, watch the Module again to see what happened.

a. "Mmm," he says, licking his lips. "Thank you. That was lovely. I'll see you
    next week. Bye now."
b. "You know what?" he says, just about to fall to the ground. "I can't taste the
    carrot juice!"
c. "That was lovely," he says, putting the glass on the bar. "The same again,
    please."

We see Meterman driving to his local. He turns to the camera and welcomes back
the viewers. He tells them that he *has got* some more sayings *up his sleeve*. He
parks his car outside the pub. "Of course I'm very well known here," he says
proudly. "But I never touch alcohol. Meterman is strictly *teetotal*."

Meterman goes into the pub and greets everybody with a loud "good morning".
He asks the young lady behind the bar if she can make him a South Pacific *Beachcomber* Scorpion. She can't. "*Never mind*," says Meterman. "I am an expert at
making cocktails. I've been making them for decades. I'll show you."

He walks behind the bar and takes a *jug*. He mixes orange juice, tomato juice,
carrot juice, *elderflower cordial*, *lime cordial*, peppermint cordial, lemon juice,
a *dash of soda* and finally an egg. He then turns to the people sitting at the bar.
"And now, ladies and gentlemen," he announces dramatically. "The *sting* in the
scorpion's *tail*." He reaches for his pocket and *produces* a small *jar*. "I never
travel without a little chili powder."

As Meterman mixes his cocktail, juice goes over his face and hat. "If you'd like to go and *tidy up, sir,*" the barmaid suggests, "I'm sure I could mix your cocktail for you."

While Meterman is leaving the room, the barmaid notices his car keys on the bar. She picks them up and puts them in her pocket. "Why don't we have some fun," she says to the other guests. Quickly they mix an unusually powerful cocktail. When Meterman comes back he drinks it all in one go.

have (got) up one's sleeve	im Ärmel, in petto haben	dash of soda	Schuss (Spritzer) Soda
teetotal	abstinent	sting	Stachel
beachcomber	Strandgutjäger; Herumtreiber	tail produce	Schwanz *hier*: hervorziehen,
never mind	macht nichts, schon gut		hervorholen (*z.B. aus der Tasche*)
jug	Krug	jar	Glas
elderflower cordial	Holundermark	tidy up	aufräumen, *hier*:
lime cordial	Limettenmark		sich säubern

II. Questions on the story. Answer them.

1. What "fun" (see last paragraph) does the barmaid have?
2. Why does she take the keys to Meterman's car?

III. What do these words and expressions mean? Complete the sentences by adding one word only.

1. If you "have something up your sleeve" you ... a plan or an idea secret until you need it.
2. If you are "teetotal" you don't drink ... .
3. If somebody drinks something "in one go", they drink everything that is in the glass without ... .

14E

Pub signs

BUYING A HOUSE

15A

Househunting ●●

David and Janet live in a flat and pay rent. They would like to buy a house of their own so they have gone to a *new development* to find out about the different houses which are for sale. The agent tells them that there are one and two-bedroom starter
5 homes for first-time buyers as well as three and four-bedroom houses with garage and garden for those who can afford more. Janet is keen to see some of the *show houses* from the inside.

Finding out about the houses for sale

Janet: Let's have a look round now.
David: Fine.
10 Janet: If it's *convenient*?
Agent: Yes, of course.

First they look around a two-bedroom *property*. Janet thinks it's lovely but a bit small so the agent shows them another house with an extra room upstairs and downstairs. Janet prefers the larger house because all the rooms are bigger. The *master bedroom*
15 is 4.7m by 3.1m and bedroom number two measures 3.35m by 2.28m.

Out in the garden Janet asks her husband for his opinion.

Janet: What do you think?

David: Oh, it's more expensive than the other. We'll have to go and talk about
the financial side of it. The first house was certainly less *spacious* and less
20   convenient. The extra space here will make all the difference to us.

Janet: Come on. Let's get some financial advice.

development	Siedlung	master bedroom	Elternschlafzimmer
new development	Neubausiedlung		(= *das größte*
show house	Musterhaus		*Schlafzimmer*)
convenient	passend, geeignet	spacious	geräumig
property	Eigentum, Besitz;		
	hier: Immobilie		

Understanding the text.

Using the information in the text finish the sentences in an appropriate way.

1. David and Janet no longer want to pay rent for a flat so they ... .
2. After they have looked around a two-bedroom house Janet asks the agent
   if they can ... .
3. Before they can make a decision the young couple ... .

*Which of the expressions (a-c) come closest to the meaning of the underlined word(s)?
Tick it.*

4. There are four-bedroom houses for those who <u>can afford more</u>.
   a) have more children   b) have more money   c) have more time

5. Janet <u>is keen to</u> see some of the show houses.
   a) doesn't want to   b) would like to   c) asks to

6. The first house <u>was</u> certainly <u>less spacious</u>.
   a) was quieter   b) was smaller   c) was cheaper

Find the English equivalent in the text for these German words and expressions.

7. Miete zahlen   9. Elternschlafzimmer
8. Wenn es Ihnen passt?   10. 3 m auf 2 m

And what about you?

11. What in your opinion are some of the differences between buying a house in
    England and buying one in Germany?
12. Where would you prefer to live? In a city, in a suburb or in the country? Can
    you say why?

Comparisons
Vergleichssätze

Die **Steigerung der Adjektive** und die **Vergleichssätze** wurden in *Part One*, Modul 3B (S. 49) bereits ausführlicher behandelt. In diesem Modul wird das Thema noch einmal kurz **wiederholt** und um die **verneinten Steigerungsformen** (mit *not*, *less/least* oder *fewer/fewest*) **erweitert**.

The hall is **bigger than** the kitchen.	Die Diele ist größer als die Küche.
The new house is **more expensive than** the old one.	Das neue Haus ist teurer als das alte.
This cottage is **less convenient than** the bungalow.	Dieses *cottage* (Landhaus) ist (für meine, unsere etc. Zwecke) nicht so geeignet wie der Bungalow.
The two-bedroom house is **not as spacious as** the three-bedroom house.	Das Haus mit zwei Schlafzimmern ist nicht so geräumig wie das Haus mit drei Schlafzimmern.

◆ Wenn **zwei Sachen oder Personen** miteinander **verglichen** werden, nimmt man entweder die **komparative Steigerungsform des Adjektivs** und das Verbindungswort *than*, oder die **Grundform (den Positiv)** des Adjektivs und die Verbindungswörter *as ... as*, *not as ... as* oder *not so ... as*.

◆ **Einsilbige Adjektive** werden durch Anhängen von *-er* gesteigert. **Drei-** und **mehrsilbige Adjektive** werden durch *more/less* gesteigert. **Adjektive mit zwei Silben** können sowohl durch Anhängen von *-er* als auch durch *more/less* gesteigert werden.

The master bedroom is **the largest** room in the house.	Das Elternschlafzimmer ist das größte Zimmer im Haus.
The five-bedroom house is **the most expensive** house.	Das Haus mit fünf Schlafzimmern ist das teuerste Haus.
The flat is **the least convenient** of all the property for sale.	Die Wohnung ist von allen Immobilien, die zum Verkauf stehen, am wenigsten geeignet.

◆ Wenn **eine Sache oder Person** innerhalb einer „Gruppe" den **höchsten Stellenwert** einnimmt, nimmt man die **superlativen Formen des Adjektivs**.

◆ **Einsilbige Adjektive** werden durch Anhängen von *-est* gesteigert. **Drei-** und **mehrsilbige Adjektive** werden durch *most/least* gesteigert. **Adjektive mit zwei Silben** können sowohl durch Anhängen von *-est* als auch durch *most/least* gesteigert werden.

The cottage has got **fewer bedrooms** than the bungalow.	Das *cottage* hat weniger Schlafzimmer als der Bungalow.
The flat has got **the fewest bedrooms**.	Die Wohnung hat die wenigsten Schlafzimmer.
The two-bedroom house has got **less space** than the five-bedroom house.	Das Haus mit zwei Schlafzimmern bietet weniger Platz als das Haus mit fünf Schlafzimmern.
The flat has got **the least space**.	Die Wohnung bietet den wenigsten Platz.

◆ **Zählbare Substantive** werden mit *fewer* bzw. *fewest* **verneint gesteigert, nicht-zählbare Substantive** mit *less* bzw. *least*.
(In Großbritannien werden allerdings die Formen *fewer/fewest* – vornehmlich in der **Umgangssprache** – zunehmend durch *less/least* **ersetzt**. So könnten die beiden ersten Beispielsätze auch lauten: *The cottage has got less bedrooms ... . The flat has got the least bedrooms.*)

Exercises

I. Look at the descriptions of these houses. Then answer the questions below using complete sentences.

Dunscombe Cottage

✳ £130,000
✳ Built in 1875
✳ 2 bedrooms, bathroom, large kitchen, lounge with fireplace, front and rear gardens, no garage
✳ 5 miles from the sea
✳ 10 miles from nearest town

Clovelly

✳ £170,000
✳ Built in 1925
✳ 4 bedrooms, bathroom, kitchen, lounge/dining area, garage, medium-size front and rear gardens
✳ 2 miles to railway station
✳ within walking distance of town centre

Parkview
* £210,000
* Built in 1985
* 4 bedrooms, 2 bathrooms, kitchen/breakfast
  room, lounge, dining room, study, double
  garage, small rear garden
* next to park
* 5 miles from town centre and railway station

1. Which house is the cheapest?
2. Which house is the most modern?
3. Which house is the most spacious?
4. Which house has got the fewest bedrooms?
5. Which house is the least convenient for the shops?

Complete these sentences comparing "Clovelly" and "Parkview". ●●

6. *Clovelly* is not only ... expensive ... *Parkview*. It is also ... convenient for the
   shops.
7. *Parkview* is more ... than *Clovelly* because it was built ... years later, in 1985.
8. Although *Parkview* is more ... than *Clovelly* it has got as many ... as *Clovelly*.
9. *Clovelly* is ... to a railway station than *Parkview* is but *Parkview* has got a ...
   garage.
10. *Clovelly* has got ... garden than *Parkview* but *Parkview*, as its name suggests,
    is much ... to a park.

Which questions about "Dunscombe Cottage" will produce these answers? ●●

11. £130,000.
12. In 1875.
13. Only two.
14. No, it hasn't.
15. Ten miles.

II. Include the information from the sentence in brackets into the first sentence.
(Be careful how you write the adjectives.) ●●

Example:
They bought a house. (It has got three bedrooms.)
They bought a **three-bedroom** house.

1. Yesterday we went for a walk. (We walked for ten miles.)
2. She lives in a small flat. (It's got two rooms.)

3. A flight to the USA can be quite tiring. (The flight lasts eight hours.)
4. They had a lovely meal in an exclusive restaurant. (It consisted of five courses.)
5. He gave a boring talk to the group. (The talk went on for one hour.)
6. She wrote a funny postcard. (It had only three words in it.)

III. What could you write in a three-word postcard? Can you give two examples?

IV. Write a short paragraph about where you live. Say where it is, how big it is and describe the rooms. The example below may help you.

Example:

I live in a two-room flat. I've got a lounge, a small bedroom, a kitchen and a bathroom. The flat is about 50m^2 so there's enough space for me and my two cats. I've got a small balcony which is south facing so in the summer I can sit outside and enjoy the sun.

15B

Getting financial advice ●●

In order to buy their house David and Janet have to *take out a mortgage* or *home loan* so they go to their bank and talk to a *mortgage adviser*. After they have filled in some forms giving information about their financial situation, they inform the
5 mortgage advisor that they want to buy a three-bedroom house and that the *asking price* is £60,000. David asks how much money they can borrow.

The mortgage advisor suggests they borrow £50,000, which would be *two-and-a-quarter times* their two *salaries*. The *repayment* would be about £350 per month. Janet wants to know what would happen if their *circumstances* changed.

10 Janet: What would happen if one of us lost our job or was made *redundant*?
            Or, well, suppose we started a family and I stopped working? What
            would happen then?
   Advisor: We can offer you insurance against accident, *sickness* or *redundancy*.
            But if you decided to start a family and if you wanted to give up work,
15   well, you will still have to pay your mortgage every month.
   David: You mean we have to think about that now?
   Advisor: That's right. Now is the time. You must decide if you can afford it.

take out a mortgage	eine Hypothek auf- nehmen	salary	Gehalt
home loan	Kredit, Darlehen zum Kauf eines Hauses	repayment circumstances	Rückzahlung(srate) Umstände, Verhältnisse
mortgage adviser	Finanzberater, *hier*: für Hypotheken	redundant	überzählig, *hier*: arbeitslos
asking price	Angebotspreis	sickness	Krankheit
(two-and-a-quarter) times	(zweieinviertel)mal, -fach	redundancy	Arbeitslosigkeit

Understanding the text.

Are the following three statements true or false according to the text?
Or does the text not say?

1. David and Janet must borrow money to buy their house.
2. The mortgage advisor says they cannot afford a house.
3. David and Janet's monthly repayment would go up if they had children one day.

Answer these questions using your own words as far as possible.

4. What does Janet mean when she talks about "circumstances" which could
   change (line 9)?
5. In what way can the mortgage advisor help David and Janet?
6. In what way can the mortgage advisor not help David and Janet?

Find the English equivalents in the text for these German words and expressions.

7. ein Formular ausfüllen
8. Gehalt
9. monatliche Rückzahlung
10. Versicherung

And what about you?

11. Do you think David and Janet should buy a house in their present situation or not? Give some reasons for your answer.
12. Would it be possible for David and Janet to buy a house in the same way in Germany? Explain your answer.

 ### Multi-word verbs/phrasal verbs (I)

Zusammengesetzte Verben (I)

We would like to **take out** a mortgage.	Wir möchten gerne eine Hypothek aufnehmen.
Can you **fill in** these forms?	Können Sie diese Formulare ausfüllen?
What would happen if I **gave up** work?	Was würde geschehen, wenn ich aufhörte zu arbeiten?

◆ Es gibt im Englischen eine ganze Reihe von sogenannten *multi-word verbs*, d.h. Verben, die aus **zwei** oder sogar **drei Teilen** bestehen (z.B. *to look after, to get on with*). Oft werden diese Verben auch *phrasal verbs* genannt.

◆ Manche *multi-word verbs* sind unkompliziert in ihrer Form und Bedeutung. Der Satz *"We filled in the form."* lässt sich z.B. problemlos mit „Wir haben das Formular ausgefüllt." übersetzen. In anderen Fällen lassen sich dagegen aus der **Grundbedeutung der Einzelwörter keine Rückschlüsse** auf die **Bedeutung** des *phrasal verbs* ziehen. So lautet z.B. die deutsche Entsprechung für *"We put off the holiday until winter."*: „Wir haben unseren Urlaub auf den Winter verschoben.". **Struktur** und **Bedeutung** dieser **zusammengesetzten Verben** werden daher am besten in **kompletten Sätzen** oder **ganzen Texten** verstanden, geübt und gelernt.

◆ Obgleich zu vielen *multi-word verbs* eine „einteilige" oder auch **längere Entsprechung** existiert (z.B. *to give up a job = to leave a job*), geben *native speakers* in der Regel der **weniger formalen Variante** den **Vorzug**. *Multi-word verbs* haben für sie den enormen Vorteil, dass sich aus einer kleinen Anzahl von Verben (z.B. *bring, give, take, put*) und Partikeln (z.B. *about, in, on, of, out, up, with*) eine ungeheure Vielzahl von Bedeutungen kombinieren lässt. Umgekehrt liegt gerade hier für den Lernenden die Schwierigkeit, so dass er versucht, die *multi-word verbs* zu vermeiden.

Mehr zu den *multi-word verbs* finden Sie in den Modulen 23A (vgl. S. 158) und 25B (vgl. S. 193).

Exercises

I. Here are some common multi-word verbs with "take". What do they mean? Match them with a German equivalent (a-e).

1. John is really good at <u>taking off</u> our boss.	a. *ähneln*
2. The plane <u>took off</u> three hours late.	b. *anfangen*
3. Does Sally <u>take after</u> her mother?	c. *mögen*
4. Mike's father <u>took to</u> Rebecca immediately.	d. *nachahmen*
5. When did Tom first <u>take up</u> jogging?	e. *starten*

II. Here are some more multi-word verbs, this time with "put". What do they mean? Match them with their more formal English equivalents (a-e).

1. The fire brigade quickly <u>put out</u> the fire.	a. perform
2. Can you <u>put</u> us <u>up</u> for a night?	b. extinguish
3. How do you <u>put up with</u> such bad service?	c. postpone
4. The school is <u>putting on</u> the play *Equus* this year.	d. provide a bed
5. We've <u>put off</u> the meeting until Friday.	e. tolerate

III. Don't mix up words. Put the words into the correct sentences. ●●

1. There is no magic ... for learning a foreign language.
2. Before you can apply for a mortgage you have to fill in this ... .

3. How much does it cost to ... a book from the library?
4. Banks ... money to people because it's good business for them.

5. Are you ... here? I thought you left five minutes ago!
6. Are you ... here? You only left five minutes ago!

7. Did you ... yourself when you fell off your bike?
8. Did you ... your luggage before you went on holiday?

Now translate your sentences into German.

If-pattern 2
Bedingungssätze (Konditionalsätze) Typ 2

What **would happen** if one of us **lost** our job?	Was würde geschehen, wenn einer von uns seinen Arbeitsplatz verlöre?
What **would happen** if I **did not work**?	Was würde geschehen, wenn ich nicht arbeitete?
If you **decided** to start a family, you **would** still **have** to pay your mortgage.	Wenn Sie sich entschließen würden, eine Familie zu gründen, müssten Sie dennoch Ihre Hypothek bezahlen.

◆ Bei **Typ 2** geht es um **Bedingungen**, die sich zwar **theoretisch erfüllen ließen**, jedoch vom Sprecher nur als **Annahme (Hypothese)** gedacht sind.

◆ Im Satzteil nach *if* steht die **einfache Form der Vergangenheit** (*Past Tense*). Bei *to be* ist in der **1. und 3. Person Singular** sowohl *were* als auch *was* möglich. Im **Hauptsatz** stehen *would + infinitive* oder auch ein anderes Hilfsverb, wie z.B. *could* oder *might* (*If they decided to start a family they might not be able to pay the mortgage any longer*. Wenn sie sich entschließen würden, eine Familie zu gründen, wären sie vielleicht nicht mehr länger in der Lage, die Hypothek zu bezahlen.).

Suppose we **started** a family and I **stopped** working. What would happen then?	Angenommen, wir gründeten eine Familie und ich hörte auf zu arbeiten. Was würde dann geschehen?

◆ An die Stelle von *"what would happen if ..."* kann auch *"suppose ..."* (*angenommen ...*) treten. Auch in diesem Fall steht das Verb in der **einfachen Form der Vergangenheit**.

IV. Complete these sentences using the correct form of the words in brackets. ●●

1. If David and Janet ... (take out) a £50,000 mortgage, they ... (have to pay back) about £350 a month.

2. If one of them ... (fall ill) or ... (be) without a job, the insurance ... (cover) their costs.

3. The insurance ... (also, pay) the mortgage if one of them ... (have) an accident.

4. But ... David's salary ... (be) enough if Janet ... (have) children and ... (stop) working one day?
5. If Janet ... (start) a family, ... she ... (be able) to go back to work?
6. ... David ... (be able, earn) more money if he ... (change) his job?
7. If they ... (get) into financial difficulties, ... Janet's parents ... (help) them?
8. If David and Janet ... (know) the answers to all these questions, they ... (be able to make) a decision more easily.

V. Now complete these sentences using the correct form of the words in brackets. ●●

One night Helen sees somebody breaking into a house. The burglar (*Einbrecher*) does not see her.

1. What ... (burglar, do) if he ... (know) that Helen could see him?
2. ... (he, run away)?
3. And if you ... (be) Helen, what ... (you, do)?
4. ... (you, phone) the police?
5. If you ... (be) near enough, ... (you, shout) to the burglar?
6. Or ... (you, wait) to see if he ... (come) out of the house?
7. And if he ... (not, come) out and you ... (not, be able) to reach the police, ... (you, follow) him?
8. If these ... (be, not) hypothetical questions, they ... (be) easier to answer.

VI. Answer the questions. Use a dictionary if you wish.

1. Would you find a coat hanger in a bedroom or a lounge?
2. Would you find a cork screw in a kitchen or a bathroom?
3. Would you find suitcases in an attic or a dining room?
4. Would you find a spade in a garden or a lounge?
5. Would you find cutlery in a kitchen or a bedroom?
6. Would you find dental floss in a bathroom or a cellar?

Where would you find these things in a house?

7. a pillow   9. a cushion
8. a mug   10. a towel

15C

Sophie Duncker – a German teacher in England

Listen carefully to what Sophie Duncker has to say about buying and renting property in England. Then answer the questions below.

I. Which ending (a-c) completes the statement best? Tick it.

1. Sophie has gone to a property auction because she ...
   a) wants to see if she can buy a house.
   b) wants to see if she can sell a house.
   c) wants to see what happens there.

2. Sophie thinks rented accommodation in Britain is normally ...
   a) attractive.   b) of low quality.   c) not easy to find.

3. If Sophie had enough money to spare (... *Geld übrig hätte*), she ...
   a) would probably buy a house.
   b) would probably buy a flat.
   c) would probably put it in a bank account.

II. Which three words from the text are defined below?

1. a written agreement between two people or organizations
2. somebody who pays rent to live in a house, flat or room
3. a person who works for a company which sells houses and land for other people

III. Match the idioms (1-4) with their explanations (a-d).

1. (to have something) on the house
2. to bring the house down
3. to get on like a house on fire
4. to have a roof over your head

a. to have somewhere where you can live
b. to make the audience clap and cheer enthusiastically
c. to eat or drink in a restaurant without having to pay
d. to understand another person very well

Now complete the sentences using one of the idioms from above.

5. It was a difficult situation for her. She was without money and did not ... but she still managed to smile.
6. It was the first time Fiona and Kevin had ever met but they ... . They talked all evening and left the party together.
7. The first night of the new Lloyd Webber musical ... . The audience clapped so long until Andrew Lloyd Webber himself came on stage.
8. After the guests were given a terrible lunch the hotel manager offered them dinner ... . It was the least he could do.

IV. Sophie says that in Germany "there isn't such a mobile market for buying houses as there is in England". Why is this? Can you give any reasons? Write a short paragraph (50–60 words).

15D

Meterman the decorator

I. Put the first sentences from the six paragraphs into their correct positions.

a. About an hour later Meterman comes downstairs.
b. At eleven o'clock the woman goes upstairs with Meterman's tea.
c. Meterman looks at the camera *sheepishly*.
d. "The meter is upstairs!" the woman replies.
e. Although it's a *bank holiday*, Meterman is working.
f. The woman who lives in the house is expecting him.

1. He is going to do some decorating. First he goes to a do-it-yourself store to buy the materials: paint, a roller, brushes, *glasspaper*, wallpaper and *paste*. Then he drives to the house where he has been asked to wallpaper a bedroom.

2. "There's something I'd just like to point out to you," she says after Meterman has carried all his materials upstairs. Meterman is quick to interrupt. "Madam, I am a professional," he warns. "I've done this sort of thing before. It's perfectly *straightforward*. Now leave it to me."

3. "Excuse me, my dear," he says to the woman. "Could I just point out to you that I will be requiring my *elevenses* today at 11 o'clock precisely." The woman would also like to point out something but Meterman isn't listening. He's looking at the colour of the kitchen walls instead. "I am an expert in colours, colours and the psychology of the *human mind*," he explains. "Now, if you painted it in green, for example, you would feel calm and relaxed. If, on the other hand, you painted it in yellow, you would be happy and *cheerful*.".

4. She knocks on the door of the bedroom. "Come in," says Meterman. "I've just finished." The woman walks in. She can't believe her eyes. *The room is a complete mess.* "Of all the *deceitful confidence tricksters* I've ever met! You can just get out my house before I ... oh!" she shouts. Meterman remains calm. "Madam, you are most *ungrateful*," he says. "I shall go downstairs and read the meter!".

5. Meterman begins to get a little bit angry now. "Madam, I am a professional," he says. "I know my meters. Once seen, never forgotten!" "Well, that's exactly what I've been trying to tell you about," the woman replies. "But you wouldn't listen to me. You've completely forgotten where the meter is. You've covered it completely with paper!".

6. *"Silly old me,"* he says.

sheepish	verlegen, „belämmert"	human mind	menschlicher Geist
		cheerful	fröhlich
bank holiday	(*in Großbritannien*) gesetzlicher Feiertag	mess	Durcheinander, Wirrwarr, Chaos
		The room is a	Das Zimmer ist ein
glasspaper	Sandpapier, Schmirgelpapier	complete mess.	„Saustall".
		deceitful	hinterlistig
paste	*hier*: Tapetenkleister	confidence trickster	Betrüger, Hochstapler
straightforward	*hier*: einfach, unkompliziert	ungrateful	undankbar
		Silly old me.	Ich Dummkopf.
elevenses	zweites Frühstück		Ich alter Trottel.

II. Which word from the text is defined or explained below?

1. a drink and something to eat in the middle of the morning
2. a day when most people in Britain do not work and most shops are closed
3. to start talking when somebody else is talking so that they cannot continue what they are saying
4. a word which Meterman often uses which means "simple and easy"

15E

Estate agents

Estate agents in England are open seven days a week

THEN AND NOW

16A

Constable country ●●

Cathy and Gavin are cycling to Flatford *Mill* in the county of Suffolk. They want to find out more about the English painter *John Constable*, who lived and worked at the Mill for much of his life.

5 Their trip does not start very well because they soon *have a row*.

Cathy: Well I don't know, we seem to *be lost*. Where's the map? They sent
             us a very good map.

Gavin: I don't know. Didn't you pack it?

Cathy: No. Didn't you?

10 Gavin: No. You are always forgetting things. You are always in such a hurry.
             Why don't you do things more slowly?

Cathy: Oh, *shut up*. It's not my fault. Why don't you *lend a hand more*?
             You always leave everything to me. You never take any *responsibility*.
             Do this, do that, do the other – and stop criticizing me. You are always
15   criticizing me. I've had enough!

After they arrive at Flatford Mill, they unpack their bags: brushes, oil paints, *turps*.
Gavin thinks that they have forgotten the *canvasses*. The two young people get into
another *argument*.

Gavin:	What about canvasses? Didn't you pack canvasses? Oh, for heaven's		

Gavin: What about canvasses? Didn't you pack canvasses? Oh, for heaven's
20   sake!

Cathy: Don't start criticizing me again. Anyway, the canvasses are here.
          Why don't you use your eyes!

Things get better for the young couple when they look around the Mill. They enjoy
seeing the house where Constable's father lived until two years before Constable
25 was born. Cathy seems to know quite a lot about the painter and his work. "That's
the cottage which he painted in *'The Haywain'*," she explains. "It's called Willy
Lott's House. And this is where he sat to paint the picture."

John Constable	*engl. Landschafts-* *maler (1776–1837)*	responsibility	Verantwortung
mill	Mühle	turps (= turpentine)	Terpentin *(zum Malen)*
have a row	einen Streit haben	canvas	Leinwand
be lost	*hier:* sich verirrt haben	argument	*hier:* Streit, Aus-einandersetzung
shut up (*coll*)	den Mund halten	"The Haywain"	„Der Heuwagen"
lend a hand (more)	(mehr) mit Hand anlegen, helfen		(*Gemälde von Constable*)

Understanding the text.

Which ending (a-c) completes the statement (1–3) best? Tick it.

1. Cathy and Gavin have gone to Flatford Mill because they seem to be
   interested in ...
   a) arguing.   b) painting.   c) reading maps.

2. Before they look around the Mill they have ...
   a) three arguments.   b) two arguments.   c) one argument.

3. The arguments between the two start because ...
   a) Gavin criticizes Cathy.
   b) Cathy criticizes Gavin.
   c) Cathy criticizes Constable's paintings.

Further questions. Answer them in your own words as far as possible.

4. What problem do Cathy and Gavin have before they get to Flatford Mill?
5. Are Cathy and Gavin going to the Mill for one day or longer? Explain your
   answer.

The Field Studies Centre at Flatford Mill

Tick the correct ending to the sentence.

6. In German the expression "it's not my fault" (line 12) means ...
    a) „es ist nicht mein Fehler".
    b) „ich bin nicht schuld".
    c) „es ist nicht recht von mir".

7. In German the expression "Why don't you lend a hand more?" (line 12) means ...
    a) „Warum tust du nicht die Hand aus deiner Tasche?"
    b) „Warum hast du nicht gepackt?"
    c) „Warum kannst du nicht mehr helfen?"

Find the English for these German words and expressions.

8. Rad fahren
9. in Eile sein
10. Verantwortung

And what about you?

11. Do you know where the county of Suffolk is? (If you don't, get hold of a map and find out.)
12. Apart from John Constable, do you know the names of any other famous English painters?

Defining relative clauses (I)

Bestimmende Relativsätze (I)

This is the house **where** Constable's father lived until 1774. That's the cottage **which** he painted in "The Haywain". Constable's paintings show a way of life **which** has mostly passed away today.	Dies ist das Haus, in dem Constables Vater bis 1774 lebte. Das ist das *cottage*, das er in seinem Bild „Der Heuwagen" malte. Constables Bilder zeigen eine Lebensweise, die es mittlerweile weitgehend nicht mehr gibt.

◆ Durch einen **Relativsatz** wird ein **Substantiv näher beschrieben;** so z.B. das Wort *house* in unserem ersten Beispiel.

◆ Ein Relativsatz, der für das **Verständnis des ganzen Satzes unerlässlich** ist, weil er die **entscheidende Information** liefert, wird als **bestimmend (notwendig)** bezeichnet. Würde bei den oben genannten Beispielsätzen der Relativsatz wegfallen, bliebe jeweils nur ein unverständliches Fragment (*This is the house.*). Im Englischen schreibt man daher diese Art von Relativsatz **ohne Komma**.

◆ In diesem Modul geht es zunächst nur um bestimmende Relativsätze, die mit den **Relativpronomen** *which* oder *where* eingeleitet werden: Das Pronomen **which** beschreibt **Sachen**. Es kann **Objekt** (*... the cottage which he painted ...*) oder **Subjekt** (*... a way of life which has mostly passed away ...*) **des Relativsatzes** sein.
Das Pronomen **where** beschreibt einen **Ort** (*... the place where he sat ...*).

(Zu den Relativsätzen siehe auch Modul 23B, S. 163.)

Exercises

I. Complete these sentences by adding the object relative pronoun "which" and an appropriate phrase from the box below. ●●

> ... I gave you this morning? ● ... I used to wear at school. ● ... they were talking about. ● ... we saw on TV last weekend? ● ... you recommended to us.

1. What's the name of the film ...
2. We once stayed at a hotel ...
3. Have you still got the key ...
4. This is the uniform ...
5. I wasn't interested in the things ...

II. Complete these sentences by adding the subject relative pronoun "which"
and the correct form of the words in brackets. (You may have to add some
words.) ●●

1. Where is the poster ... (hang/here/yesterday)?
2. A dictionary is a book ... (explain/meanings/words).
3. What's the title of the book ... (begin/sentence/*"At the little town of Vevey,*
   in Switzerland, there is a particularly comfortable hotel.")?
4. She works for a firm ... (design/computer software).
5. This is the jacket ... (used to/belong/grandfather).

III. Add the relative pronoun "where" and an appropriate phrase from the box below
to complete these sentences. ●●

> ... I can send a fax? ● ... they serve German beer. ● ... we can get
> something quick to eat? ● ... we used to lie. ● ... you bought it.

1. If it doesn't work take it back to the shop ...
2. Do you know a nice place ...
3. There's a pub not far from here ...
4. Is there anywhere in the village ...
5. This photograph shows the beach ...

Valley Farm

IV. *Translate into English. Use relative clauses which begin with "where" or "which". (Don't use commas!)* ●●

    1. Dies ist die Stadt, in der ich aufgewachsen bin.
    2. Wo sind die Bilder, die ich dir gestern gezeigt habe?
    3. Hier ist der Ort, wo ich einen Autounfall hatte.
    4. Wie heißt die Sendung, die wir gestern angesehen haben?
    5. Ich habe die Stelle, die ich wollte, nicht bekommen.

V. *Complete the sentences using your own ideas.*

    1. I would like to live in a place where ... .
    2. I would like to have a job which I ... .

VI. *In Part One, Module 2B (page 31) the word "always" was introduced as a signal word for the present simple. Here, in Module 16A, we can see that "always" is also used with the present continuous. What feeling is expressed by sentences 1 and 2? Choose from the four possibilities (a-d).*

                             a. worry (*Besorgnis*)
    1. You're always forgetting things!   b. pleasure (*Freude*)
    2. You're always criticizing me!   c. anger (*Zorn*)
                             d. satisfaction (*Genugtuung*)

VII. *Choose one of the words in each of the brackets to form correct sentences.* ●●

    1. That picture (reminds/remembers) me (of/on) the holiday we (had/made) in England last year.
    2. Did you receive a (prize/price) for (getting/becoming) the best (mark/note) in the class?
    3. Can you explain (to me/me) the difference between "bag" and "pocket"?
    4. (When/Whenever) I was small we (have lived/lived) in a small house in the (country/county).
    5. I (ride/drive) my bike (in/to) work every day because I enjoy (to get/getting) the exercise.
    6. You speak English very (good/well). Who (taught/learnt) you?
    7. The statistics (is/are) interesting but (it/they) can be (easy/easily) misinterpreted.

16B

How Flatford Mill has changed ●●

Later in the day Cathy and Gavin meet Edward Jackson, the director of the Flatford
Mill Centre. They ask him to tell them more about the Mill in Constable's time.
Mr Jackson tells them that Constable's father owned Flatford Mill and that Consta-
5 ble worked there for a year learning the business of *grinding corn*. Mr Jackson then
points out the bell on the top of the Mill. He tells the visitors that when the water
level was right, they used to ring that bell to tell everyone that they were going to
mill. "They also used to ring the bell if there was a danger of *flooding*," Mr Jackson
adds. "That happened quite often in winter. They would ring the bell and the people
10 round about would know that they had to get their cows and sheep to safety."
Mr Jackson then shows Cathy and Gavin the *alterations* and improvements which
have been made to Flatford Mill. At Valley Farm, for example, Cathy and Gavin see
that many of the rooms have been converted into accommodation for guests. "This
used to be the *pantry* where they kept bread and dry food," Mr Jackson explains.
15 "We've turned this room into a bedroom." Then he opens the door to another
room. "This used to be the *buttery* where they stored the *butts* – or barrels – of beer.
We've made this into a bathroom." Finally Mr Jackson shows them upstairs.
"We've converted the room up these stairs into a double bedroom," he says. "The
stairs are from the 14th century. As you can see, we haven't changed them at all."
20 Mr Jackson finishes his tour of Flatford Mill by telling Cathy and Gavin that over
5,000 visitors come to the Mill every year. "Over the last 10 years we have doubled
the number of visitors who come to stay," he says proudly. "And we have doubled
the number of people who work here."

grind (corn)	(Getreide) mahlen	alteration	Veränderung
(ground, ground)		pantry	(Trocken-)Speisekammer
mill	(Getreide) mahlen	buttery	*eine Art Vorratsraum für*
flood	Überschwemmung;		*Bier*
	überschwemmen	butt	Fass

Understanding the text.

Are these statements true or false according to the text? Or does the text not say?

1. Although John Constable was a good painter he knew nothing about farming.
2. Many years ago people used to make bread at Flatford Mill.
3. Nowadays tourists can spend the night at Flatford Mill.
4. Flatford Mill is becoming more and more popular with tourists.

Cathy and Gavin meet
Edward Jackson

Further questions. Answer them using your own words as far as possible.

5. Why was the level of the water so important for the people at Flatford Mill?
6. What function did the bell on the top of the Mill have in Constable's time?
7. What shows the popularity of Flatford Mill as a tourist attraction today?

What is the English for the following German words or expressions?

8. Überschwemmung   9. mahlen (*two words*)   10. verdoppeln

And what about you?

11. Could you imagine spending a week at Flatford Mill? Say why or why not.
12. Do you think people living in Suffolk at the beginning of the nineteenth century had an easy life? Give some reasons for your answer.

The Mill

Past tense forms

Vergangenheitsformen

Constable **worked** for a year at the Mill.	Constable arbeitete ein Jahr in der Mühle.
They **used to grow** a lot of corn around here.	Sie bauten früher hier in dieser Gegend eine Menge Getreide an.
Did they **use to bring** the corn here by river?	Brachten sie früher das Getreide auf dem Flussweg hierher?
The horse **would walk** along the path.	Das Pferd ging gewöhnlich den Weg entlang.
He **would watch** the sky carefully.	Er hatte die Angewohnheit, den Himmel genau zu beobachten. (Er beobachtete den Himmel stets genau.)

◆ Wenn man über ein **in der Vergangenheit abgeschlossenes Ereignis** berichtet, nimmt man in der Regel als Verb die **einfache Form** – oder seltener die Verlaufsform – **der Vergangenheit** (siehe dazu *Part One*, Module 3B, S. 51, und 7B, S. 113).

◆ In diesem Modul kommen zwei weitere Verbformen hinzu. Eine ist bereits in *Part One,* Modul 10B vorgekommen: *used to + infinitive* (vgl. S. 165). Bei der zweiten Verbform handelt es sich um *would + infinitive*. Beide Konstruktionen werden verwendet, um über **vergangene Gewohnheiten** zu berichten:

– Die Konstruktion *used to + infinitive* existiert **nur als Vergangenheitsform**. Die **Frageform** lautet: *"Did ... use to + infinitive?"* Zur Bildung der **Verneinung** kommt ein *not* dazu: *"... did not use to + infinitive"*.

– Die Form *would + infinitive* leitet keinen Bedingungssatz ein. In dem Satz *"He would watch the sky carefully."* erinnert sich der Sprecher z.B. an Gewohnheiten des Malers Constable aus einem anderen Jahrhundert. Da *would* in der Regel **häufig wiederholte Handlungen der Vergangenheit** zum Ausdruck bringt, wird bei der Übertragung ins Deutsche bisweilen ein *immer* oder *stets* ergänzt.

Exercises

I. Check your past tense verb forms. Complete this dialogue using the correct forms of the words in brackets. ●●

1. When ... (you, go) to Flatford Mill?
    We ... (go) last summer, in September.

2. ... (it, be) busy?
    No, because the children ... (be) back at school.

3. How long ... (you, be) there for?
    We only ... (stay) for a week.

4. ... (you, have) accommodation at the Mill?
    Yes, we ... (have) a room in Valley Farm.

5. ... (you, enjoy) the course?
    Yes. We ... (learn) a lot and ... (make) many new friends.

6. ... (you, come) back to Germany after the course?
    No, we ... (fly) to Ireland and ... (do) some more painting.

7. What ... (you, think) of Ireland?
    We ... (think) it was lovely. We're going back next year.

II. Complete these sentences about Flatford Mill by using the correct forms of the words in brackets. ●●

1. What ... (they, used to, grow) around Flatford Mill?
    It was mostly barley.

2. How ... (they, used to, bring) the corn to the Mill?
    By barge (*Lastkahn*).

3. Why ... (they, used to, ring) the bell up there?
    It had two functions really.

4. ... (it, not, used to, warn) people about flooding?
    Yes, and it ... (used to, tell) everybody that they were going to mill.

5. ... (Constable, used to, work) at the Mill?
    Yes, he did. He ... (used to, help, grind) the corn.

III. Complete the sentences below by adding "would" and one of the verbs from the box. ●●

> go ● have ● be ● play ● think ● come

1. When I was small we used to live in a small flat. My brother and I didn't have a room of our own so we ... in the kitchen most of the time.
2. My father used to work at nights. He ... home at six in the morning and sleep until midday.
3. The whole family ... lunch together and then in the afternoon my dad ... out with us somewhere.
4. We ... in the park or go cycling together.
5. Later, when I was a teenager, I ... often ... about the good times we had in our old flat.

The present perfect simple

Die einfache Form des Perfekts

Hier soll noch einmal etwas ausführlicher das *Present Perfect* wiederholt werden, mit dem wir uns bereits mehrmals beschäftigt haben und dessen Anwendung Lernenden häufig besondere Probleme bereitet. (Vgl. dazu auch *Part One*, S. 64 und 156, *Part Two*, S. 13.)

Have you **made** many changes?	Haben Sie viele Veränderungen vorgenommen?
We**'ve turned** this room into a bedroom.	Wir haben aus diesem Raum ein Schlafzimmer gemacht.
We **haven't changed** the stairs at all.	Wir haben die Stufen überhaupt nicht verändert.

◆ Das *Present Perfect* ist **keine Vergangenheitsform**, sondern – wie der Name bereits sagt – **eng** mit der **Gegenwart** verbunden.

◆ Die oben genannten Beispielsätze zeigen, dass das *Present Perfect* sehr häufig verwendet wird, um über die **Folgen eines Ereignisses** zu sprechen, das in der Vergangenheit stattgefunden hat. So ist z.B. bei dem Satz *"We've turned this room into a bedroom."* das in der **Gegenwart sichtbare Ergebnis** („das umgebaute Schlafzimmer") für den Sprecher wichtiger als die Arbeit selbst, die dafür in der Vergangenheit geleistet wurde.

Will man **dagegen** den in der **Vergangenheit abgeschlossenen Vorgang** zum Ausdruck bringen, geschieht dies durch die *Past Tense* (häufig in Verbindung mit einer **entsprechenden Zeitangabe**): *"We turned this room into a bedroom last year."*.

IV. Read the situation and then write a sentence in the present perfect simple.
(The words in brackets will help you.) ●●

1. Why can't Jack open his suitcase?
    He ... (lose) the key.

2. Is Sally in the office today?
    No, she ... (go) to Italy for a week.

3. Is there something wrong with the car?
    No, we ... (run out) of petrol, that's all.

4. Can I borrow some money?
    Sorry. I ... (spend) all the spare money I had.

5. Why is Mike not playing football this weekend?
    Don't you know? He ... (break) his leg.

6. Wayne looks different, doesn't he?
    Yes, he ... (lose) some weight.

7. This room used to be yellow, didn't it?
    Yes, we ... (paint) it blue.

8. Sandwich?
    No, thanks. I ... (just, have) lunch.

V. Present perfect or past simple? Use the correct form of the words in brackets to
complete the sentences. ●●

1. Last night Joanna ... (tell) me that Cathy ... (not, speak) to Gavin for the last
    three days. I wonder why.

2. ... (you, manage, save) money last month?

3. My brother ... (buy) himself a new computer last weekend so he ... (give) me
    his old one.

4. Jack ... (not, be) to an art exhibition once this year.

5. ... (Mike, be) at work yesterday? I ... (not, see) him.

6. I ... (not, feel) well on Friday so I ... (go) home a bit earlier.

7. My boyfriend's parents ... (not, have) a holiday last summer because they ...
    (be) away at Whitsun (*Pfingsten*).

8. Rebecca ... (have) three job interviews so far this month but she ... (not, hear)
    whether she ... (be) successful yet.

since/for + present perfect or past tense

since/for + Perfekt oder Vergangenheitsform

I've been director at Flatford Mill **for ten years**. (= I still am)	Ich bin seit zehn Jahren Direktor von Flatford Mill.
I **was** director at Flatford Mill **for ten** years.	Ich war zehn Jahre lang Direktor von Flatford Mill.

◆ Für Vorgänge, die **in der Vergangenheit begonnen haben** und **bis in die Gegenwart andauern**, wird gleichfalls das *Present Perfect* verwendet. Häufig stehen in diesen Fällen die Wörter *for* und *since* zur Bezeichnung eines bestimmten Zeitraumes bzw. Zeitpunktes (vgl. *Part One*, Modul 10B, S. 163).

◆ Jedoch, **Vorsicht**: *for* und *since* sind **nicht automatisch Signalwörter** für den Gebrauch des Perfekts. Sie können auch in Verbindung mit der *Past Tense* stehen, wenn ein **in der Vergangenheit abgeschlossener Vorgang** ausgedrückt werden soll. Wenn es z.B. heißt *"I was director at Flatford Mill for ten years."*, so will der Sprecher damit zu verstehen geben, dass er mittlerweile nicht mehr Direktor ist.

VI. Match the sentences to their "meanings".

1. We lived in England for five years.
2. We've lived in England for five years.

   a. and we still do
   b. and now we don't

3. I was a friend of Fiona's for many years.
4. I've been a friend of Fiona's for many years.

   a. but we're not friends now
   b. and I am a friend of hers today

5. She was married to Kevin for 8 years.
6. She's been married to Kevin for 8 years.

   a. and she's still married to Kevin
   b. and now she's married to Rick

7. We thought about emigrating to Australia.
8. We've thought about emigrating to Australia.

   a. and we might do it one day
   b. but we gave up the idea

VII. Match the two sentences with the phrases (a-f). (Three phrases go with sentence
1 and three with sentence 2.)

	a. at Christmas.
	b. since 1996.
1. We have not been to London ...	c. yet.
2. We went to London ...	d. last summer.
	e. for over ten years.
	f. on the 25 April.

VIII. Doctor, doctor!

Patient: Doctor, doctor! I've swallowed a film.
Doctor: Mmm, I see. I think we should see how it develops.

Patient: Doctor, doctor! I've swallowed a sheep.
Doctor: Oh dear. You must be feeling very baaaaaad.

16C

Edward Jackson – Director of the Field Studies Centre

Edward Jackson is the Director of the Field Studies Centre at Flatford Mill. Listen
carefully to him talking about the work which goes on at the Centre. Then answer
the questions on page 55.

Some young people learn more about pond life

I. Are these statements about the Centre true or false according to the interview?
Tick the appropriate box.

	T	F
1. The Centre offers courses on the environment.		
2. The Centre only runs classes for schoolchildren.		
3. Edward Jackson is the owner of Flatford Mill.		
4. He is a teacher at the Centre.		
5. He is very interested in bird watching.		

II. Which ending (a-c) best finishes these statements about John Constable?

1. John Constable knew the area around Flatford Mill ...
   a) quite well.   b) well.   c) extremely well.

2. Through his paintings Constable shows us ...
   a) that life in England at the beginning of the 19th century was changing dramatically.
   b) that he did not want life in England to change.
   c) that he wasn't really interested in life around him.

3. During his lifetime Constable was ...
   a) a well-known artist throughout Europe.
   b) misunderstood as an artist.
   c) highly admired as an artist.

III. Read what Edward Jackson says at the end of his interview. What does he mean?
Choose one of the alternatives below.

"Environmental issues are increasingly important to us nowadays. The way that we live in and use the environment is quite critical to our future and we have recognized this over the last 10, 20 years. And so our job is to encourage young people to have an awareness and understanding, and hopefully an empathy, for the environments in which they live and also the environments in which other people live so that they can appreciate it and learn to cherish it and look after it for future generations."

a) There is no future for us if we do not look after the environment.
b) If we understand the environment, we can look after it.
c) Future generations must look after the environment more than the present generation.

16D

Meterman the painter

I. Put the seven paragraphs into the correct order. Start with paragraph d.

a. First Meterman unpacks his things. He seems to know a lot about the different materials which painters need. "This is the *easel*, and this the canvas," he explains. "These are the brushes, nice thick ones for *oils*, and here are the tubes of paint. This is the palette where you mix the colours and here is the turpentine for cleaning the brushes."

b. Meterman pauses for a second and looks into the camera. "What a shame. I was quite struck by that picture."

c. Meterman then walks up to a younger woman and asks her what she is drawing. "Oh no," she says looking embarrassed and hiding her picture from him. "You really mustn't see." Meterman goes back to his seat and continues working on his self-portrait. "The artist at work," he says to the camera. And then, looking over at the young girl again, he adds: "When it's finished I'm going to give it to her."

d. Meterman is attending a weekend painting course. He's late for one of the classes. Everybody else is working hard when he comes in. "You'd better sit at the back of the class," says the teacher.

e. It's break time. While the other participants are chatting Meterman adds a mini self-portrait to the teacher's picture. He then goes to the young woman again and offers her his picture. "I've got something for you, too," she says, handing him a picture of himself sitting naked on a chair. "Oh, I say, a portrait of Meterman. That's very fine indeed. It will go in my sitting room."

f. Before he starts working, Meterman walks around the studio looking at what the other course participants are doing. One man is painting a landscape *in pastel*. A younger man is doing a *sketch* in charcoal. Another woman is using *acrylic paints*. Meterman has some advice for her. "My dear lady. Slowly. Slowly. Rome wasn't built in a day, you know."

g. At that moment the teacher discovers Meterman has drawn on her watercolour. She is very angry. "What have you done? How *dare* you appear in my picture!" she says smashing her canvas over Meterman's head.

easel	Staffelei	acrylic paints	Acrylfarben (*chemisch*
oils	Ölfarben		*hergestellte Farben*)
in pastel	in Pastellfarben	dare	sich getrauen, wagen
sketch	Skizze		

II. It is good to know what proverbs mean but you should be careful not to use them too often. Link the proverbs (1-5) with their explanations (a-e).

1. Rome wasn't built in a day.
2. Never look a gift horse in the mouth.
3. Familiarity breeds contempt.
4. Don't count your chickens before they are hatched.
5. Many hands make light work.

a. if you know somebody well you begin to dislike them
b. a lot of people helping to do a job make it easier
c. never say no to something which you get for free
d. it can take a long time to do something properly
e. do not make plans on the basis of what you expect to happen

Are any of these proverbs the same in German?

III. Puns (= a play on words)

Meterman is playing with words when, at the end of the story, the teacher hits him over the head with her painting and he says, "I was quite struck by that picture." Can you explain what the pun is exactly?

16E

London galleries

11 *The National Gallery*

TRAFALGAR SQUARE, LONDON, WC2N 5DN TELEPHONE 071 839 3321/3526

OPENING HOURS
Monday-Saturday 10-6,
Sunday 2-6.
No entry charge.

✕ ♿ ⊖ ⇌
Train: Charing Cross Tube:
Charing Cross, Leicester
Square, Embankment,
Piccadilly Circus Bus: 3,6,9,
11,12,13,15,15a,24,29,30,53,
77,77a,88,159,168,170, 176,
177, 184.

THE NATIONAL COLLECTION
of Western Painting from
c1260-1920, with over two
thousand paintings -
including works by Leonardo,
Rembrandt, Constable and
Van Gogh. The Sainsbury
wing (opened July 1991)
contains the early
Renaissance collection,
temporary exhibition galleries
for major exhibitions, a large
lecture theatre, shop and
restaurant. 1992 loan
exhibitions include
Rembrandt, Manet, and
Edvard Munch.

Rembrandt 'A Woman Bathing in a
Stream'

12 *National Portrait Gallery*

ST MARTIN'S PLACE, LONDON, WC2H OHE TELEPHONE 071 306 0055

OPENING HOURS
Monday-Friday 10-5,
Saturday 10-6.
No entry charge.

⊖ ⇌
Tube: Charing Cross or
Leicester Square. Train:
Charing Cross. Bus: To
Trafalgar Square

**THE NATIONAL PORTRAIT
GALLERY**
was founded in 1856 to
collect the likenesses of
famous British men and
women. The collection is the
most comprehensive in the
world starting with the
Tudors and ending with the
present day. Each year the
gallery holds between four
and six temporary
exhibitions.

'Elizabeth I' Marcus Gheeraerts, the
Younger c1592

13 *Tate Gallery*

MILLBANK, LONDON, SW1P 4RG, TELEPHONE 071 821 1313

Thomas Gainsborough 'Giovanna
Baccelli' exh. 1872

OPENING HOURS
Monday-Saturday 10-5:50,
Sunday 2-5:50. Entrance to
collection free, with
admission charges for major
exhibitions.

✕ ♿ ⊖ ⇌
Tube: Pimlico (Victoria line)
Bus: 88, 77A, C10 (other
buses in area include 2,3,36,
159,185, 507) Train: Vauxhall.

FOUNDED IN 1897
the Tate Gallery houses the
national collections of British
painting, including the
Turner Collection, and of
international 20th century
painting and sculpture.
Displays from the collection
change annually and are
supplemented by a full
programme of special loan
exhibitions, free lectures,
films and talks.

THE ARTS FESTIVAL   UNIT 17

17A

During the rehearsals ●●

The Sevenoaks Summer Festival begins soon so there are rehearsals every day. What are the actors and musicians doing?

The director watches carefully during rehearsals

Some actors are running through a scene from the play *"Equus"*. The play is about
5 Alan Strang, a boy of 17, played by Geoffrey, who *blinds* six horses in one night. The *psychiatrist*, played by Andy, tries to find out why the boy does such a *horrific* thing. The psychiatrist is assisted by a *nurse*, who is played by Helen. During the rehearsal the *director* explains what he wants the actors to do.

Director: Helen, remember the *ritual*. When you go to the chair, I'd like you
10   to face the chair, pause and then turn slowly and sit.
Helen: Right.

(They rehearse part of the scene.)

Director: Let's stop there for a moment, please. Geoffrey, I'd like you
               to be more like an angry child.
15 Geoffrey: Do you want me to be more aggressive?

Director: Yes, good.
Andy: How do you want me to react to him?
Director: I want you to look at him all the time.
Andy: OK.
20 Director: That's coming along fine. You are doing really well. I'd like to go
                from the beginning again, please. Can you get into positions?

The orchestra is getting ready for a concert. The *conductor* is explaining what he wants them to do.

Conductor: Stop. Well done. That's very good. Let's pause there for a moment.
25   Don't forget to listen to each other. Let's see if you can do it better.
                So if we could try that with just the *woodwind* and the *brass*. I'd like
                you to play from the same *bar*. After two *beats* ... one, two ... .

rehearsal	Probe	director	Regisseur(in)
"Equus"	*Titel eines Theaterstücks*	ritual	Ritual
	von Peter Shaffer	conductor	Dirigent(in)
	(lat. equus = Pferd)	woodwind	Holzblasinstrument
blind	blenden, das Augenlicht	(instrument)	
	nehmen	brass (instrument)	Blechblasinstrument
psychiatrist	Psychiater(in)	bar	Taktstrich
horrific	schrecklich, abscheulich	beat	Takt(-schlag)
nurse	Krankenschwester		

Understanding the text.

Which verb in the brackets best completes the sentence? Underline it.

1. The actors are (performing/rehearsing/writing) a scene.
2. The director is (praising/criticizing/worrying) them.
3. The musicians are (talking about/practising/performing) a piece of music.
4. The conductor is (encouraging/watching/annoying) them.

Underline one of the words or expressions in brackets to complete the sentence.

5. A (conductor/director) is a person who decides how actors and actresses should perform in a play or film.
6. A (conductor/director) is responsible for how an orchestra plays a piece of music. He or she stands in front of the musicians while they are playing.
7. I'm very interested in (art/the arts): music, drama, literature and painting. But I suppose my favourite is ballet.
8. I'm very interested in (art/the arts) and I regularly go to exhibitions. In fact I was in the Tate Gallery only (*erst*) last week.

What's the English for these German words?

9. Theaterstück
10. Blasinstrumente

And what about you?

11. Do you think it's easy being a director or a conductor? Give reasons for your answer.
12. Are you interested in the arts? When did you last go to the cinema or to the theatre for example?

 Verb + object + infinitive with "to"

Verb + Objekt + Infinitiv mit "to"

I'd like you to be more like an angry child.	Ich möchte, dass du dich mehr wie ein zorniges Kind verhältst.
I want you to look at him all the time.	Ich möchte, dass du ihn die ganze Zeit über ansiehst.
Do you **want me to be** more aggressive?	Möchten Sie, dass ich aggressiver bin?

Hier vergleichen wir nun den Satzbau des Deutschen mit dem des Englischen. Der deutsche Satz „*Ich möchte, dass du ihn ansiehst.*" entspricht z.B. dem englischen Satz "*I want you to look at him.*". Im Englischen wird somit eine andere grammatische Struktur verwendet als im Deutschen: **Verb + Objekt + Infinitiv mit "to"**.

Diese für deutsche Ohren recht ungewöhnlich klingende Konstruktion folgt auf eine Reihe von Verben. Zu den wichtigsten gehören:

to advise (*raten*)	to persuade (*überreden*)
to allow (*erlauben*)	to recommend (*empfehlen*)
to ask (*bitten*)	to remind (*erinnern*)
to encourage (*ermutigen*)	to teach (*lehren*)
to expect (*erwarten*)	to tell (*sagen, auffordern*)
to invite (*einladen*)	to want (*wollen*)
to order (*befehlen*)	I would like (*ich möchte*)

Getting ready for a concert

Exercises

I. Complete Helen's sentences by using the correct form of the words in brackets.
(The statements are made in the past tense, but there is one exception.) ●●

1. The director ... (teach, we, speak) loudly and clearly.
2. He ... (encourage, we, think) carefully about our roles.
3. He ... (want, we, give) the best performance we could.
4. He ... (advise, I, practise) certain scenes at home.
5. Once he said to Geoffrey: "Don't ... (expect, the audience, understand) the play as well as you do."

II. Read the sentence and write a second sentence with the same meaning.
The first words have been given. ●●

1. A passer-by told us that we should ring for a doctor.
   A passer-by advised ... .

2. I didn't really want to go out with Shirley but in the end I said yes.
   Shirley persuaded ... .

3. Mike asked Helen if she would like to have dinner with him.
   Mike invited ... .

4. Simon told Alex that he shouldn't forget the shopping.
   Simon reminded ... .

5. Fiona said it would be great if Daryl came to the party.
   Fiona would like ... .

III. Translate the following sentences into English.
Exercises I and II on page 62 will help you.

1. Ich möchte, dass du mich heiratest.
2. Er wollte, dass sie das Spiel gewinnt.
3. Sie haben gebeten, dass wir pünktlich kommen.
4. Sie hat nicht erwartet, dass es schneit.
5. Wir haben ihm gesagt, dass er später anrufen soll.

H The gerund or the infinitive after certain verbs

Das Gerund oder der Infinitiv nach bestimmten Verben

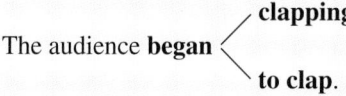

The audience **began** clapping. / to clap.   Das Publikum begann zu klatschen.

Auf eine Reihe von Verben kann sowohl das **Gerund** als auch der **Infinitiv** folgen, **ohne** dass sich dabei in der Regel die **Bedeutung ändert**. Zu diesen Verben gehören u.a. *to begin, to continue, to propose* (*vorschlagen*), *to start*.

Andy, **remember to look** at Geoffrey all the time.   Andy, denk daran, Geoffrey die ganze Zeit über anzusehen.
I **remember meeting** him at last year's summer festival.   Ich erinnere mich daran, ihn beim Sommerfestival des letzten Jahres getroffen zu haben.

Einige Verben haben jedoch **unterschiedliche Bedeutung**, je nachdem, ob sie mit einem **Gerund** oder mit einem **Infinitiv** verbunden werden. Zu den wichtigsten gehören *to remember, to forget, to stop*:

◆ Die Konstruktion mit dem **Gerund** hat **rückblickenden Charakter**:

to remember doing sth = *sich daran erinnern, dass man etw. getan hat*
to forget doing sth = *vergessen, dass man etw. getan hat*
to stop doing sth = *aufhören, etw. zu tun*

◆ Bei der Konstruktion mit dem **Infinitiv** schaut man **in die Zukunft**:

to remember to do sth = *daran denken, etw. zu tun*
to forget to do sth = *vergessen, etw. zu tun*
to stop to do sth = *unterbrechen/innehalten, um etw. zu tun;*
stehen bleiben, um etw. zu tun

IV. Rewrite the sentences in the first person and with the verb "remember". ●●

1. When he was a child Malcolm fell off his bike and broke a tooth.
   "I can remember ... ."

2. When Julie was young she sprayed perfume in her eyes and had to go to hospital.
   "I can remember ... ."

3. David once fell into the pond while feeding the ducks.
   "I can remember ... ."

4. When she was seven Tracy drove her mother's car to the shops.
   "I can remember ... ."

V. Complete the sentences using a gerund or infinitive construction.

1. I can never forget ... (see) my daughter for the first time.
2. Don't forget ... (ring) your grandma tonight, will you?
3. Did you forget ... (put) some sugar in this tea?
4. They will never forget ... (go) on holiday for the first time together.

VI. What's the difference? Translate into German.

1. He stopped to smoke.
2. He stopped smoking.

17B

Feelings and impressions

After the show

A group of boys have just watched a *puppet show*, in which "*the goodie*" is an old *wizard* with a bad memory and "*the baddie*" is a *gigantic alien* monster. Which of
5 the characters did the boys like best?

1 Boy: I like the wizard because he kept forgetting things.
2 Boy: I like the alien because he was enormous.
3 Boy: I like Ben because he was brave.
4 Boy: I like the dog because he was funny.

10 The children seem to be quite excited after the show. How did the show make them feel?

1 Boy: It made me feel excited.
2 Boy: It made me laugh.
3 Boy: It made me feel nervous.
15 4 Boy: It made me *giggle*.

At the exhibition

Some young people are visiting the Festival art exhibition to see the work of
Harvey Daniels, who was a painter and print-maker. Which exhibits do they like
best and why?

20 1 Visitor: I like these two paintings. I prefer this one as I like the way he uses the
blues. He uses many different colours. I find this exciting.
2 Visitor: I like this picture the most. I like the way he uses light and dark. I think
it is a very balanced picture and I find the dark colours mysterious.
3 Visitor: I like this print very much. I like the way he paints the different *shapes*.
25   The colours are very strong and I find it lively and fun.

During the interval

A large audience is watching the performance of "Equus". At the interval some of
them talk about their reactions to the play.

1 Man: I thought it was superb; a brilliant production.
30 1 Woman: I found it quite *disturbing*; a rather shocking experience.

2 Woman: I found it quite shocking, too; a very powerful performance.
2 Man: Oh, I didn't think it was so shocking, but I thought the *lighting* was
           very effective.
1 Man: The costumes were quite simple – except the horses' heads –
35   but they are very dramatic.
1 Woman: The actors were excellent: *convincing* and very professional.
2 Woman: The *set* was very simple – rather like a boxing ring.

puppet show	Puppentheater	shape	*hier*: Figuren, Formen
"the goodie"	„der Gute"	interval	Pause
wizard	Zauberer, Magier	disturbing	*hier*: beunruhigend
"the baddie"	„der Böse"	lighting	Beleuchtung
gigantic	riesig, gewaltig	convincing	überzeugend
alien	fremd, außerirdisch	set	*hier*: Bühnenbild
giggle	kichern		

Understanding the text.

True or false or the text doesn't say?

	True	False	Doesn't say
1. The boys didn't enjoy the puppet show.			
2. Harvey Daniels paints and makes prints.			
3. The performance of "Equus" was sold out.			

Answer these questions using your own words as far as possible.

4. Did all the boys react positively to the puppet show? Explain.
5. What do the three visitors to the exhibition have in common in their reactions to Harvey Daniels' paintings?
6. Do any of the people talking about "Equus" express the same opinion?

What's the English equivalent for the following German words and expressions?

7. Ausstellung
8. Aufführung
9. Pause
10. außer (ausgenommen)

And what about you?

11. Which of the three events – a puppet show, an art exhibition or a theatre performance – would you like to go to? Why?
12. Do you think it is good to show your emotions to other people? Or do you think it is better to keep your feelings to yourself? Write a short comment of about 50 words giving your opinion.

Verb + object + infinitive without "to"
Verb + Objekt + Infinitiv ohne "to"

The show **made me feel** excited.	Die Vorstellung hat mich aufgeregt.
It **made me feel** nervous.	Sie hat mich nervös gemacht.
It **made me laugh**.	Sie brachte mich zum Lachen.

Einige Anwendungsmöglichkeiten für den Infinitiv ohne *"to"* wurden bereits in *Part One* behandelt: nach allen unvollständigen Hilfsverben (z.B. *I can't help you.*) sowie nach den Fügungen *had better* (*We'd better go now.*) und *would rather* (*I'd rather stay at home than go to their party.*).
(Vgl. dazu Modul 2A, S. 27; Modul 4A, S. 60; Modul 10A, S. 159.)

Es gibt im Englischen aber auch die **Konstruktion Vollverb + Objekt + Infinitiv ohne *"to"***. Diese lässt sich u.a. mit *make* und *let* bilden:
Das Verb ***make + object + infinitive without "to"*** bedeutet *jemanden (veran)lassen, bringen zu ..., zwingen* (*The film made me cry.* Der Film brachte mich zum Weinen.).
Das Verb ***let + object + infinitive without "to"*** bedeutet *(zu)lassen, jemandem erlauben zu ...* (*They let us decide.* Sie lassen/ließen uns entscheiden.).

Exercises

I. Match the two halves of the sentences. ●●

1. Peeling onions makes you ...   a. feel uncomfortable.
2. Drinking alcohol can make you ...   b. want to have a drink.
3. Watching a funny film makes you ...   c. giggle.
4. Hot weather makes you ...   d. cry.
5. Eating peanuts makes you ...   e. feel tired.
6. Tickling somebody makes them ...   f. feel good.

II. Rewrite these sentences using the verb "let". The first words are given in brackets.

1. Clare didn't allow me to read the letter.   (Clare ... .)
2. My parents never said I could stay out late.   (My parents ... .)
3. The school does not permit us to use dictionaries.   (The school ... .)
4. I drove Simon's car yesterday.   (Simon ... .)

III. Put the parts of the sentences into the correct order.
   Make sure the adverb is in the right position. ●●

1. acting/very much/she/likes
2. at/were you/on Saturday night/the party/?
3. well/the piano/plays/he
4. she/to work/walks/every morning
5. rehearse/he/all day/does/?
6. to/recently/have you been/the theatre/?

*IV. Don't mix up -ed adjectives (they describe people's reactions) and
     -ing adjectives (they describe things). Look at the example and complete
     the sentences below using the correct word from the box.*

Example:
She was annoyed when he didn't arrive on time.
It's annoying when you miss a train.

> excited   •   exciting

1. Were you ... when you passed your driving test?
2. Do you find New Year's Eve ...?

> shocked   •   shocking

3. The pictures of the aeroplane crash were ... .
4. They were ... when they heard of the accident.

> convinced   •   convincing

5. He was ... that somebody had stolen his wallet.
6. Your arguments are not particularly ... .

> interested   •   interesting

7. Was it ... to live abroad for a year?
8. Are they ... in travelling?

*V. Which sentence (1-6) below describes which underlined word in the text?
    Match them.*

"We saw a new production of 'Much Ado About Nothing' last weekend. It was
a really good <u>cast</u> and I thought the <u>direction</u> was excellent. Shirley O'Connor
gave a brilliant <u>performance</u>. The <u>set</u> was superb, too, and the <u>costumes</u> were
wonderful. It was given a great <u>review</u> in the paper."

1. the clothes which the actors and actresses wear
2. all the actors and actresses
3. the buildings and furniture on the stage
4. the way the performance was organized by the director
5. comments by somebody who watched the play
6. the way an actor or actress plays their part

VI. Read this short extract from the play "Equus".
Who do you think the people are talking about?

ACT ONE

12

[DALTON *comes in to the square: heavy-set, mid-fifties.*]

DALTON: Dr Dysart?

DYSART: Mr Dalton. It's very good of you to come.

DALTON: It is, actually. In my opinion the boy should be in prison.
Not in a hospital at the tax-payers' expense.

DYSART: Please sit down.

[DALTON *sits.*]

This must have been a terrible experience for you.

DALTON: Terrible? I don't think I'll ever get over it. Jill's had a
nervous breakdown.

DYSART: Jill?

DALTON: The girl who worked for me. Of course, she feels responsible in a way. Being the one who introduced him in the first place.

DYSART: He was introduced to the stable by a girl?

DALTON: Jill Mason. He met her somewhere, and asked for a job.
She told him to come and see me. I wish to Christ she never had.

DYSART: But when he first appeared he didn't seem in any way
peculiar?

DALTON: No, he was bloody good. He'd spend hours with the
horses cleaning and grooming them, way over the call of duty. I
thought he was a real find.

DYSART: Apparently, during the whole time he worked for you, he
never actually rode.

DALTON: That's true.

DYSART: Wasn't that peculiar?

DALTON: Very . . . *If* he didn't.

DYSART: What do you mean?

[DALTON *rises.*]

DALTON: Because on and off, that whole year, I had the feeling the
horses were being taken out at night.

DYSART: At night?

17C

Jonathan Carter and Eileen Williams – dedicated to the arts

Listen to Jonathan Carter and Eileen Williams talking about the Sevenoaks Summer Festival. Then answer the questions below.

I. Which expression in the brackets completes the sentences? Underline it.

1. Jonathan says the Festival is organized for the (pupils' parents/town community).
2. When he is planning the programme for the Festival Jonathan likes to choose a (wide variety/small number) of events.
3. Eileen makes it clear that publicity for the Festival is (very/not so) important.
4. Jonathan says that many of the performers at the Festival are from the (professional/amateur) world.
5. For Jonathan one of the highlights of the Festival is to see (young/old) people enjoying themselves.

II. Complete the following sentences using a word from the interview.
   The first letter is given.

1. A v _ _ _ _ is a place where an event is taking place.
2. If you give a d _ _ _ _ _ _ _ to an organization, you give it money because you support what it does.

3. Many young people prefer pop music to c _ _ _ _ _ _ _ music.

4. A v _ _ _ _ _ _ _ _ is somebody who does some useful work but does not get paid for it.

5. The word s _ _ _ _ is used to describe the teachers in a school or a company's employees.

6. If you study d _ _ _ _ you learn about how to act in, direct and produce plays.

7. A v _ _ _ _ _ _ _ _ is somebody who plays the violin well.

8. A r _ _ is a line of seats in a cinema or theatre.

17D

Meterman – composer, conductor and singer

I. In five of the six paragraphs one sentence does not belong there. In one of the six paragraphs two sentences do not belong there. Can you find all seven sentences?

1. Meterman is driving along singing the Meterman song. He turns to the camera. He eats a sandwich. "My latest composition is almost completed," he says. "I'm just waiting for the last note. And inspiration could strike any minute now."

2. Suddenly inspiration strikes. It begins to rain. Meterman stops his car, gets out and lays his music on the bonnet of his van. "Now I can *initial* my masterpiece," he announces. "W. A. M., Wolfgang Amadeus ... Meterman! In fact tonight one of my pieces is being performed by an excellent *choir* down in the *village hall*."

3. Meterman enters the village hall in the middle of a rehearsal. He likes the sound of the choir but he does not think much of the conductor. Perhaps all the tickets have been sold. Immediately he thinks of an elegant way of getting rid of him. He decides to switch off the stage lights.

4. As soon as the lights go out, the choir stops singing. It's nearly time for lunch. The conductor goes behind the stage to find out what is happening. "For goodness' sake," he says to Meterman. "What do you think you're doing?" Meterman opens a door pretending to look for the problem. "Perhaps you might help me find the *fuse box*, my dear sir?" he asks politely. The guitar was a present from his uncle. He lets the conductor go in front of him but as soon as he has gone through the door, he pushes him through and locks the door. Now the conductor can't get back onto the stage. Meterman can take control.

5. The church bells ring. Meterman stands in front of the choir and takes out his *baton*. "Now I have some music here which you might enjoy singing," he says. "I composed it myself, actually." The choir sings:

> Meterman is my name
> Reading meters is my game
> I know everyone
> Everyone knows me
> Read your meter and
> Have a cup of tea.

6. A few minutes later the conductor appears. He has managed to escape through a window at the back of the village hall. A bird flies past his head. He listens to the choir and seems pleased. "Well, I must say, that really was quite good!" he says walking up to Meterman. "Congratulations! Now I honestly think that what it needs is a soloist."

Meterman joins the choir by taking up position in the middle of the front row. Now he's exactly where he wanted to be: centre stage!

composer	Komponist(in)	village hall	Gemeindesaal
initial	unterzeichnen (*mit Initialen*)	fuse box	Sicherungskasten
choir	(Gesangs-)Chor	baton	*hier*: Taktstock

II. One word – two meanings. Which words from the text are being described?

1. an argument and a number of people in a line
2. something you write down to remind yourself what to do and part of a piece of music
3. the front of a car and a type of hat

Are the pairs of words pronounced in the same way?

III. Complete the sentences using the correct words from the box.

1. It's not easy to ... a bike when you cycle over ice.
2. Can you please ... that you have got everything with you before you leave the plane.

3. I've got a lot of ... at the moment so I can't go out at the weekend.
4. I have an interesting ... but it doesn't pay well.

5. Did you see the ... on that shop window? It said "Please come in and browse."
6. Can I make a ... of your telephone number?

7. The lights are not on in the library. ... it's closed today.
8. After a long drive through the night they ... arrived in England.

Now translate the sentences into German.

17E

Entertainment

GARRICK 0171 494 5085/312 1990
(no bkg fee)
Some Experiences You Never Forget
WINNER OF 19 MAJOR AWARDS
The Royal National Theatre production
J B Priestléy's
AN INSPECTOR CALLS
"THRILLING...MUST BE SEEN" *D.Mail*
"One of the most intoxicating,
theatrically imaginative
experiences of the 1990s" *Eve.Stand.*
"TWO HOURS OF ENTHRALLING
VISUALLY STUNNING DRAMA" *D.Tel*
Mon-Fri 7.45, Sat 5.00 & 8.15, Wed mat 2.30

 0991 992 015

GIELGUD THEATRE 0171 494 5065/
0171 312 1990
"BOB HOSKINS's
STAGE COMEBACK IS AN
ELECTRIFYING HIT" *S. Express*
JAMES CALLIS
"an astonishing performance" *Gdn*
OLD WICKED SONGS
directed by **Elijah Moshinsky**
An "EMOTIONAL PUNCH
THAT LEAVES YOU
REELING WITH PLEASURE...
A RIVETING NIGHT"*Eve Std*
Mon-Sat 7.30pm, Thurs mat 2.30pm
Sat mat 4pm.
Running Time 2hrs 15 mins
MUST END 11 JAN

 0991 992 016

HAYMARKET 0171 930 8800 cc 344 4444
Grps 930 8800/413 3321
Tue - Sat 8pm Mats Thur & Sat 3pm
LYNN REDGRAVE
"TRULY BREATHTAKING
The most impressive performance
on any London stage" *Spectator*
SHAKESPEARE FOR MY FATHER
"UNFORGETTABLE. A PIECE
OF THEATRE HISTORY" S.Tms
ENDS TONIGHT

JESSICA LANGE
TOBY   IMOGEN
STEPHENS   STUBBS
in TENNESSEE WILLIAMS'
A STREETCAR NAMED DESIRE
directed by **PETER HALL**
Red Price Prevs from Wed

 0991 992 042

HER MAJESTY'S 24hr 494 5400 (bkg fee)
CC 0171 344 4444/420 0000 (bkg fee)
Grps 0171 494 5454/413 3311/436 5588.
ANDREW LLOYD WEBBER'S
AWARD WINNING MUSICAL
THE PHANTOM OF THE OPERA
Directed by HAROLD PRINCE
NOW BOOKING TO MAY 97
Eves 7.45, Mats Wed & Sat 3.00
Apply to Box Office Daily for Returns

 0991 992 020

LYRIC 0171 494 5045
cc 420 0100/344 4444 (bkg fee)
"THE MOST UNPRETENTIOUSLY
ENJOYABLE SHOW IN LONDON" *Tms*
BY JEEVES
THE ALAN AYCKBOURN &
ANDREW LLOYD WEBBER MUSICAL
"...HAD THE AUDIENCE
BUCKLING UP WITH LAUGHTER" *Ind*
Eves 7.45, Mats Wed & Sat 3pm
Concessions available

 0991 992 019

NATIONAL THEATRE 0171 928 2252:
Grps 0171 620 0741; 24hr cc bkg fee
0171 420 0000.
OLIVIER Today 2.00 & 7.15, Mon 7.15
(PREVIEWS) GUYS AND DOLLS Based
on a story and characters of Damon
Runyon. Music and lyrics by Frank
Loesser. Book by Jo Swerling & Abe
Burrows
LYTTELTON Today 2.15 & 7.30 JOHN
GABRIEL BORKMAN Henrik Ibsen in a
new version by Nicholas Wright. Mon 7.30
DEATH OF A SALESMAN Arthur Miller
COTTESLOE Ton't, Mon 7.30 (PREVIEWS)
THE CRIPPLE OF INISHMAAN Martin
McDonagh.

 0991 992 034 (Olivier)

 0991 992 033 (Lyttelton)

NEW LONDON Drury Lane WC2
BO 0171 405 0072 CC 0171 404 4079
24hr 0171 344 4444/0171 420 0000.
Groups 0171 413 3311/436 5588
THE ANDREW LLOYD WEBBER/
T.S. ELIOT INTERNATIONAL
AWARD-WINNING MUSICAL
CATS
Eves 7.45 Mats Tue & Sat 3.00.
LATECOMERS NOT ADMITTED WHILE
AUDITORIUM IS IN MOTION. PLEASE
BE PROMPT. Bars open at 6.45.
LIMITED NUMBER OF SEATS AVAIL
DAILY FROM BOX OFFICE

 0991 992 022

OLD VIC 928 7616/312 8034
THE PETER HALL COMPANY
Simon Ward   Carol Drinkwater
Deborah Grant   Robert East
Barbara Murray   Richard Todd
OSCAR WILDE'S MASTERPIECE
AN IDEAL HUSBAND
"GREAT & GLORIOUS" *S.Tms*
Mon-Sat 7.30, Mats Wed & Sat 3.00
LAST 7 WEEKS

 0991 992 023

THE WEATHER IS CHANGING   UNIT 18

18A

On the beach

We see a family of four on the beach in summer. While the children are playing, the parents sit in their deck chairs and talk about the weather. The father reads in his newspaper that it has been the hottest July since *records* began. His wife doesn't
5 mind. She thinks that since they had the highest snowfall for 30 years in the previous winter they deserve a hot summer. Suddenly the children, who have had their faces painted, come running up.

Father: Here comes trouble.
Girl: Hi, Mum. You look like a grilled tomato.
10 Boy: And Dad looks like a boiled *lobster*.
Father: Thanks very much. Do you want to know what you look like?
Girl: Okay ...
Father: You look like a *tribe* of Zulu *warriors*.

(The boy and girl pretend to dance like Zulu warriors.)

15 Mother: I hope it will *come off* when you wash.
Boy: But seriously. You shouldn't *lie out in the sun* so much. All your
           generation think about when you are on holiday is getting a suntan.
           You ought to wear a hat!

Girl: You think it looks healthy but really it doesn't look good.
20 Mother: All right. That's enough. Don't forget we've been sunbathing for years
          and years and if you're careful there is really no harm in it.
    Boy: You can't be serious. Everyone knows the sun's rays are more harmful
          nowadays. Haven't you heard about the hole in the *ozone layer*?
    Father: Of course I've heard about the hole in the ozone layer. All I'm saying
25   is that a little sunbathing does no harm at all. And it's ridiculous to go
          around completely covered up.

record	Aufzeichnung	lie out in the sun	*hier*: in der Sonne
lobster	Hummer		liegen
tribe	Stamm	ozone layer	Ozonschicht
warrior	Krieger		
come off	ab-, heruntergehen		
	(*Farbe etc.*)		

Understanding the text.

Which ending (a-c) best completes the statement (1-5)? Tick it.

1. England has had ...
    a) a hot summer and a mild winter.
    b) a hot summer and a cold winter.
    c) a mild summer and a cold winter.

2. The parents are happy to ...
    a) sit in the sun.   b) avoid the sun.   c) play in the sun.

3. The children think their parents should ...
    a) have their faces painted.
    b) read more about the environment.
    c) cover up their skin.

4. The children seem to be a bit ...
    a) funny.   b) disrespectful.   c) serious.

5. The parents ...
    a) listen carefully to what their children say.
    b) ignore what their children say.
    c) make fun of what their children say.

Further question. Answer in your own words as far as possible.

6. Do you remember what happens at the end of the television scene? How do we
    know that the children "won" the argument?

What's the English for these German words and expressions?

7. Liegestuhl   9. lächerlich
8. Ozonschicht   10. schädlich

And what about you?

11. Do you like to have a suntan? Why/Why not?
12. Can you explain what the problem is with the "hole" in the ozone layer?

---

to lie/to lay – to rise/to raise

They **lay** on the beach all day.	Sie lagen den ganzen Tag (über) am Strand.
He **laid** the newspaper on the table.	Er legte die Zeitung auf den Tisch.
The sun **rose** over the top of the hill.	Die Sonne ging über dem Berggipfel auf.
She **raised** her hand and wanted to wave.	Sie hob ihre Hand und wollte winken.

Die Verben *to lie/to lay* bzw. *to rise/to raise* kann man leicht miteinander ver-
wechseln. *To lie* (*liegen*) und *to rise* (u.a. *sich erheben*) sind **unregelmäßig** (*lie
– lay – lain*; *rise – rose – risen*) und **intransitiv**, d.h. nach ihnen darf **kein direktes Objekt** (Akkusativ, Objekt im 4. Fall) stehen. Die Verben *to lay* (*legen*) und
to raise (u.a. *heben*) sind dagegen **regelmäßig** (*lay – laid – laid* (nur die Schreib-
weise ist unregelmäßig!); *raise – raised – raised*) und **transitiv**, d.h. auf sie folgt
ein direktes Objekt.

Exercises

I. Which verb form in the brackets is correct? Underline it.

1. They (rose/raised) from the table and left the room.
2. She (rose/raised) her glass and said cheers.
3. Do you like it when the temperature (rises/raises) above 30°C?
4. When he gets angry he (rises/raises) his voice.
5. We used to (rise/raise) with the sun and go to bed at dusk.
6. Men used to (rise/raise) their hats when they passed women in the streets.

Now translate your sentences into German. You will need more verbs in German than in English.

II. Put the words in the box into the correct sentence.

> "lie"   •   "lay"

1. Don't throw the book on the floor. ... it on the table!
2. Don't ... in bed all day. Get up!

> "lay"   •   "laid"

3. He fell on the floor and ... completely still.
4. She ... her hand on his shoulder.

> "has laid"   •   "has lain"

5. The ship ... on the ocean floor for over 200 years.
6. She ... down her passport on this table and forgotten it!

III. Translate into English. Exercises I and II will help you.

1. Das Schloss liegt im Zentrum der Stadt.
2. Sie hob die Hand, um die Frage zu beantworten.
3. Die Sonne geht im Osten auf.
4. Er legte seine Tasche auf den Tisch.
5. Die Zahl der Unfälle ist gestiegen.
6. Der Hund legte sich auf den Boden.

A view of the River Thames in London

IV. One word, many meanings. Match a question (1-4) with an appropriate answer (a-d). ●●

1. What does he look like?
2. What is he like?
3. Would you like tea?
4. Do you like tea?

a. I'd prefer coffee.
b. He's short and fair.
c. Yes, I love it.
d. He's a bit serious.

Match the descriptions below with the questions (1-4) above.

5. When you ask this question you want to find out what somebody wants to have at the moment of speaking.
6. When you ask this question you want to find out about somebody's character.
7. When you ask this question you want to find out what somebody likes in a general way.
8. When you ask this question you want to find out about somebody's appearance.

V. Which question produces this answer? Write it down.

1. Oh, she's really nice. You'd like her.
2. Yes. In fact I've been to Germany every summer for the last five years.
3. Well, he's quite tall and he's got black hair.
4. I'll have a pint of bitter, please.

VI. Look at the table and answer the questions. ●●

AROUND BRITAIN					
24 hrs to 5 pm: b = bright; c = cloud; d = drizzle; ds = dust storm; du = dull; f = fair; fg = fog; g = gale; h = hail; r = rain; sh = shower; sl = sleet; sn = snow; s = sun; t = thunder					
	Sun hrs	Rain inches	Max C	F	
Belfast	-	0.01	8	46	du
Birmingham	-	0.01	2	36	fg
Buxton	-	0.02	2	36	fg
Cardiff	3.7	0.01	7	45	s
Edinburgh	-	-	7	45	c
Falmouth	-	-	9	48	du
Folkestone	8.0	-	7	45	s
Glasgow	-	0.01	8	46	d
Hastings	7.4	-	6	43	s
Leeds	0.7	-	5	41	fg
London	7.2	-	11	52	s
Manchester	1.8	0.01	6	43	b
Morecambe	1.9	0.01	7	45	b
Newcastle	0.4	-	3	37	du
Norwich	7.1	0.01	9	48	s
Oxford	2.3	-	6	43	fg
Poole	6.1	-	9	48	s
Sandown	7.0	0.01	8	46	s
Scarborough	-	0.01	2	36	fg
Torquay	3.3	0.01	9	48	s
Ventnor	7.5	-	9	48	s
Weymouth	6.4	-	8	46	s

1. Where was it the warmest in Britain yesterday?
2. Which place had the most sunshine?
3. Which three places were the coldest?
4. Was it dull in both Glasgow and Belfast? Explain.
5. Which place had the most rain?
6. Was the weather the same in Leeds and Oxford? Explain.

18B

The Thames Barrier ●●

With the construction of the Thames Barrier Londoners no longer live in fear of
floods from the Thames. At times of danger the great gates are raised to create a
barrier from one side of the river to the other. At other times the gates rest unseen
5 on the riverbed.

Keith Cleverly, Manager of the Thames Barrier Visitors Centre, explains to some
visitors why there has always been a risk of flooding in London. One reason, he says,
is the *surge tides*. Another is that the water level of the Thames is rising at the rate
of 75 centimetres every hundred years. Another point, Keith suggests, is that the
10 Thames is getting narrower. In Roman times it was 800 metres wide at West-
minster. Today it measures 250 metres. Also the south-east of England is gradually
sinking. Ever since the last Ice Age, Keith says, England has been sinking and
north-west Scotland has been rising.

Steve East, Administration Manager, explains that it took just eight years to build
15 the Thames Barrier. Work started in 1974 and was completed in 1982. He adds that
the risk of flooding in London is *considerable*, above all when there is a surge tide.
The visitors ask how they know when there is a surge tide.

1 Visitor: How do you know? I mean, how can you tell that there is going to be one?
Steve: It's all based on computer *prediction* in our control room over there.

20 1 Visitor: How much *notice* do you get?

Steve: Usually we get about 12 hours' warning of a surge tide, sometimes more,
            sometimes less, it depends.

2 Visitor: And how long does it take to close the Barrier?

Steve: It takes just 30 minutes to close the Barrier. That's to say, we can close it
25   in 30 minutes if necessary.

2 Visitor: How often do you have to close the Barrier?

Steve: It varies. On average about four times a year.

surge tide	Springflut	prediction	Vorhersage
considerable	beträchtlich, beachtlich	notice	*hier:* Vorwarnung

Understanding the text.

Complete these sentences using the information in the text.

1. The Thames Barrier was built in order to ... .
2. If you go to Woolwich in London you won't always see the Thames Barrier gates because ... .
3. The people who operate the Barrier rely on computers to ... .
4. We can see that the Thames Barrier was not a waste of money because ... .

Further questions. Answer them using your own words as far as possible.

5. Is the Thames Barrier very new to London? Explain.
6. Does it seem to you as if the Barrier is very effective? Say why/why not.

Write down the English for the following German words and expressions.

7. ... es ist unterschiedlich
8. Wie lange dauert es, die "Thames Barrier" zu schließen?
9. durchschnittlich
10. viermal pro Jahr

And what about you?

11. Can you think of any other natural catastrophes which can affect a city? Explain.
12. Have you ever been to London (or any other large city where English is spoken)? Say when you went and what you did there.

The present perfect continuous
Die Verlaufsform des Perfekts

Ever **since** the last Ice Age the south-east of England **has been sinking**.

Seit Beginn der letzten Eiszeit sinkt der Südosten Englands (ab).

The manager **has been talking** to visitors all morning.

Der Manager spricht schon den ganzen Vormittag (über) mit Besuchern. (*oder*: Der Manager hat den ganzen Vormittag über ... gesprochen.)

In diesem Modul soll noch einmal die **Verlaufsform des Perfekts** wiederholt werden. (Vgl. *Part One*, Modul 10B, S. 162 und *Part Two*, Modul 14A, S. 13.) Sie drückt aus, dass eine **Handlung noch nicht beendet ist** oder **eben erst beendet wurde**. Im Gegensatz zum Gebrauch der einfachen Form des Perfekts möchte der Sprecher bei der Verlaufsform nicht das Ergebnis, sondern das **Andauern** oder den **Ablauf** einer Handlung **betonen**.
Ebenso wie die einfache Form des Perfekts steht auch die Verlaufsform oft in Verbindung mit *since* und *for*.

Exercises

I. Complete these mini-dialogues by using the present perfect continuous form of the verb in brackets. ●●

1. How long ... (you, live) here?
   Oh, for about five years, I think.

2. He ... (work) on the translation all morning.
   I know. At that rate he'll never finish it.

3. What ... (you, do) all day?
   Lots of things. Do you really want to know?

4. We ... (walk) around the city for over an hour now.
   You're right. Shall we go somewhere and have a cup of coffee?

5. I ... (read) this book the whole evening but I'm still not enjoying it.
   Aren't you? That surprises me.

6. Why ... (he, ring) me every day for the last week?
   Ask a stupid question ... .

II. Which of the verb forms (present perfect simple or present perfect continuous) in the brackets is more appropriate? Underline it. ●●

1. I'm really tired because I (have been driving/have driven) non-stop for ten hours.
2. I've got some bad news: I (have been crashing/have crashed) your car this morning.
3. Hi, Tracy. I haven't seen you for ages. What (have you been doing/have you done) since we last met?
4. Do you know what's happened? I (have been losing/have lost) my new watch somewhere.

III. Past tense or present perfect tense? Translate into English. The verbs in brackets will help you. ●●

1. Wie lange wartest du schon auf meinen Anruf? (*to wait*)
2. Als ich 16 war, habe ich ein Jahr lang eine Schule in Schottland besucht. (*to go*)
3. Wir waren noch nie in Großbritannien. (*to be*)
4. Wann sind Sie zum letzten Mal im Kino gewesen? (*to go*)

The question words "what" and "how"

Die Fragewörter "what" und "how"

What colour are his eyes?	**Welche** (**Was für eine**) Farbe haben seine Augen?
What happened last Friday?	**Was** geschah letzten Freitag?
What time is it?	**Wie** spät ist es?
(*or*: **What**'s the time?)	
What's the capital of Scotland?	**Wie** heißt die Hauptstadt von Schottland?
How are you?	**Wie** geht es dir (Ihnen)?

Das englische Fragewort ***what*** kann man im Deutschen mit *was* bzw. *welche* oder *wie* übersetzen. Auch entspricht nicht jedes *wie* im Deutschen einem ***how*** im Englischen. Da sich die korrekte Anwendung nicht durch Regeln, sondern nur aus dem **Sprachgebrauch** heraus lernen lässt, liegt hier eine Fehlerquelle für Lernende, die Deutsch als Muttersprache haben.

IV. Translate the questions into English. Be careful with the question word. ●●

1. Wie heißen Sie?   Tony O'Neill.
2. Wie ist sie?   She's very quiet.
3. Wie lange dauert der Flug? (*to take*)   About an hour.
4. Wie heißt „Lineal" auf Englisch?   The word is "ruler".
5. Wie schaut er aus?   He's tall and thin.
6. Wieviel Uhr ist es?   It's nearly four.
7. Wie alt ist sie?   Twenty-two.
8. Wie komme ich zum Flughafen? (*to get*) The easiest way is by train.

V. Environmental problems. Which words in the box go with which definitions (1-6) below?

> air pollution ● flooding ● hurricanes ● overpopulation ●
> starvation ● waste disposal

1. when people have so little to eat that they die
2. very strong winds which cause great damage
3. when a place which is usually dry is covered with water
4. when dangerous substances like carbon dioxide get into the air
5. throwing away material which you no longer want or need
6. when there are too many people in one place

VI. Look at the six environmental problems in exercise V. Which one do you think is the most serious? Why? Write a short comment (about 50 words) explaining your point of view.

18C

William Richardson – an RNLI coxswain

Listen carefully to what William Richardson says about the work he does and answer the questions below.

I. Which sentence (a-c) best completes the statement? Tick it.

1. As coxswain William Richardson is ...
   a) one of the team on a boat.
   b) in charge of the team on a boat.
   c) training to become part of the team on a boat.

An RNLI lifeboat in action

2. If there is an emergency out at sea ...
    a) 6 men go out on the lifeboat.
    b) 18 men go out on the lifeboat.
    c) 12 men go out on the lifeboat.

3. If someone is rescued by the Royal National Lifeboat Institution (RNLI) it costs them ...
    a) a lot of money.   b) a small charge.   c) nothing.

4. William Richardson seems to have a good knowledge ...
    a) of the weather and the English coastline.
    b) of the fish and birds along the coast.
    c) of what ships are transporting.

5. The job of the RNLI is to ...
    a) make money.   b) save people's lives.   c) offer training courses.

II. Further questions. Can you answer them using your own words?

1. How is the RNLI financed?
2. William Richardson mentions a "lifeboat man's nightmare". What is this nightmare exactly?
3. William Richardson also talks about "salvage". What is salvage and why does it play such an important role during emergencies at sea?

William Richardson at the helm
(*am Steuer*)

III. Complete this text using the words from the box below.

> bay • changeable • Channel • lane • station • tip

The lifeboat ... at Dungeness stands on the ... of the Kent coast, looking across the ... to Dover and out across the English ... to the coast of France. This is the busiest shipping ... in the world, with some of the most difficult and ... weather.

IV. These words are difficult to pronounce.
Can you remember how to say them? ●●

1. coxswain   4. knots
2. buoy   5. dinghy
3. salvage

18D

Meterman the meteorologist

I. In each paragraph two words have been taken out. Which words are they?
The first letter has been given.

Meterman has gone to the b... . It looks like rain but as a meteorological expert Meterman is sure that the sun will begin to shine again very soon. He looks up at the s... and thinks for a second. "In about nine minutes," he says. "Fingers crossed."

On his way to a quieter part of the beach, Meterman stops to tell the viewer what he's got with him: a beachball, a b... and spade, suntan l..., sun hat, a little mat and a rubber ring.

Meterman sees two boys building a sand castle and decides to build one himself. Soon an a... begins about who has made the best one. "My castle's got four towers," Meterman says. "And a special gateway and a bridge with *seaweed*." The boys refuse to give in. "All I'm saying is my castle has got the biggest tower and my castle is the best," one of them r... .

The boys run off when their father calls for them. Meterman looks into the camera. "Children are so c... these days," he says. "But still, if they want to *take on* an expert, I'll show them what an expert can do." He goes back to his van to f... a large bucket and spade. Then he builds a huge castle and destroys the children's castle. "That'll teach them," he says. "Now, it's time for my little *snooze*. I think I'll take forty winks in the sun."

Soon the boys are back. They see what Meterman has done and decide to take revenge. In the meantime Meterman finds himself running out into the w... to rescue a young woman from *drowning*. He c... her to the beach and has to *administer* the kiss of life.

Suddenly Meterman wakes up. He has been d... . He is lying on the beach covered in sand from head to f... . The tide is coming in and it has begun to rain. Meterman looks at the camera. "It never rains but it pours!"

seaweed	Seetang	snooze	Schläfchen
take on	es aufnehmen mit, herausfordern	drown	ertrinken
		administer	*hier*: verabreichen

II. Match the expressions with their explanations.

1. to keep your fingers crossed
2. to have forty winks
3. to give somebody the kiss of life
4. "it never rains but it pours"

a. you wish something will happen as you would like it to happen
b. one unfortunate event will probably be followed by another unfortunate event
c. a short rest during the day
d. you put your mouth on somebody's mouth and breathe into their lungs to make them start breathing again

18E

At the seaside

"*Actually I sell solar sun-beds.*"

GETTING AROUND   UNIT 19

19A

A tour of Gravesend ●●

The statue of Pocahontas in front of St George's Church

Paul, who needs a *wheelchair* to get around, wants to show some visitors Gravesend, his home town. He begins his tour at Windmill Hill. Since it's uphill all the way, he decides to take his car.

5 First Paul drives along Clarence Place. Then he turns left up Rouge Lane and carries on to the top of Windmill Hill. From the top of the hill there's a good view of the Thames. Paul explains some of the sights.

Paul: London is up that way and Southend is down that way, on the north side of the river.

10 Woman: What is opposite us, on the other side?

Paul: That's Tilbury over there. It's the port for London. On this side is the *county* of Kent. On the other side is the county of Essex.

Woman: How do you get across?

Paul: There's a ferry that goes across the river from Gravesend to Tilbury and
15   there's a tunnel and a bridge further up the river. If you look between the trees you can just see the bridge in the distance.

Paul then takes his visitors to Gordon Promenade, Gordon Gardens and Khartoum Place, which are all named after *General Gordon*. Then he shows them the statue of *Pocahontas*, who died and was buried in Gravesend.

get around	herumkommen, -fahren (*im Sinne von*: beweglich sein)	Pocahontas	*(1595–1617); Angehörige eines Indianerstammes, die sich um den Frieden*
wheelchair	Rollstuhl		*zwischen den Ureinwohnern Amerikas und den*
wheelchair user	Rollstuhlfahrer		*europäischen Siedlern*
county	Grafschaft		*bemühte*
General Gordon	*brit. General (1833–1885), schaffte im Sudan den Sklavenhandel ab*		

Understanding the text.

True, false or the text doesn't say? Tick a column.

	True	False	Doesn't say
1. Gravesend is the town where Paul lives.			
2. Gravesend is in Kent.			
3. Gravesend is 20 miles from London.			

Further questions. Answer them in your own words as far as possible.

4. Why does Paul drive up to the top of Windmill Hill?
5. How can we see that a lot happens in the area around Gravesend?

Find the English for the following German expressions.

6. Heimatstadt
7. Aussicht
8. Hafen
9. Sehenswürdigkeiten
10. Fähre

And what about you?

11. Apart from getting around, what other sort of problems do you think people in wheelchairs have in their day-to-day lives?
12. What places of interest would you show visitors if they came to see your home town? Write three sentences giving some examples.

Prepositions of place and direction

Präpositionen des Ortes und der Richtung

We'll start **at** the top of Windmill Hill.

If you look **between** the trees, you can see the bridge.

There's a ferry that goes **across** the river.

Wir werden (oben) auf dem *Windmill Hill* beginnen.

Wenn Sie zwischen den Bäumen hindurchschauen, können Sie die Brücke sehen.

Es gibt eine Fähre, die über den Fluss führt. (Es gibt eine Fähre über den Fluss.)

◆ **Präpositionen des Ortes** beschreiben etwas **Statisches**, **Präpositionen der Richtung** etwas **Bewegliches**.

Die nachfolgende Übersicht nennt die wichtigsten Präpositionen beider Gruppen. Die schematischen Darstellungen zu den einzelnen Wörtern bzw. „Gegensatz"-Paaren sollen es erleichtern, sich die **räumliche Bedeutung** der einzelnen Präpositionen vorzustellen.

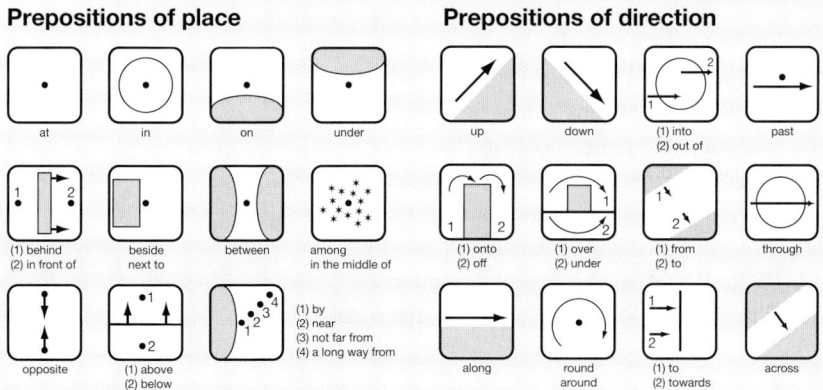

◆ Ähnlich wie im Deutschen besitzen auch im Englischen zahlreiche der oben genannten Präpositionen neben der räumlichen eine **zeitliche** oder **übertragene Bedeutung**, z.B. *He left the office **at** two o'clock **on** Friday afternoon. Who are you talking **to**?*

Exercises

I. Look at the map of Gravesend on the opposite page. These directions will take you from the train station to the Tilbury passenger ferry. Use the words and expressions in the box to complete the text. ●●

> along   ●   at   ●   on   ●   into   ●   next to   ●   on   ●   opposite   ●   up to

Leave Gravesend station and turn right ... Clive Road. Walk ... the roundabout and turn left. You should be walking ... Stone Street now. ... the end of Stone Street you will see Princes Street. It's ... you. As you go along Princes Street you will see St George's Church and the statue of Pocahontas ... your left. At the end of Princes Street turn right and ... the other side of West Street you will see the ferry pier. It is ... the town pier.

II. Look at the map again. Write down a short paragraph explaining the way from the train station to the tourist information office (Parrock Street).

III. Use the prepositions "at", "in" and "on" to complete the following sentences. ●●

1. Do people in Britain drive ... the left?
2. Look at those lambs ... that field!
3. Do you take sugar ... your tea?
4. There's a front door and an entrance ... the back.
5. Is your flat ... the ground floor?
6. We live ... the end of the street ... the left.
7. Would you like to live ... the country?
8. The weather forecast is always ... the second page.

IV. The words "in", "on" and "at" are also prepositions of time. Use one of these words to complete the sentences below. ●●

1. The course begins ... September and ends ... July.
2. The plane arrives ... 11 o'clock.
3. John Constable was born in England ... the end of the 18th century.
4. The wedding is ... 2 September.
5. We usually go out ... Friday evenings.
6. Do you ever work ... the weekend?
7. I'm going out and I'll be back ... twenty minutes.
8. I'll phone you ... Wednesday afternoon ... about 2 o'clock.

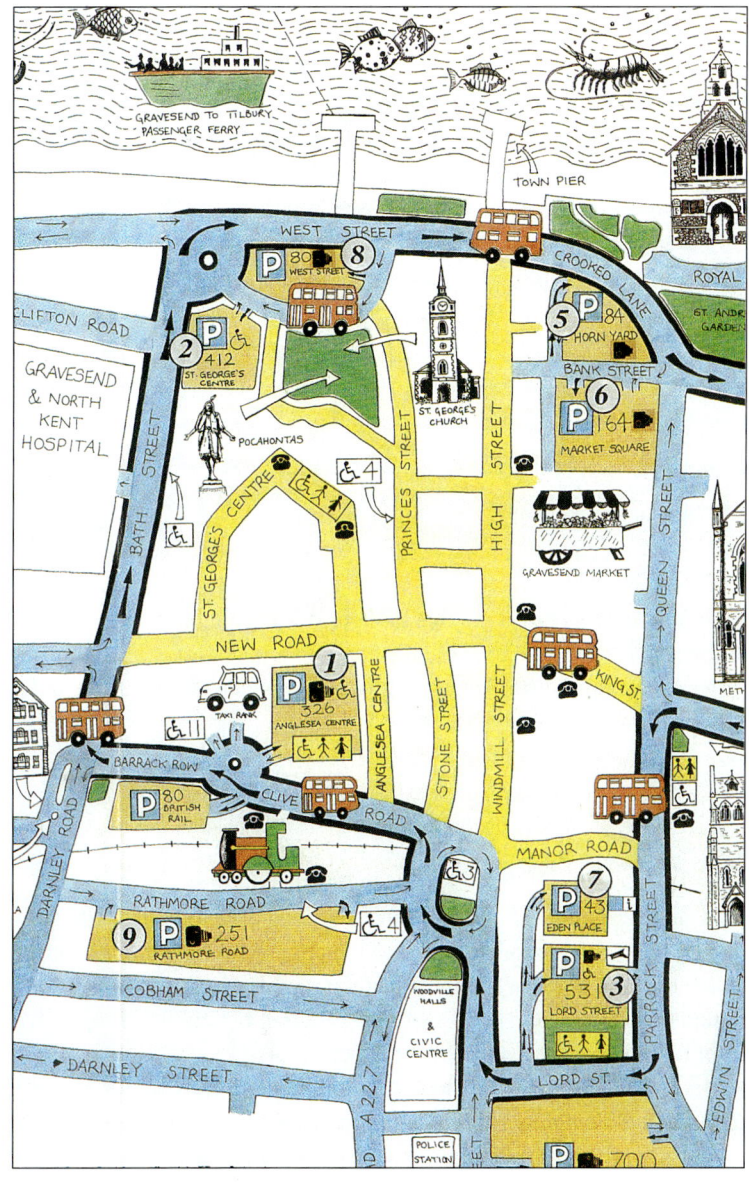

V. Many prepositions in English are very simple and you know them already.
Which prepositions are missing in these sentences? ●●

   1. The Channel Tunnel goes ... England to France.
   2. Are you for or ... a speed limit on motorways?
   3. We went to London ... train.
   4. You're very quiet. What are you thinking ...?
   5. You never told me that you were born ... Ireland.
   6. Did you use to have your own room ... home?
   7. We'll be ... holiday for the last two weeks in June.
   8. My daughter gave me this book ... my birthday.

VI. Which word in the box goes with which sentence below?
(Be careful, though. There are six sentences but eight words.)

> a driver ● a dog ● a hot-air balloon ● a cyclist ●
> a river ● a ship ● a train ● a tree

   1. He slid on the ice, fell off and broke his arm.
   2. It flows through the capital and then into the Mediterranean.
   3. It sails at 6.30.
   4. It was moving so much that we thought it was going to break.
   5. She had to brake hard to avoid driving into a lamppost.
   6. It was travelling at 100 kph through a tunnel when the fire broke out.

19B

Disability awareness ●●

Paul thinks that Gravesend is in many ways a special place because it makes it easy
for *disabled people* to get around. Some of the pavements have *slopes* and many of
the buses have access for wheelchairs. The town centre is good, too. There are several
5 disabled toilets and you can get a special key for them. Very few shops have steps
and a lot of them have automatic doors or open fronts.
The centre of Gravesend, King Street, has been completely *pedestrianized*. The
crossing places all have *dots* for blind people and the traffic lights make a *beeping
noise* to tell them when they should cross the road. People with *guide dogs* can take
10 them into shops or other public places.
Paul feels very strongly that the public needs to be made more *aware* that disabled
people are quite normal. Sometimes, however, they do have special *needs*. When he

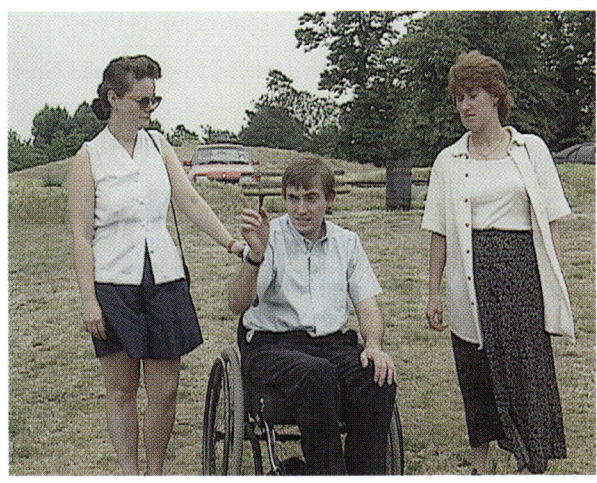

Paul with his visitors on the top of Windmill Hill

returns to the car park, for example, Paul sees that there's not enough space for him to get back into his car. "Oh no. Look at that," he says. "They must have seen the
15   sticker. They really shouldn't park so close." At that moment a woman runs up. She apologizes for parking too close to Paul's car. "Sorry about that," she says.

disability	*sinngemäß:* Bewusstsein	dot	Noppe
awareness	für Probleme der Behin-	beeping noise	*hier:* Piepton
	derten	guide dog	Blindenhund
disabled people	Behinderte	be aware	sich bewusst sein,
slope	Hang, Abhang; *hier:*		wissen, (er)kennen
	Abschrägung	(make sb aware	(jmdm. bewusst
pedestrianize	in eine Fußgängerzone	that ...)	machen, dass ...)
	umwandeln	need	Bedürfnis

Understanding the text.

Complete these sentences in a logical way using the information in the text and your own words as far as possible.

1.   Gravesend seems to be different from many other English towns. It ... .
2.   Blind people find it easy to cross the roads in Gravesend because ... .
3.   Paul, who sits in a wheelchair, wants other people to understand that disabled people are normal but ... .

Further questions. Answer them in complete sentences.

4. What makes it easy for people in wheelchairs to get around Gravesend?
5. Paul talks about disabled people's special needs. What need does Paul have which the woman in the car park was obviously not aware of?

Which word from the text is it?

6. the part of the street which people walk on
7. a way in or an entrance
8. to say sorry

Find the English for these German words.

9. Parkplatz
10. Aufkleber

And what about you?

11. Would you say most people are aware of disabled people's needs? Give a reason for your answer.
12. Do you think Gravesend is like most German towns and cities in the services which it provides for disabled people? Say why or why not.

Paul shows his visitors the centre of Gravesend

H ### Quantifiers

Mengenbezeichnungen

Many of the buses have access for wheelchair users.	Viele der Busse haben Einstiegsmöglichkeiten für Rollstuhlfahrer.
There are **several** disabled toilets.	Es gibt einige Toiletten für Behinderte.
There are **a lot of (lots of)** disabled car parking places.	Es gibt viele Parkplätze für Behinderte.

Zu den wichtigsten Mengenbezeichnungen (siehe dazu auch *Part One*, Modul 5A, S. 74) im Englischen gehören:

some   *einige, manche; etwas* (bei positiven Aussagen)

any   *einige, manche; (irgend)etwas* (bei Fragen und Verneinungen)

(Mit *some* und *any* gibt es eine Reihe von Wortzusammensetzungen, wie z.B. *somebody*, *anybody*, etc.; vgl. dazu *Part One*, S. 74.)

much   *viel* (in der Regel nur bei nicht-zählbaren Begriffen in Fragen und Verneinungen)

many   *viele* (in der Regel nur bei zählbaren Begriffen in Fragen und Verneinungen)

a lot of ⎫
lots of ⎭   *viel(e)* (bei nicht-zählbaren und zählbaren Begriffen in positiven Aussagen)

a little   *etwas, ein wenig* (nur bei nicht-zählbaren Begriffen)

a few   *einige, ein paar* (nur bei zählbaren Begriffen)

several   *einige* (nur bei zählbaren Begriffen)

every   *jede/r/s* (in einem ganz allgemeinen Sinn)

each   *jede/r/s (einzelne)*

Exercises

I. Add "some" (somebody/something/somewhere) or "any" (anybody/anything/anywhere) to complete the sentences. ●●

1. Does ... live near the post office?
2. He left without saying ... to anybody.
3. Can you help me? I've got ... in my eye.
4. ... must be at home because the light's on.
5. Have you read ... novels by Joseph Conrad?

6. We've got ... milk, but not very much.
7. The restaurant should be ... near here, I think.
8. Did ... phone while we were out?

II. Put in "much", "many" or "a lot of"/"lots of" to complete the sentences. ●●

1. There wasn't ... traffic on the motorway, was there?
2. Do you need ... eggs to make an omelette?
3. We didn't have ... rain this year.
4. ... people work from home nowadays.
5. How ... times have I told you not to do that?
6. No more for me, thanks. I've had ... too much to eat.
7. There's not ... room but you can squeeze in.
8. Some people have ... luck.

III. Match the answer (a or b) to the question (1–6). ●●

1. How many bottles would you like?
2. How much do you want?
3. Any problems?   a. Only a few.
4. Have you got some time?   b. Only a little.
5. How many can I offer you?
6. Are there any tickets left?

IV. Underline the word in brackets which best completes the sentence. (Use each word twice.) ●●

1. The government believes (each/every/several) schoolleaver should train for a job.
2. (Each/Every/Several) student in the class wants to do as well as they can.
3. There are (each/every/several) places in the town where you can hire bicycles.
4. We play squash (each/every/several) Tuesday.
5. The college offers (each/every/several) courses for people whose first language is not English.
6. They've got three daughters and (each/every/several) of them plays a musical instrument.

V. Where would you see these signs? Choose from the expressions in the box below. Then match the signs to the explanations (a–f).

> inside a shop • at an airport • in a park • on a packet of cigarettes • on a shop window • in a car park

1. SHOPLIFTERS WILL BE PROSECUTED

2. NOTHING TO DECLARE

3. PAY AND DISPLAY

4. PENALTY FOR DROPPING LITTER – £100

5. THIS PACKET CARRIES A GOVERNMENT HEALTH WARNING

6. SALE STARTS TODAY

a. You must buy a ticket and put in a place where it can be seen.
b. If you steal something you will be taken to court.
c. Things are being sold at a cheaper price.
d. You have nothing with you which you have to pay duty on when you bring it into another country.
e. If you drop rubbish on the ground you will have to pay a fine.
f. What is inside is bad for your health.

VI. There are words in English which sound like their meaning. The most obvious example is "moo", which is the noise cows make. Match the verbs in the box with the sentences below.

> clang • clink • clip-clop • crackle • creak

1. when two pieces of glass knock together
2. when dry wood burns
3. when a door which needs oil on it is opened
4. when horses walk along a road
5. when church bells ring loudly

19C

Jackie Hails and Mike Bishop – two views on disabled sport

Jackie Hails

Listen carefully to Jackie Hails and Mike Bishop talking about sports for disabled people. Then answer the questions below.

I. Which of the two speakers, Jackie or Mike, seems more positive about sport for the disabled? Give a reason for your answer.

II. What does Jackie Hails say? Answer the questions.

1. What does she mean exactly when she talks about disabled people having "access" to a sports centre?
2. What is the main advantage for physically handicapped people of being able to use a swimming pool?

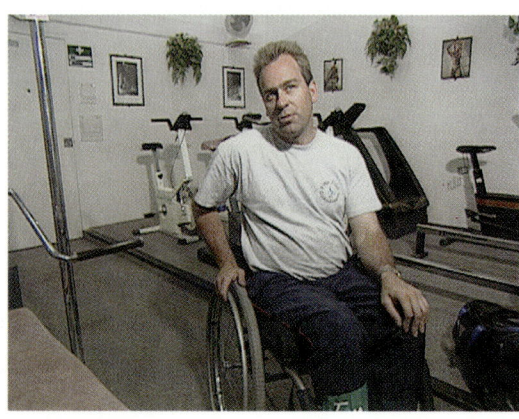

Mike Bishop

III. What does Mike Bishop say? Answer these questions.

1. Which reasons does Mike give for playing basketball?
2. What does Mike say about the status of disabled athletes when compared to non-disabled athletes?

IV. Match the beginnings (1–5) and ends (a–e) of the sentences up.

1. As far as I'm concerned, ...
2. As luck would have it, ...
3. If the worst comes to the worst, ...
4. If all else fails, ...
5. With one thing and another, ...

a. I'll have to send them a registered letter.
b. I just haven't had time to tidy up my study.
c. the London Marathon is a second-class race.
d. I got stuck in a bad traffic jam and missed the game.
e. I'll have to resign from the team.

V. These words are difficult to pronounce. Practise them. ●●

physical / ˈfɪzɪkl /
physiotherapy / fɪzɪəʊˈθerəpɪ /
physicist / ˈfɪzɪsɪst /
physician / fɪˈzɪʃn /
physics / ˈfɪzɪks /

What is the difference in meaning between a "physicist" and a "physician"?

19D

Meterman the philanthropist

I. Read through the story about Meterman and what happened to him when he helped a blind couple for the day. What do you think the blind couple thought about him? Choose one of the alternatives.

a) They thought he was polite, helpful and efficient.
b) They thought he was polite, friendly but inefficient.
c) They thought he was unfriendly and uncooperative.

Meterman is in the mood for helping people. He wants to *spread* a little sunshine. Today he is visiting a couple who are blind.

As soon as he arrives at the couple's house, he asks them how he can help. The couple say that they are going to take the dogs to the park. Would Meterman like to come along and keep an eye on them? Before they leave, the couple ask Meterman to go into the kitchen to pick up their purse and keys. It takes Meterman a little bit longer than they expect. "He must *be as blind as a bat* – or *as deaf as a post*," they mutter to themselves.

Out on the street Meterman seems to forget that blind people and their guide dogs are very independent. "Mind the *kerb*," shouts Meterman as the couple approach the road. The guide dogs are not impressed. "He's doing our job," says one. "Why doesn't he *stick to* reading meters?" says the other.

Eventually the five of them reach a park bench and sit down. "There we are," says Meterman relaxing in the sun. "Well, this is very nice, isn't it? Wide open spaces for the doggies to have a free run. Well, would anyone like an ice-cream?" The dogs *prick up their ears*. "Do you think he'll get one for us?" says one. "No, I doubt it. They never do. It's a dog's life," says the other.

On his way back from buying the ice-creams Meterman notices a boy up in a tree. He's trying to get his ball down. As he is having trouble Meterman offers to help. "I'll get it down for you," he says giving the ice-creams to another boy to hold.

Soon Meterman himself is stuck in the tree. The dogs have run back to their owners. The boys have eaten the ice-creams and the blind couple will have to go home without Meterman's "assistance"."Help! Help!" shouts Meterman holding on to a thick *branch*. It's no use, though. There's nobody there to lend him a helping hand.

philanthropist	Menschenfreund, Philanthrop	kerb	Rinnstein, Randstein
spread (spread, spread)	verbreiten	stick to	*hier*: bleiben bei
be as blind as a bat	blind wie ein Maulwurf sein (*bat* = Fledermaus)	prick up one's ears	die Ohren spitzen
be as deaf as a post	stocktaub sein (*post* = Pfosten)	branch	Ast, Zweig

II. Look at these expressions with the word "dog" in them.
Match them with their explanations.

1. a dog's life
2. let sleeping dogs lie
3. to go to the dogs
4. you can't teach an old dog new tricks

a. old people do not want to learn new things
b. something is losing its good qualities
c. if you disturb something which is OK you may cause problems
d. a miserable and unpleasant way of life

III. Put these expressions into the correct sentences to show their meaning.
Use the correct forms.

- not to take a blind bit of notice of sb
- to turn a blind eye to sth
- the blind leading the blind

1. You want me to help you with your computer! I don't know anything about computers! It would be like ... , wouldn't it?
2. It's terrible. She ... me when I'm talking. She completely ignores me.
3. She often ... to her husband's heavy drinking.

Which of these three expressions is informal?

19E

The way to Gravesend

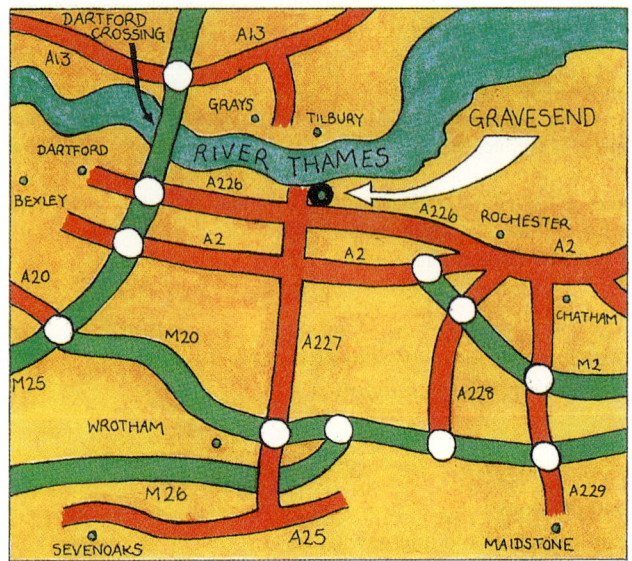

"Getting to Gravesend"

By Car—Gravesend is clearly signposted
from the M2, M20 & M25. Direct access is
provided by the A2, A226 & A227.

By Bus—Regular services to Gravesend are
run by Kentish Bus and Maidstone & District
bus companies. Timetable information is
available directly from these companies &
other local operators

By Train—Gravesend BR station is in the
heart of the town and is barely 2 minutes
from the shops

By Ferry—Ferries run regularly between
Gravesend and Tilbury with bus and rail
connection to Grays BR station

THE BRITISH PASSION UNIT 20

20A

Having a flutter

What do these three men think about the rights and wrongs of *gambling*?

1 Man (at the races): As a matter of fact I know a lot about *horse racing*. I go to as many races as I can. I read all the articles in the newspapers. I follow the results
5 carefully. So when I *bet on* a horse I'm very well informed about the horse, the trainer, his rider and his chances of winning. I don't think it's wrong to gamble, *especially* if it's part of a wider interest – like mine.

2 Man (in a casino): I don't want to say how much money I gamble in an evening because I don't think it's right to gamble as much as I do – but then it's part of life,
10 isn't it? I mean life's a gamble, isn't it? *Take me* – I'm young, single, no *responsibility* for a family or anything. I earn a good salary, can spend it how I like, can't I? Now for someone with a wife and kids, a house and a mortgage and all those other *expenses*, well for someone like that, it would not be right to gamble because they have other responsibilities. If you take me, apart from the new Porsche, well, I've
15 got no responsibilities.

3 Man (at home): I don't gamble because I can't afford to. I don't have enough money left at the end of each month to gamble with. If you have responsibilities, I think it is wrong to take risks with money. I'm responsible for the house, I'm responsible for paying the mortgage each month and I have other household payments to make.
20 I'm responsible for looking after my family. What would my wife say if I told her I had *lost all the money on a horse* that month or on the roulette wheel?

have a flutter	spielen, wetten (*häufig bezogen auf Pferde-rennen*)	Take me, ...	Nehmen Sie (Nimm) mich zum Beispiel, ...
		responsibility	Verantwortung, *hier*: Verpflichtung
gamble, *v/n*	spielen; Glücksspiel		
horse racing	Pferderennen	expenses	Ausgaben, Kosten
bet on	eine Wette abschließen auf, setzen auf	I lost all the money on a horse.	Ich habe das ganze Geld bei einer Pferdewette verloren.
especially	insbesondere		

Understanding the text.

Which ending (a–c) best completes the statement (1–3)? Tick it.

1. The first man thinks ...
   a) that he should not gamble.
   b) that it is OK for him to gamble.
   c) that gambling is bad for him.

2. The second man thinks ...
   a) that gambling is acceptable if you can afford it.
   b) that gambling is good for you.
   c) that gambling is wrong.

3. The third man ...
   a) thinks that gambling is right.
   b) thinks that his wife should let him gamble.
   c) might gamble if he had the money.

Further questions. Answer them in full sentences using your own words as far as possible.

4. Do the first and second man have different opinions about gambling? Explain.
5. Do the second and third man have different opinions about gambling? Say why/why not.

Which word from the text is being described?

6. the money you get every month for doing your job
7. the amount you pay to the bank for borrowing money from them for buying a house

Find a word in the text which has the opposite meaning of the following.

8. married
9. husband
10. to save (money)

And what about you?

11. Do you think people gamble for any other reasons apart from the ones mentioned in the text? Give some examples.
12. What do you personally think about gambling?

Stative verbs

Zustandsverben

I **know** a lot about horse racing.	Ich weiß eine Menge über Pferderennen.
I **don't think** it is wrong to gamble.	Ich glaube (denke) nicht, dass es falsch ist zu spielen.

◆ Die Verlaufsform ist eine Besonderheit der englischen Grammatik, die Lernenden immer wieder Schwierigkeiten bereitet.

Durch die Verlaufsform hat der Sprecher die Möglichkeit, dem Verb eine zusätzliche Bedeutung zu geben. Das heißt, er kann zum Ausdruck bringen, dass er eine Handlung als zeitlich begrenzt oder als nicht abgeschlossen betrachtet; er kann ihren Ablauf betonen oder unterstreichen, dass etwas zum Zeitpunkt des Sprechens geschieht.

Es gibt jedoch im Englischen eine kleine **Gruppe von Verben**, die **üblicherweise nicht in der Verlaufsform** verwendet werden können. Diese Verben nennt man **Zustandsverben**, weil sie Zustände – und **keine echten Handlungen** – ausdrücken. Zu den wichtigsten Zustandsverben gehören:

– Verben des **Glaubens, Denkens** und **Meinens**, wie z.B.:

to believe (*glauben*), to know (*wissen*), to mean (*bedeuten*), to think (*glauben, denken, meinen*), to understand (*verstehen*)

– Verben der **Gemütsbewegung** und des **Wünschens**, wie z.B.:

to hate (*hassen*), to like (*mögen*), to love (*lieben*), to need (*brauchen*), to want (*wollen*)

– Verben der **Sinneswahrnehmung**, wie z.B.:

to feel (*fühlen, spüren; sich anfühlen*), to hear (*hören*), to look (*aussehen*), to see (*sehen, wahrnehmen*), to smell (*riechen*), to sound (*klingen*), to taste (*schmecken*)

– Verben, die eine **Tatsache** zum Ausdruck bringen, wie z.B.:

to belong (*gehören*), to consist (*bestehen*), to contain (*beinhalten*), to have (*haben, besitzen*), to own (*besitzen*)

◆ **Einige** der oben genannten **Verben** haben jedoch **weitere Bedeutungen** und können dann als **echte Tätigkeitsverben** selbstverständlich auch in der **Verlaufsform** gebraucht werden. Dies gilt z.B. für **to think of sth** (*an etw. denken*), **to feel** (*sich fühlen; betasten*), **to look at sth** (*etw. betrachten*) oder **to see sb** (*jmdn. treffen*).

The horses approach the finishing line

Exercises

I. Add the correct form of the words in brackets to complete the sentence. ●●

1. Be careful. This bottle ... (contain) a dangerous drug.
2. Excuse me? How much ... (cost, the return fare to Birmingham)?
3. Have you seen this book? It ... (look) really old.
4. Who ... (want) another drink?
5. Where ... (you, come) from? The USA or Canada?
6. I ... (not, understand) this exercise. You try it.

II. Say it in English. Use the present perfect simple form of the verb. ●●

1. Hast du deinen Computer schon lange?
2. Ich wollte immer schon einen Hund.
3. Wie lange kennen wir uns schon?
4. Früh aufzustehen habe ich seit meiner Kindheit gehasst.

III. Complete these pairs of sentences using the correct form of the words in brackets.
One verb is in the present simple. The other is in the present continuous. ●●

to look
1. What's happening? What ... (you, look) at?
2. Your car ... (look) new. Is it new?

to think
3. This is my latest poem. What ... (you, think) of it?
4. You're quiet. What ... (you, think) about?

to see
5. We're not in tonight. We ... (see) some friends of ours.
6. I ... (see) the notice but I can't read the writing.

to feel
7. I ... (feel) something in my shoe.
8. I ... (feel) tired. I'll have to go to bed.

Now translate your sentences into German.

 Preposition + gerund

Präposition + Gerund

You can learn a language **by reading** a lot.	Man kann eine Sprache lernen, indem man viel liest.
She **insisted on paying** the bill.	Sie bestand darauf, die Rechnung zu bezahlen.
We've got no **time for arguing**.	Wir haben keine Zeit zum Diskutieren.
I'm **responsible for looking** after my family.	Ich bin dafür verantwortlich, mich um meine Familie zu kümmern.

In *Part One*, Modul 12A (S. 187) steht eine einfache, aber **wichtige Regel** der englischen Grammatik: folgt auf eine **Präposition** ein **Verb**, steht **immer** das **Gerund**. Dies gilt für **alle Präposition+Verb-Kombinationen**, d.h. für:

◆ **allein stehende Präpositionen** (*He left the room without speaking.*)
◆ die **Verbindung Verb + Präposition** (*I'm looking forward to hearing from you.*)
◆ die **Verbindung Substantiv + Präposition** (*She had no intention of hurting him.*)
◆ die **Verbindung Adjektiv + Präposition** (*He's fond of driving his car.*)

IV. Complete the sentences using a preposition from the box below and the correct form of the verb in brackets. ●●

> about ● of ● at ● for ● of ● at ● in ● about ● of

1. Are you afraid ... (tell) the truth?
2. He's bad ... (cook) but good ... (do) the washing-up!
3. They're excited ... (go) on holiday.
4. Are you fond ... (cycle)?
5. They're interested ... (travel) to exotic countries.
6. Is he happy ... (stay) at home by himself?
7. She was proud ... (get) the best mark in the test.
8. Are you responsible ... (make) this mess?

V. Put the nouns from the box and the prepositions from the box into the correct sentences below. Use the correct form of the word in brackets.
(Be careful, however. One noun must be followed by an infinitive, not a preposition and gerund.) ●●

> intention ● job ● opportunity ● point ●
> prospect (*Aussicht*) ● reason ● way ● wish

> of ● for ● in

1. We had no ... (make) fools of ourselves but I think that's the impression we left behind.
2. The ... (work) in a company from nine to five every day doesn't interest her.
3. There's no ... (find) out what happened exactly, is there?
4. He's got the ... (clear) up when everybody's left.
5. It was not my ... (live) alone.
6. There must surely be a ... (behave) like that.
7. There's no ... (wait). The bus isn't going to come, is it?
8. Do you know about the ... (study) abroad?

VI. Can you remember these verb + preposition combinations?
Complete these sentences using the correct form of the words in brackets.
You will have to find the preposition yourself. ●●

1. I must apologize ... (ring) you so late.
2. Have you succeeded ... (give up) smoking?
3. We're thinking ... (start) a drama club.
4. We insist ... (pay) for the food.
5. We'd like to thank you ... (be) so patient.
6. We're looking forward ... (see) you in the summer.
7. They're talking ... (emigrate) to New Zealand.
8. Do you object ... (wait) so long?

VII. How would you react? Choose two of the following situations and write down
what you would do.

1. You see somebody you know stealing something from a shop.
2. You see another student cheating in an exam.
3. Two days before the end of your holiday you run out of money.
4. A stranger stops you at the airport and offers you a lot of money to take a suitcase.

20B

A day at the races ●●

Bob and Tessa enjoy betting on horses but do they always win? Bob explains: "I like betting. It makes the races more exciting. If I win on one race, I put more money on the next." Tessa is more *cautious*. "If I lose money on two races, then I stop betting," she admits. "I sometimes *back* an outsider. Here's an outsider, 'Radical Exception'. *The odds are* 20:1. It means that if you put £1 on, you will get £20 back – if he wins." Tessa and Bob are sitting together with Irene and George a few minutes before the next race begins. They talk about which horses they are going to back.

Bob: Have you *made up your mind* yet?
Tessa: I haven't decided yet. I may back "Fort Knox" or I may back "Sooty Tern" or I may back both of them.
Bob: And you, George? Have you decided?
George: No, I can't make up my mind. I may put my money on "Broughtons Turmoil" or I may go for "Twin Creeks" or I might put my money on "Lorins Gold".
Bob: Irene? What about you? You've made up your mind?

"I wish I hadn't bet
on the wrong horse."

Irene: I'm still *working out* the odds.
Tessa: OK, I've made up my mind. I'm going to put £50 on an outsider –
          this one – "Sweet Allegiance". I think he's got a good chance of winning.
20   The odds are 66:1. Could you work that out for me?
George: £50 on a 66:1? I think you're mad. Well, if you win you'll get ... £3,300.
          Well, I don't think you'll win.
Irene: What would you do with the money if you won?
Tessa: If I won £3,300, I'd take you all out to dinner tonight and with the rest
25   I'd go on a holiday. Come on. Let's *place our bets*.

After the race the four friends find out if they've won or not. Bob is satisfied. He
says he won £28 for a £4 bet. Tessa is disappointed. She wishes she had backed
"Balance of Power". "I wish I hadn't *thrown* my £50 *away on* that *pathetic* 'Sweet
Allegiance'," she says. George also wishes he hadn't bet on the wrong horse. Irene
30 seems much happier. "Actually I put £20 on 'Balance of Power'. I won £140. Come
on. I'll buy you a drink!"

cautious	vorsichtig, umsichtig	work out	berechnen, kalkulieren
back sth/sb	*hier*: auf etw./jmdn. setzen	place a bet	eine Wette platzieren
		throw away on	*hier*: verschleudern für
the odds are ...	die Quote liegt bei ...	pathetic	*hier*: lächerlich,
make up one's mind	sich entschließen		jämmerlich

Understanding the text.
True or false according to the text? Tick the correct box.

	True	False
1. Bob won the most money.		
2. Tessa lost the most money.		
3. Irene won less than Bob.		
4. George did not bet.		

Further questions. Answer them in complete sentences using your own words as far as possible.

5. Why does Tessa put so much money on "Sweet Allegiance"?
6. What were the odds for the horse which Bob backed? Explain your answer.

Find a word in the text which has the same meaning as the following.

7. careful
8. crazy

What's the English for the following German expressions?

9. Hast du dich entschlossen? (*two expressions*)
10. jmdn. zum Essen einladen

And what about you?

11. Would you bet on horses? Say why or why not.
12. What would you do if you won £3,300?

Who won and who lost?

Revision of helping verbs
Wiederholung der Hilfsverben

I **may** put my money on "Broughtons Turmoil".	Ich kann (könnte) mein Geld auf „Broughtons Turmoil" setzen.
I **might** put my money on "Lorins Gold".	Ich könnte mein Geld (vielleicht) auf „Lorins Gold" setzen.
May (Might) I come in? – Of course you **may**. / No, you **may not**.	Kann (Könnte) ich (vielleicht) hereinkommen? – Natürlich können Sie (kannst du). / Nein, Sie können (du kannst) nicht.

◆ Die unvollständigen Hilfsverben *can, could, will, would, shall, should* und *must* wurden bereits in *Part One* vorgestellt und geübt (vgl. 2A, 4A, 9B und 13A).

In diesem Modul kommen zwei weitere dazu: *may* und *might*. Beide Hilfsverben drücken u.a. eine **Möglichkeit** aus, wobei bei *might* die Wahrscheinlichkeit, dass etwas geschieht, etwas geringer ist als bei *may*. *May* und *might* verwendet man außerdem, um eine **Erlaubnis** zu erbitten bzw. zu erteilen. *May not* drückt ein **Verbot** aus.

Hier nun noch einmal im **Überblick** die **wichtigsten Regeln** zum Gebrauch der **Hilfsverben**:

◆ Hilfsverben haben besondere Eigenschaften. Sie sind **unvollständig**, d.h. sie bilden die **3. Person Singular ohne -s** und können nur **in Verbindung** mit einem **Vollverb ohne *to*** verwendet werden (*She can help you.*). Die **Frageform** eines Hilfsverbs wird durch **Umstellen** von **Subjekt und Hilfsverb** gebildet (*Must we go now?*). Zur Bildung der **Verneinung** verwendet man *not* (*He may not come.*).

◆ Nicht nur in ihrer Struktur spielen Hilfsverben eine Sonderrolle in der englischen Grammatik. Auch in ihrer **Bedeutung** weisen sie einige **Besonderheiten** auf. Sie bringen die **Meinung**, die **Einstellung** oder die **Auffassung des Sprechers** zum Ausdruck. Daher auch die Bezeichnung **modale Hilfsverben** (von *Modus* = Art und Weise). Mit Hilfsverben drücken wir aus, was wir für möglich, wahrscheinlich, notwendig, verboten, erlaubt oder empfehlenswert halten. Ein Hilfsverb kann etwas **Vergangenes**, **Gegenwärtiges** oder **Zukünftiges** beschreiben.

Exercises

I. Look at these six sentences. They all contain the word "could".
Do these sentences refer to something in the past,
present or future? Tick the appropriate box.

	past	present	future
1. I could read when I was five.			
2. Could you pass the butter?			
3. I was wondering if we could meet tomorrow.			
4. Could I have another coffee, please?			
5. She could do well if she worked hard.			
6. Unfortunately nobody could come yesterday.			

II. What meaning is being expressed with these helping verbs?
Choose from the box below.

> ability (*Fähigkeit*) ● advice (*Ratschlag*) ● necessity (*Notwendigkeit*) ●
> offer (*Angebot*) ● permission (*Erlaubnis*) ● suggestion (*Vorschlag*)
> ● possibility (*Wahrscheinlichkeit*) ● prohibition (*Verbot*) ● request (*Bitte*)

Example:
Would you pass the salt, please? – request

1. I could take you to the airport if you want.
2. It could rain later.
3. Can you type quickly?
4. We must leave at six.
5. You can't park here.
6. May I use your phone?
7. Shall I open the window?
8. You should take the train.

III. Are these sentences expressing permission or possibility? Say which.

1. May I open the window, please?
2. We may have time later for lunch.
3. You may borrow the book but please bring it back.
4. I think it might snow. It's turned very cold suddenly.

IV. Rewrite these sentences using "might". ●●

1. Perhaps it will be warm enough to go swimming.
2. Perhaps she's right. You never know.
3. I don't know if I can come to the party. I'll see.
4. Perhaps we'll go away over Christmas this year.

 Zero if-sentences

| **If** I **win** on one race, | Wenn ich in dem einen Rennen gewinne, |
| **I put** more money on the next. | setze ich mehr Geld im nächsten. |

Bei Typ 1 der Bedingungssätze (vgl. *Part One*, Modul 12A, S. 189) denken wir üblicherweise an die Zeitenfolge: *will* im Hauptsatz und einfache Form der Gegenwart im *if*-Satz (*If you put £1 on, you will get £20 back.*).
Es gibt im Englischen aber auch Bedingungssätze, die **ohne *will* im Hauptsatz** gebildet werden. Diese sogenannten *zero if-sentences* drücken **keine** spezifische Bedingung aus, sondern bringen eine **allgemein gültige Situation** zum Ausdruck, z.B.: *My parents get angry if (= whenever) I smoke at home.* (Meine Eltern ärgern sich (jedes Mal), wenn ich zu Hause rauche.). Bei einem *zero if-sentence* steht in **beiden Satzhälften** die **einfache Form der Gegenwart**.

V. Form four complete sentences. ●●

1. He never says sorry	a.	if you ring before 10.
2. She gets angry	b.	if she comes by bus.
3. He doesn't answer the phone	c.	if he's late.
4. She always arrives early	d.	if you talk about her hair.

VI. Complete these sentences using the correct forms of the words in brackets.
(Three are zero if-sentences and three are if-sentences type 1.) ●●

1. We ... (miss) the bus if we ... (not, hurry).
2. Grass ... (grow) quickly if it ... (rain) a lot.
3. If you ... (not, put) milk in the fridge, it ... (go) bad.
4. They ... (not, go) away if there ... (be) a lot of traffic.
5. The dog ... (bark) if anybody ... (come) to the door.
6. If she ... (work) hard, she ... (do) well in her exams.

20C

Josh Gifford and Mandy Madden – crazy about horses

Josh (middle) returns from an early-morning canter

Listen carefully to Josh Gifford and Mandy Madden talking about the racing business and answer the questions below.

I. Which three things does Josh talk about? Tick them.

1. the dangers of horse racing
2. why he likes getting up early
3. the joy of training a Grand National winner
4. when he met his wife
5. why he does not gamble

II. What does Mandy Madden, one of Josh's stable girls, say about her job? Tick the appropriate sentence.

1. The work is OK, especially in winter.
2. She is overworked and badly paid but she gets free accommodation.
3. She loves her job and wouldn't want to do anything else.

III. Answer these questions using your own words.

1. Josh talks about a "fairy story". What does he mean?
2. Mandy Madden says horses are like a "disease" for her. Why is this?

IV. Which seven words from the text are being defined or explained?
The first letter has been given.

1. what horses jump over during a race – f_ _ _ _
2. an informal word for "young man" – l_ _
3. you have to make sure it is not too much if you are a jockey – w_ _ _ _ _
4. if you fall off a horse and land on your shoulder you can easily break it –
    c_ _ _ _ _ _ _ _
5. a serious disease which can kill you – c_ _ _ _ _
6. a person who takes your money when you bet on horses – b_ _ _ _ _ _ _ _
7. a very strong interest in something – p_ _ _ _ _ _

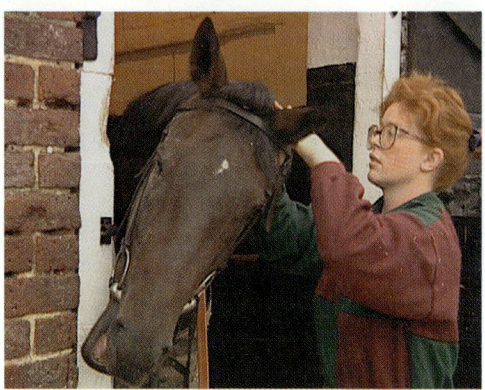

Mandy Madden

20D

Meterman the gambler

I. Read about what happens to Meterman when he goes to a bingo hall.
What sort of impression does he leave on the people there?
Choose from one of the alternatives below (1–3).

1. He shows everybody how much he knows about bingo.
2. He shows everybody what a fool he is.
3. He shows everybody that he can play bingo better than he can read meters.

Meterman goes into a bingo hall. "I'm not a gambling man myself," he explains
to the camera. "When a man has responsibilities like me, then I think it is wrong
to gamble." Soon, however, Meterman *warms to* the idea. He decides to *toss
a coin* to see if he should play a quick game of bingo. If it's heads, he'll play.
He tosses. It's heads.

Meterman explains the game to the viewers. "It's perfectly straightforward," he says. "You have cards with numbers on and if you get a whole row of numbers, you win."

Meterman buys his card and sits down at a table where some people are already playing. Soon he thinks he has won. He stands up and shouts: "Bingo! Yes! Bingo! I've won, I've won, I've won!"

A man comes up and checks his card. "Sorry, sir," he says. "False *claim* on the red page." The game continues. Again, Meterman thinks he's won. "Bingo! Yes! Yes!" he shouts loudly. "This time it is definitely a win!" He points at his card. "Look at this, look at this, look ... that way, that way, that way and that way."

This time the man has had enough. He escorts Meterman out of the bingo hall. For a second Meterman gets angry. "*Frankly* I find this rather boring. It bores the pants off me if you'll pardon the expression," he says. "Bingo isn't like it used to be you know. And you know whose fault it is?" He looks at the man calling the numbers. "It's his – the caller!"

Outside Meterman has an idea. He goes to the *public address system* and announces that the caller is needed on the phone. The caller leaves the hall and this gives Meterman a chance to take over.

As soon as Meterman begins to call out the numbers the men and women in the hall get annoyed. "Off, off, off!" they shout angrily. For the second time Meterman is escorted out of the hall. Outside he talks to the viewers. "I've lost £10!

I wish I'd never come here in the first place. And now I'*m skint*!" At that moment he finds a £1 coin in his pocket. He decides to put it into a *fruit machine*. Perhaps he can win his £10 back.

It looks as if it's not been Meterman's lucky day. Nothing has come of the money he has put in the machine. He turns, walks out of the bingo hall and goes across the car park to his car. Suddenly back in the bingo hall £20 fall out of the fruit machine. It could have been Meterman's lucky day after all.

warm to sth	sich für etw. erwärmen	public address	Lautsprecheranlage
toss a coin	eine Münze werfen	system	
claim	Anspruch, Forderung	fruit machine	Spielautomat
frankly	offen gesagt	be skint (*coll*)	pleite sein

II. Which four expressions below mean "it bores me very much"?
Tick them. (If you don't know have a guess!)

a. it bores me to death
b. it bores me to sleep
c. it bores me stiff

d. it bores me to tears
e. it bores me cold
f. it bores the pants off me

20E

The National Lottery

"I put £10 on the National Lottery every week. I think of
it as a kind of investment. I know that one day I'll win at least
enough to cover what I pay."

MEET THE POLICE

21A

What had happened earlier? ●●

A driving offence

A man was stopped by the police after he had driven over some red lights. He was
asked to show the police officers his *driving licence* but he was only given a *verbal*
5 *warning*.

A burglary

One morning a woman came back home and saw that someone had broken into her
house. The *burglar* had smashed a window and stolen some electrical equipment.
The woman phoned the police and they came immediately.

10 **A raid on a disco**

Some young people had been enjoying themselves at a disco when the music
suddenly stopped and a group of police officers came in. They had received some
information about the possibility of drugs being used there. They *searched* a few
people and then *arrested* a young man.

15 **A visit to a police station**

Two visitors to Britain went to a police station because one of them had lost her air-
line bag. The girls had been travelling on a bus when they realized that the bag was
missing. They asked the police officer *on duty* if anybody had handed the bag in or
seen it anywhere. The policeman did not have the bag but he was very helpful and
20 *understanding*.

driving licence	Führerschein	search	durchsuchen
verbal warning	mündliche Verwarnung	arrest	festnehmen
burglary	Einbruchsdiebstahl	on duty	Dienst habend
burglar	Einbrecher	understanding	verständnisvoll
raid, *n/v*	(Polizei-)Razzia; eine		
	Razzia machen in		

The police come to see what has happened

Understanding the text.

Answer the questions using full sentences.

1. In which of the four situations did somebody do something wrong?
2. In which of the four situations did somebody have a very bad experience?
3. In which situation(s) do we not know what really happened?

Write down what had happened before ...

4. the man in the car was stopped.
5. the woman came back home.
6. the police raided the disco.
7. the girls went to the police station.

Find a word in the text which means the same as the following.

8. to call   9. at once   10. to discover

And what about you?

11. What sort of electrical equipment (line 8) are burglars usually interested in and why?
12. Would you get a verbal warning if you drove over red lights in Germany? Explain.

The past perfect simple and continuous

Die Vorvergangenheit (einfache Form und Verlaufsform)

One morning a woman came back home and saw that someone **had broken** into her house. Some young people **had been enjoying** themselves at a disco when the music suddenly stopped. They asked the police officer on duty if anybody **had handed** the bag **in**.

Eine Frau kam eines Morgens zurück nach Hause und sah, dass jemand in ihr Haus eingebrochen hatte. Einige junge Leute hatten sich in einer Disco vergnügt, als die Musik plötzlich abbrach. Sie fragten den Dienst habenden Polizeibeamten, ob jemand die Tasche abgegeben habe.

♦ Mit dem **Past Perfect** (einfache Form und Verlaufsform) bezeichnet man **Vorgänge** oder **Handlungen**, die bereits **vor einem bestimmten Zeitpunkt** in der **Vergangenheit geschahen**. Daher auch der Name „**Vorvergangenheit**".
Die **einfache Form** beschreibt das **Ergebnis einer Handlung**, die in der **Vorvergangenheit stattfand** (*They had all gone out so there was nobody at home.*).
Die **Verlaufsform** dagegen betont den **Verlauf einer Handlung** in der **Vorvergangenheit** (*The man was out of breath because he had been running.*).
Das **Past Perfect** wird oft **zusammen mit** dem **Past Simple** verwendet, um hervorzuheben, dass eine Handlung **vor** einer anderen Handlung in der Vergangenheit geschah.

♦ Den **Zeitunterschied** zwischen den beiden Handlungen „**signalisieren**" häufig Wörter wie *before* (bevor, ehe), *after* (nachdem) und *when* (als): *After everything had gone quiet, the police searched some people.*

♦ Das *Past Perfect* findet oft Anwendung in Zusammenhang mit der **indirekten Rede**, wenn das **Verb des einleitenden Satzes** in der **Vergangenheit** steht (*They asked the police officer if anybody had handed the bag in.*). (Die indirekte Rede wird im Modul 22A, S. 140, ausführlicher behandelt.)

♦ Die **einfache Form** des *Past Perfect* bildet man mit **had** und dem **Partizip Perfekt** (der dritten Form des Verbs; *Past Participle*); die **Verlaufsform** mit *had been* + **-ing Form** des Verbs. Die **Frageform** wird durch **Umstellung** gebildet (*Had he arrived when you left?*). Zur Bildung der **Verneinung** nimmt man das Wort *not* (*We had not been talking long when he phoned.*). In der **gesprochenen Sprache** wird *had* üblicherweise mit dem **persönlichen Pronomen zusammengezogen** (*They did not notice that we'd gone out.*).

Exercises

I. Read the situation and then write a sentence using the past perfect simple. ●●

Example:
When I got to the top of the mountain I felt sick. (ski)
I had never skied before.

1. When I stood up my mouth went dry. (give a speech)
2. When the engine started I began to feel a little nervous. (ride a motorbike)
3. I suddenly regretted my decision when everybody looked at me. (tell a joke in public)
4. When I saw how much my guests were eating I knew there was not enough food. (cook for twenty people)
5. I wanted to go home when I heard the words "your plane is now ready for boarding". (fly)
6. I went red and looked at my feet when they read out my name. (win a prize)

II. David, Samantha, Kevin and Fiona went to the cinema.
Write down the answers to the questions by using the words in brackets.
(You will have to add some words.) ●●

1. Why did David fall asleep during the film? (see/before)
2. Why did Samantha have two packets of sandwiches during the film? (not/eat/anything at home)
3. Why did Kevin try to kiss Fiona during the film? (fall in love/her/the day before)
4. Why did Fiona make a phone call during the film? (not told/parents/be out with friends)

III. Answer the questions by using the past perfect continuous form of
the verb in brackets. ●●

1. Why did it feel so warm in the room?
    People ... (dance).
2. Why did he look so red?
    He ... (run) for over an hour.
3. Why did the child wake up in the night shouting?
    It ... (dream).
4. Why did she look so tired on Saturday?
    She ... (work) hard all week.

IV. Read the situation and then write a sentence using the past perfect continuous form of the verb. ●●

Example:

We were cycling. After ten minutes it started to rain very heavily.

either: We had been cycling for ten minutes when it began to rain.

or: After we had been cycling for ten minutes, it began to rain.

1. The group was playing in front of a large audience. After half an hour the lead singer felt ill.
2. We were living in our new house. After six months the heating stopped working.
3. The train was travelling through Scotland. After fifteen minutes she saw that she was on the wrong train.
4. He smoked. After 40 years he decided to give it up.
5. They gave up everything and went to live in Spain. After six months they got very homesick and came back to Germany.
6. She was at work sitting in front of her computer. After five minutes she realized that it was an hour later than she thought.

V. Complete the sentences below by using either the past continuous form or the past perfect continuous form of the verb in brackets. (Be careful, in one sentence you will need a simple form.) ●●

1. Clare was in her car outside the school. She ... (wait) for her son.
2. Mike ... (wait) at the bus stop for half an hour so he decided to walk rather than wait any longer.
3. When Tim and Alison arrived at the party most of the guests ... (eat). Jane said that she would cook something else for them.
4. When Tim and Alison arrived at the party most of the guests ... (eat). Jane said that they should sit down and help themselves.

21B

Neighbourhood watch ●●

Neighbourhood watch is an organization run by the *residents* and neighbours in a
particular street or area together with the police. It works to stop crimes such as
burglaries, *theft* and car crimes. In this Module a group of people are learning how
5 to start a neighbourhood watch group. A police officer is talking to them.
He tells them that if they see anyone acting *suspiciously*, they should call the police.
A woman in the group asks what "suspiciously" means exactly. The officer explains:
"Well, if you see someone *hanging about* with no particular reason for being there.
If you see someone *trying car doors* or walking up the sides and backs of houses and
10 in any way acting *furtively*, *secretively* or suspiciously, then please contact the police
and inform other neighbourhood watch members."
Later in the meeting the police officer goes on to talk about the *security* of houses.
"It is important to have good locks on windows and doors, at the front, at the side
and at the back of the house. If you have a *driveway* or *path*, put down *gravel*
15 instead of a hard surface. That way anyone who comes can be heard easily. A dog,
especially a dog that *barks* loudly, is always a good way to *deter* a criminal."
The officer suggests that people go round their houses checking carefully. "At the
front of the house, check front door and windows and make sure you have really
secure locks. At the side of the house, check again. Do you have any small windows
20 which could *provide entry*? Is it a dark area, where a burglar might *hide*? Install a
light which goes on when someone walks past. At the back of the house, check doors
and windows again."
The police officer has one last piece of advice. "If you are out all day, don't leave
milk outside the front door. That's as good as writing a letter to the burglar telling
25 him that you are out. Ask a neighbour to take the milk in for you."

neighbourhood watch	*von Nachbarn* *organisierter* „Wachdienst"	furtive	heimlichtuerisch; verstohlen
		secretive	geheimnistuerisch; geheimnisvoll
resident	Einwohner(in), Bewohner(in)	security	Sicherheit
theft	Diebstahl	driveway	Zufahrts-, Auffahrtsweg
suspicious	verdächtig, Verdacht erregend	path	Weg
hang about (around)	„herumlungern", herumstehen	gravel	Kies
		bark	bellen
try car doors	ausprobieren, ob die Autotüren unverschlossen sind	deter	abschrecken
		provide entry	Zugang verschaffen
		hide (hid, hidden)	sich verstecken

The police explain what a neighbourhood watch group can do

Understanding the text.

Which ending (a–c) completes the statement (1–6) best? Tick it.

1. Neighbourhood watch is a group of people ...
   a) who work for the police.
   b) who help the police.
   c) who steal cars and break into houses.

2. If a neighbourhood watch member sees somebody trying car doors he or she should ...
   a) ring the police.
   b) offer the person some help.
   c) arrest them.

3. The advantage of having gravel in front of your house is that ...
   a) dogs can bark more loudly.
   b) people can be heard more easily.
   c) windows can be checked more quickly.

4. Installing a light outside your house which goes on when someone walks past could ...
   a) make some burglars afraid.
   b) make your locks more secure.
   c) make entry into your house easier.

5. It's not good to leave milk outside your front door because it shows ...
   a) that you get up late.
   b) that you are not at home.
   c) that your neighbours don't like you.

Answer this question by choosing one of the four alternatives (a–d) below.

6. Which two main things does the police officer talk about during his meeting
   with the neighbourhood watch group?
   a) car security and guard dogs
   b) lighting around the house and securing windows
   c) house security and observing the neighbourhood
   d) the work of the police and prison officers

Find a word in the text which means the opposite of the following.

7. soft   8. large   9. light   10. first

And what about you?

11. Why in your opinion do people steal cars?
12. Would a police officer in Germany give the same sort of advice as the police
    officer in England did to the neighbourhood watch members? Say why/why not.

A bobby on the beat

H Adverbs of manner

Adverbien der Art und Weise

He was acting **suspiciously**.	Er verhielt sich verdächtig.
Check the windows **carefully**.	Überprüfen Sie die Fenster sorgfältig.
Are the doors locked **securely**?	Sind die Türen fest verschlossen?

◆ Es gibt **verschiedene Adverbien** (Umstandswörter): Adverbien des **Ortes** (*Your room is* ***upstairs***.), der **Zeit** (*I'll see you* ***later***.), der **Häufigkeit** (*She* ***often*** *goes swimming*.), des **Grades** (*They checked everything* ***very*** *carefully*.) und der **Art und Weise** (*We were looking for a dog that barks* ***loudly***.).

◆ Durch **Adverbien der Art und Weise** werden **Verben näher bestimmt**; sie beschreiben, wie etwas geschieht (*He spoke slowly and clearly*.). Das Adverb wird vom Adjektiv abgeleitet. Man bildet es in der Regel durch **Anhängen von -ly**. Eine Reihe von **Besonderheiten** bei der Bildung von Adverbien müssen dennoch beachtet werden:

Adjektiv	Adverb	
happy	happ**ily**	**-y** wird zu **-i**
nice	nic**ely**	Schluss **-e bleibt**
sim**ple**	sim**ply**	**Wegfall** von **-e** bei Endung **Konsonant + -le**
automat**ic**	automat**ically**	Endung **-ic + -ally**
friendly	**in a friendly way**	wenn das **Adjektiv auf -ly** endet, nimmt man die Wendung **"in a ... way/manner"**
good	**well**	**Ausnahme**

(Zu Adjektiven und Adverbien vgl. auch *Part One*, Modul 5B, S. 79.)

Exercises

I. Match an adjective (1–8) with a noun (a–h) to form eight pairs. ● ●

Example:
suspicious behaviour

Adjective	Noun
1. suspicious	a. applause
2. loud	b. arrival
3. happy	c. behaviour
4. slow	d. laugh
5. enthusiastic	e. rain
6. heavy	f. run
7. temporary	g. smile
8. unexpected	h. work

II. Answer these questions using the pairs from exercise I. Use the nouns as verbs and the adjectives as adverbs. The first one has been done for you. ● ●

1. What did you see when you looked out of the window?
   We saw two young men. They were behaving suspiciously.

2. How did the audience react when the actors came back onto the stage?
   They ... .

3. Has Joanna got a permanent job at the bank?
   No, she ... .

4. What happened when you told her she had won first prize?
   She didn't say much. She just ... .

5. Did they like the joke?
   Yes, they did. They all ... .

6. Did you know your parents were coming?
   No. They ... .

7. Why didn't you come out and see us?
   I couldn't leave the house. It ... .

8. Did you really do a half-marathon?
   Yes, but I ... . It took me over two hours.

III. Look at the four examples of the verb "rob" and "steal" and answer the questions below.

- Somebody stole my bike.
- My bag has been stolen.
- Three masked gunmen robbed a bank last night.
- On her way home she was attacked and robbed.

Which one of the following statements is not true? Mark it with a cross.

1. The object of the verb "to rob" is a person or place.
2. The object of the verb "to steal" is a thing.
3. The verb "to rob" is regular.
4. The verb "to steal" is regular.

Now put in "robbed" or "stole/stolen" to complete these sentences. ●●

5. Last night a gang ... the post office.
6. Yesterday morning our car radio was ... .
7. Every year hundreds of banks are ... .
8. Last weekend somebody ... my bike and left it outside the station.

IV. Match the crime in the box with its correct definition (1–6) below.

arson ● assault ● bribery ● burglary ● forgery ● shoplifting

1. Going into somebody's house and stealing something.
2. Going into a shop and stealing something.
3. Physically attacking another person.
4. Setting a house or other building on fire.
5. Giving somebody money to persuade them to do something for you.
6. Copying something to make other people think it is the original.

Now give the German equivalents for the words in the box.

V. Read this text and complete the sentences on page 134 by underlining the correct word in brackets. ●●

Last week at Winchester crown court two men were charged with drug trafficking. During the trial one of the men was found guilty and the judge sent him to prison for two years. (He will probably be released after 18 months.) The second man was found guilty of possessing small amounts of heroine. He was acquitted and left the court room smiling and waving to his family and friends.

1. The German word for "court" is („Halle"/„Gericht"/„Platz").
2. In German you say („Versuch"/„Probe"/„Prozess") for "trial".
3. If you are found "guilty" of a crime the judge thinks you (saw/thought about/carried out) the crime.
4. If you are "acquitted" of a crime you (can/must/do not) go to prison.

21C

Jonathan Dyer and Julia Buchan – on the beat in Farnham

Listen carefully to two British police officers talking about their work and then answer the questions below.

PC Dyer

PC Buchan

I. What is this interview mainly about? Choose one sentence from below.

1. It's about why women make such good police officers.
2. It's about the role of men and women in the British police force.
3. It's about why British police officers think that they are the best in the world.
4. It's about how dangerous it can be as a police officer on the streets of Farnham.

II. Complete the sentences by choosing the most appropriate ending.

1. PC (= Police Constable) Dyer thinks the British police ...
   a) should not patrol the streets.
   b) should be a normal part of British life.
   c) should have guns with them all the time.

2. PC Dyer thinks female police officers are ...
   a) just as good as male police officers.
   b) not trained well enough for all police work.
   c) not strong enough to handle conflict situations.

3. As soon as PC Buchan was expecting a baby she ...
   a) left the police.
   b) got another job.
   c) stopped doing patrol work.

4. PC Buchan says that British police officers no longer carry truncheons. Today they have asps. PC Buchan says that the advantage of the asp is that it is ...
   a) sharp and very dangerous.
   b) easy to handle.
   c) large and threatening.

III. At the end of the interview PC Dyer mentions an old saying that "in heaven all the policemen would be British". What does he mean exactly?

21D

Meterman the detective (Part 1)

I. As you read the story about Meterman at Monchelsea Place, answer the questions between the paragraphs.

On his way to read the meter in Monchelsea Place Meterman bumps into the local vicar. "Good morning, vicar," he says politely. "Your electricity consumption is nicely down this quarter I'm happy to report. I'm afraid it won't be such good news at the manor house next door, though." When the vicar has gone, Meterman turns to the camera and explains what he has just said. He tells the viewers that because the owner of the manor, Lady Boughton or dear Lady Bea, is as poor as a church mouse, she has to allow tourists into her house.

(Why does Lady Bea use so much electricity?)

As he walks past the manor Meterman looks through the windows and notices that some of the tourists are behaving very suspiciously. "I shouldn't be surprised if there's some dirty business going on here," he remarks. He is right. Suddenly there's a loud cry from inside the house. It's Lady Bea. "The music box! The music box! It's gone! Stolen! I've been robbed!" she cries. Meterman is quickly on the scene. Fortunately he has come prepared for some detective work. He pulls out a hat and pipe and looks straight into the camera. "This is a job for Sherlock Meterman," he announces. "Everyone keep calm and don't move." He orders the tourists to wait in the drawing room. Then he tells the maid to lock all the doors.

(Why does Meterman ask the maid to lock all the doors?)

Meterman goes into the drawing room to interview the tourists. "I saw the vicar," one of them reports. "And he was behaving most strangely. He was picking things up and putting them down, and he was most rude to me. Most unlike a vicar!" Meterman wants to know more. "And where is this vicar now?" he asks. "Has he *vanished into thin air*?"

At that moment the vicar from the local church comes in. Meterman does not hesitate. "Arrest that man and *secure him*!" he says at once. The maid is *overwhelmed* by Meterman's heroic actions. "Hero, eh? Yes, you're right," Meterman says to her. He thinks for a second. "I should be famous. I should be in the newspapers. Perhaps I should ring them first. (He picks up the phone and dials.) Connect me to the 'Daily Splash' immediately."

(Was Meterman right to arrest the friendly vicar?)

Meterman is just about to phone the police when he is interrupted by another vicar. It's not the real vicar, however. It's one of the tourists dressed as a vicar. He is holding a gun and pointing it straight at Meterman. "Oh no, you don't," he warns Meterman. "You're coming with me!" And with that he pulls Meterman and the maid into another room.

vanish	verschwinden	secure sb	jmdn. festnehmen
vanish into thin air	sich in Luft auflösen	overwhelm	überwältigen

II. What do you think will happen to Meterman?
Choose one of the alternatives (1–4) below.

1. He will die and there will be no more Meterman stories.
2. He will shoot the criminal and marry the maid.
3. He will be a hero and have his name on the front of the "Daily Splash".
4. He will work together with the criminal and steal Lady Bea's silver.

III. Link up the two halves of the similes.

1. as poor as
2. as gentle as
3. as dry as
4. as deaf as
5. as cool as
6. as red as

a. a beetroot
b. a post
c. a church mouse
d. a cucumber
e. a bone
f. a lamb

(Remember that these expressions are easy to understand but should be used carefully. They are informal and often humorous and you have to know in which situation you can use them appropriately.)

21E

Behind bars

"Sid, this place may not be as tough as we thought."

REPORTING THE NEWS   UNIT 22

22A

What did she say? ●●

This morning Katie, who is a *trainee reporter* with a local newspaper, visited Mrs Brown. Mrs Brown was the *victim* of a burglary and Katie wanted to find out what had happened.

5 Katie: What time did it happen?
  Mrs Brown: It was about half past one in the morning, *dear*. I know because
                of the little clock that I have.
  Katie: What did you hear?
  Mrs Brown: I heard a *crash*. I came downstairs and there he was.
10 Katie: What did the *intrudor* look like?
  Mrs Brown: Well, it's difficult to say, really, dear. He had a *stocking* or
                something over his face. He looked horrible.
  Katie: Can you remember his voice?
  Mrs Brown: His voice? Yes, he had a very *unpleasant* voice.
15 Katie: What did he say to you?
  Mrs Brown: He told me to be quiet.
  Katie: What happened next?
  Mrs Brown: He told me to sit on a chair.
  Katie: How do you feel now?

20 Mrs Brown: Oh, very *upset*. It'll take me a long time to *get over* this. I'll dream
                about it for months, I'm sure.
   Katie: I think you are very brave.

When she got back to the office Katie told her boss what questions she had asked
and what Mrs Brown had told her.

25 "I asked a lot of questions. I asked her what time it had happened. I asked her what
she had heard. I asked her what the intrudor had looked like. I asked her if she could
remember his voice. I asked her what he had said to her. The man told her to sit on
a chair and then he tied her up. It was a terrible experience. She said she felt very
upset and that it would take her a long time to get over it. She said that she would
30 dream about it for months. I tried to cheer her up by telling her that she was very
brave."

trainee reporter	Volontär(in), Praktikant(in) *im Medienbereich*	intrudor	Eindringling
		stocking	Strumpf
		unpleasant	unangenehm
victim	Opfer	be (feel) upset	durcheinander sein
dear (*coll*)	mein(e) Liebe(r)	get over sth	über etw. hinweg-
crash	Krachen		kommen

Understanding the text.

Are these statements true or false according to the text? Or does the text not say?
Tick the appropriate column.

	True	False	Doesn't say
1. Katie wants to write an article about a burglary.			
2. The burglary took place in a rich lady's house.			
3. Mrs Brown did not know about the burglary until after it had happened.			
4. Mrs Brown seems quite relaxed about everything.			
5. Katie tried to help Mrs Brown feel better.			

Further question. Answer it in full sentences.

6. What effect has the burglary had on Mrs Brown?

Replace the words in brackets with other words of the same meaning.

7. It's (difficult) ... to say. (line 11)
8. I heard a (crash) ... . (line 9)
9. When she (got back) ... to the office ... . (line 23)
10. It was (a terrible) ... experience. (line 28)

And what about you?

11. Why is a burglary such a terrible experience for the victim?
12. What is the job of a reporter in a situation such as Katie's?

Reported speech
Indirekte Rede

"You **are** very brave."	„Sie sind sehr mutig."
I **told** her that she **was** very brave.	Ich sagte ihr, dass sie sehr mutig sei.
	(..., sie sei sehr mutig.)

◆ In der direkten Rede wird wörtlich wiedergegeben, was jemand gesagt hat. Diese Sätze stehen meist in Anführungszeichen (*inverted commas*). Im Englischen sehen Anführungszeichen anders aus als im Deutschen: "..." statt „...".

In der **indirekten Rede** wird **berichtet**, was jemand gesagt hat, **ohne** den **genauen Wortlaut** des **Sprechers** wiederzugeben. Wenn das **Verb** des **einleitenden Satzes** in der **Vergangenheit** steht (*She said that ...*), werden in der indirekten Rede oft **andere Zeitformen** verwendet. Das heißt, beim Wechsel zur indirekten Rede erfolgt eine **„Verschiebung" der Zeitebene**. Dieses Merkmal der englischen Grammatik wird normalerweise *"backshift of tenses"* genannt.

present	⟶	past
past	⟶	past perfect
present perfect	⟶	past perfect
future ("will")	⟶	conditional ("would")

◆ **Komma** und **Anführungszeichen entfallen** in der indirekten Rede (*I said, "You are very brave." I told her that she was very brave.*).

◆ Außer *tell* und *say* gibt es eine Reihe von **anderen Verben**, die die **indirekte Rede einleiten** können, u.a. *to add* (*hinzufügen*), *to claim* (*behaupten*), *to explain* (*erklären*), *to report* (*berichten*), *to reply* (*erwidern*).

◆ Das Wort *that* (*dass*) ist **häufig entbehrlich**. Dies hängt jedoch davon ab, mit **welchem Verb** man die indirekte Rede **einleitet**: *She said (that) she had heard a crash. She added that he had ransacked* (plündern) *the house.*

◆ **Personalpronomen** (*I, you etc*) und **Possessivpronomen** (*my, your etc*) der **1. und 2. Person** müssen in der indirekten Rede **verändert** werden (*"I was upstairs in my bedroom," she replied. She replied that she had been upstairs in her bedroom.*).

Katie receives some instructions from her boss

Exercises

I. Imagine you met Daniel, a friend of yours. Daniel told you a lot of things:

1. "I was on holiday last month. I flew to Spain."
2. "My sister has had a baby. It was born on June 20."
3. "I am not enjoying my job. I'm looking for another one."
4. "I bought a second-hand car at the weekend."
5. "My girlfriend has fallen in love with someone else."
6. "My father was in hospital for a week."

The next day you tell another friend of yours what Daniel said to you.
Put Daniel's sentences into reported speech. Start with "He told me that ..."
or "He said that ...". ●●

II. The verbs "say" and "tell" are easy to mix up. There is an important
grammatical difference between them. Look at these examples and the
explanation below.

> a. He told **me** (that) he was tired.
> b. He said (that) he was tired.

The verb "to tell" is normally followed by a personal pronoun
(me, you, him, her, us, them).

Now complete these four sentences by adding "said" or "told". ●●

1. Mike ... us he had been offered a new job.
2. Sue ... it was a nice hotel but we didn't enjoy it.
3. William ... I could borrow his car if I wanted to.
4. Anne ... him she couldn't come to the party.

Reported questions
Indirekte Fragesätze

"What time **did** it **happen**?"   „Wann ist es passiert?“
I **asked** her what time it **had**   Ich fragte sie, wann es passiert sei.
happened.

◆ Bei der Wiedergabe von **Fragen in der indirekten Rede** findet in der Regel
  gleichfalls eine **„Zeitverschiebung“** (*"backshift of tenses"*) statt, wenn das
  Verb des einleitenden Satzes in der **Vergangenheit** steht.
◆ Das **Fragewort bleibt**, und die **Wortstellung** entspricht der eines **Aussa-
  gesatzes** (d.h. Subjekt-Verb-Objekt): *I asked her what he had said to her.*
  Bei **Fragen ohne Fragewort** verwendet man *if* oder ***whether*** (*ob*): *I asked
  her if she had seen him.*
◆ Wie im Deutschen steht auch im Englischen nach indirekten Fragen **kein
  Fragezeichen** (*"What time did you see him?" the reporter asked. The
  reporter asked what time she had seen him.*).

*III. Imagine that a reporter interviewed you about a day in your life.
These were some of her questions:*

1. "When do you get up?"
2. "Where do you work?"
3. "Do you drive to work?"
4. "What time do you finish work?"
5. "Do you spend your evenings at home?"
6. "Are you the sort of person who stays up late?"

*Later you tell one of your friends what the reporter asked you. Put her
questions into reported speech. Start with "She asked me ... ."* ●●

Reported commands, advice, requests

Indirekte Befehle, Ratschläge, Bitten

He said: "Sit down!"	Er sagte: „Setzen Sie sich hin!"
He **told her to sit** on a chair.	Er forderte sie auf, sich auf einen Stuhl zu setzen.

Befehle, Ratschläge und **Bitten** werden in der **indirekten Rede** durch eine **Verb + Objekt + Infinitiv mit *"to"*-Konstruktion** wiedergegeben (vgl. dazu auch Modul 17A, S. 61). Bei **Verneinungen** tritt ein *not* zwischen Objekt und Infinitiv (*He told her not to move.*).

Für Befehle oder Ratschläge verwendet man als **einleitendes Verb** in der Regel *to tell* oder *to advise*, für Bitten *to ask* oder *to invite*.

IV. Imagine that somebody is giving you advice about finding a job.
    This is the advice:

1. "Read all the local papers."
2. "Apply for as many jobs as possible."
3. "Be polite on the phone."
4. "Arrive for the interview on time."
5. "Smile at the interviewer."
6. "Don't worry if you are not successful the first time."

The next day you tell somebody about the advice you were given.
Put the sentences above into reported speech. Start with "She told me ... ."
or "She advised me ... ." ●●

V. Which remarks match which statements? Link them. ●●

- Good luck! I hope it goes well.
- Have a good holiday.
- Oh, that's a shame.
- Oh, we'd love to.

1. I'll ring you when we get back from Canada.
2. We won't be able to come to the party, I'm afraid.
3. Would you and Steve like to come round for dinner?
4. I've got an important exam tomorrow.

VI. Which statements would produce these remarks? ● ●

1. .?. .   No, I didn't get a ticket unfortunately.
2. .?. .   Really? Congratulations!
3. .?. .   Nothing serious, I hope.
4. .?. .   Have a good journey!

22B

Gathering information

Katie is visiting a small firm which makes *rocking horses*. She is going to write an article about it for the newspaper. First she meets the owners, Mark and Tony Stevenson.

5 **In the office**

Mark: Hi, I'm Mark Stevenson. This is my *twin brother* Tony.
Tony: Hello.
Katie: Thank you for inviting me along.
Mark: Oh, that's all right. You are very welcome. Perhaps you would like
10   to start with a tour of the *workshop*?
Tony: Yeah, and come back later and have a look at the horses?
Katie: Fine, that sounds good.

In the workshop

Mark: So this is the workshop where the horses start their lives.
15 Katie: (looking at a hole in the horse's body:) Is this where you fit the time
            capsule in?
Mark: Yes it is. The time capsule goes right into the middle of the horse.

In the carving shop

Mark: Mind the step, Katie. It's quite steep.
20 Katie: Oh, thanks. I see what you mean.
Mark: This is the carving shop.
Katie: Are all your horses carved by hand?
Mark: Yes, indeed, they are. We employ 16 *craftsmen*.
Katie: What kind of wood is used for the horses?
25 Mark: This horse is made from *walnut* and this one at the back is made
            from English oak and the painted horses are made from *tulip* and *beech*
            in the legs. And the tropical *hardwood* like mahogany comes from
            sustainable forests.

Katie: And the eyes?
30 Mark: The eyes are made for us in Germany.

In the finishing shop

Mark: We have been incredibly lucky over the last 14 years. All sorts of people
have bought horses from us. And we have been given *awards* by the
British Toy and Hobby Manufacturer's Association and the Toy *Guild*.
35 Katie: I think they are lovely, just gorgeous. I'd love to have one for my little
niece and nephew.
Tony: If you want one for Christmas, you'd better *get your order in right away*.
We've got a full *order book*.

A summary of the story ●●

40 Mark Stevenson greeted Katie and introduced her to his twin brother, Tony. Katie
thanked them for inviting her along. Mark suggested starting with a tour of the workshop. Tony added that they could come back to look at the horses afterwards. Katie
agreed.
In the workshop Katie wanted to know how they put the time capsule into the horse.
45 Mark showed her how it was done. As they were going into the carving shop Mark
warned Katie about the step. Katie enquired what kind of wood was used for the
horses. Mark explained that the horses were made from walnut, oak, tulip and beech
wood. He added that the mahogany came from sustainable forests and that the eyes
were made in Germany.

50 In the finishing shop Katie admired the gorgeous horses and expressed an interest in
    buying one herself for her niece and nephew. Tony smiled and advised her to place
    her order immediately.

gather information	Informationen sammeln, zusammentragen		*Holz herausge-schlagen wie nach-wächst. Dies deckt*
rocking horse	Schaukelpferd		*sich jedoch in*
twin brother	Zwillingsbruder		*Bezug auf Maha-*
workshop	Werkstatt		*goni nicht mit der*
capsule	Kapsel, Behälter		*Realität.*)
carving shop	Schnitzwerkstatt	award	Preis, Auszeich-
craftsman	*hier*: Kunsthand-werker	British Toy	nung
		British Toy	*etwa*: Vereinigung
walnut	Nussbaumholz; Walnuss(baum)	and Hobby Manufacturer's	der britischen Spielzeug- und
tulip	Tulpenbaum(holz)	Association	Hobbygeräte-
beech	Buche(nholz)		Hersteller
hardwood	Hartholz	guild	Innung
sustainable forests	nachhaltig bewirt-schaftete Wälder (*„nachhaltig"* in *der vereinfachten Bedeutung: es wird nur so viel*	get one's order in right away order book	in Auftrag geben, eine Bestellung aufgeben sofort, auf der Stelle Auftragsbuch

Understanding the text.

Complete the sentences by underlining one of the expressions in the brackets.

1. Katie has gone to the Stevensons' firm to find out more about (the British toy
   industry/small firms in Britain/how twins work together).
2. On her tour of the company Katie sees how (hard/easy/cheap) it is to make
   rocking horses.
3. Katie also sees that the horses are made almost totally by (hand/machine/eye).
4. The Stevensons are obviously very proud of (each other/Katie/their work).
5. Business must be going well because the company has lots of (new employ-
   ees/prizes/orders).

Further questions. Answer them using your own words as far as possible.

6. The horses have a hole in them for a "time capsule" (lines 15–16). What do you
   think is a time capsule and what is its purpose?
7. How can we see that the Stevensons' rocking horses have a good reputation?

What are the English equivalents for these German expressions?

8.   Vorsicht Stufe!
9.   Wir haben wahnsinnig viel Glück gehabt.
10. Sie sollten lieber gleich bestellen.

And what about you?

11. Would you like to have your own company? Say why/why not.
12. Do you think making traditional toys like rocking horses has a future?

H   Verb patterns

Das Verb und seine Ergänzungen

Katie **thanked them for inviting** her along.	Katie dankte ihnen dafür, dass sie sie eingeladen hatten.
Tony **advised her to place** her order immediately.	Tony riet ihr, die Bestellung sofort aufzugeben.

◆   **Ausführlich formulierte Texte** oder **Dialoge** kann man durch geeignete **Verben verkürzen**, anstatt sie in der indirekten Rede detailliert wiederzugeben. Nehmen wir das folgende Beispiel:
   "I was wondering if you'd like to come to a party with me on Saturday evening?" she asked. "Yes," he replied. "I'd love to."

   Der Inhalt dieses Mini-Dialogs lässt sich in einem einfachen Satz wiedergeben: *"She invited him to a party."* oder *"He accepted her invitation to a party.".*

◆   Zur korrekten und präzisen Wiedergabe von Aussagen benötigt man jedoch nicht nur Verben. Man braucht auch Kenntnisse darüber, wie diese **Verben** in einem Satz **grammatikalisch verwendet** werden. Im Folgenden ein **Überblick** über einige wichtige „**Konstruktionsmöglichkeiten**".

   –   **Verb + Objekt + Infinitiv mit *"to"*** (vgl. Module 17A, S. 61 und 22A, S. 143), wie z.B. bei:

      to advise, to ask, to order, to recommend, to remind, to tell sb to do sth

         He **advised us to call** again later.
         She **told me to keep** quiet.

- **Verb (+ Objekt) + Nebensatz mit *"that"*** (vgl. Modul 22A, S. 140), wie z.B. bei:

to admit, to answer (sb), to complain (to sb), to explain (to sb), to promise (sb), to recommend (to sb), to reply (to sb), to say (to sb), to suggest, to tell sb that ...

(Mit Ausnahme von *to answer* und *to reply* ist *that* in allen anderen Fällen entbehrlich.)

> She **promised her (that)** she would be on time.
> They **told us (that)** they were going away the next day.
> He **suggested (that)** they should come later.

- **Verb (+ Präposition) + -ing Form (Gerund)** (vgl. Module 9A, S. 138 und 12A, S. 187), wie z.B. bei:

to admit, to apologize for, to insist on, to recommend, to suggest doing sth

> She **apologized for asking** so many questions.
> He **suggested coming** later.

- **Verb + Infinitiv mit *"to"***, wie z.B. bei:

to agree, to expect, to promise, to offer, to refuse to do sth

> She **expects to be** back on time. (... *damit rechnen, dass* ...)
> She **promised to be** on time.

Hinweis: Für den Lernenden empfiehlt es sich, **Verben** stets **zusammen** mit ihren **möglichen Ergänzungen** zu **lernen** und dabei auch ein gutes **einsprachiges** Wörterbuch zu benutzen. Und man sollte auch beachten, dass es bei einer Reihe von Verben – wie z.B. bei *to tell* oder *to promise* – **nicht nur eine Konstruktionsmöglichkeit** gibt.

Exercises

I. Report the direct speech using the verbs given. ●●

"Why don't you accept the job?" I asked him.
1. I suggested that ... .
2. I advised him ... .
3. I recommended to him that ... .
4. I told him ... .

II. Report the direct speech using the verbs given. ●●

"I'll ring you tomorrow," he said to her.
1. He said ... .
2. He told ... .
3. He explained ... .
4. He promised ... .

III. Report the direct speech using the verbs given. ●●

"You must get up earlier," she said to him.
1. She told ... .
2. She ordered ... .
3. She asked ... .
4. She suggested that ... .

IV. Rewrite these six sentences using the verbs given. ●●

1. Clare said: "My son never rings me."
   Clare complained ... .
2. "It was me," said Tony. "I broke the tea pot."
   Tony admitted ... .
3. "I'm sorry I'm late," said Alex to his boss.
   Alex apologized ... .
4. "Shall we have a game of cards?" Julia asked.
   Julia suggested ... .
5. "No. I'm not giving you the money," Jack said to Rose.
   Jack refused ... .
6. "Don't forget to ring Tom," Karen said to her son.
   Karen reminded ... .

V. Adverbs and adjectives. Complete the sentences by using one word from each box. ● ●

bitterly ● completely ● incredibly ●
reasonably ● seriously ● surprisingly

disappointed ● easy ● ill ● lucky ● cheap ● different

1. We expected the meal to be very expensive but it turned out to be ... .
2. We had waited ten hours to get tickets so when we found out that the concert was sold out we were ... .
3. When we got back home after a year in New Zealand we saw that everything here was ... .
4. The car turned over three times and crashed into the back of a lorry but nobody was injured so we were ... .
5. My wife's mother is ... . We visit her every day in hospital.
6. Everybody had told me that the exam would be very difficult but on the day it seemed ... .

VI. Write a short text about the job(s) you have done or do. Say what the job is (was), where you do (did) it and what you like (liked) about it. Write about 50 words. Use a dictionary if you wish.

22C

Roger Perkins and Andrew Cruickshank – two journalists

Listen carefully to Roger Perkins and Andrew Cruickshank talking about their work on "The Sevenoaks Chronicle". Then answer the questions below.

I. Which things do Roger and Andrew talk about during the interview? Tick four of the eight alternatives.

   a. a typical lead story
   b. how many hours a week he works
   c. the biggest story that had ever happened
   d. his qualifications for becoming editor
   e. a typical human interest story in the paper
   f. the number of women reporters
   g. writing a leader for the paper
   h. why he lives in Sevenoaks

Roger Perkins

II. Answer these questions using your own words as far as possible.

1. Roger Perkins talks about "the biggest story" ever on October 17, 1987. What was the story?
2. What sort of stories interest the readers of "The Sevenoaks Chronicle" most and why?
3. Roger Perkins talks about writing the leading article every week. Why does he like writing "the leader" so much?

III. Which eight parts of a newspaper are being described below? Choose an expression from the box.

> obituary ● horoscope ● crossword ● advertisements ● letters page ●
> gossip column ● weather forecast ● review

1. These bring a newspaper a lot of money.
2. This is an article about somebody who has just died.
3. This tells you if you can expect a good day or not.
4. This contains the opinions of the readers.
5. This informs you about famous people.
6. This provides information on the day's weather.
7. This describes a book, a film, or an art exhibition and what the writer thinks of it.
8. This is a game using words.

22D

Meterman the detective (Part 2)

*I. Two words in each paragraph are missing. Select them from the box below
and put them into the right part of the text.*

> valuables • keys • story • hostage • handle •
> freedom • ladder • pounds

As Scoop Malone, top reporter from the "Daily Splash", is making his way to
Monchelsea Place to find out more about the ... story, Meterman is begging the
"vicar" to let him go.
"You must keep the girl," he *pleads*. "Let me go. You'll get a lot of money for
her! Half a million ... in *ransom money* perhaps. No one would pay that much for
a poor Meterman. Let me go!"

The "vicar", however, has another idea. "So Meterman. You want to go free, do
you? Well, the price of ... is your van. And for you, young lady," he says turning
to the maid, "I want you to get all the tourists to put all the ... into the van. The
porcelain, the silver, the pictures, the antiques, the *bric-a-brac*. Everything, in
fact, must go into the van. Do you understand?"

The maid rushes to the drawing room where Scoop Malone is talking to the
tourists. She asks them to help her get everything into Meterman's van. In the
meantime the "vicar" orders Meterman to give him the ... to his van. As the
tourists are packing up Meterman's van with expensive antiques, silver and other
precious things Meterman and the "vicar" climb out of a window and down
a ... . "Come faster! Faster you idiot!" the criminal shouts nervously. "Come
down here and wait while I see *if the coast is clear.*"

As Meterman walks towards his van, he does not notice a *rake* lying on the
ground. Without realizing it he steps on the end of it and the ... *flies up* and
hits the "vicar" on the nose. He falls to the ground unconscious. Meterman and
the other tourists are free. Lady Bea has her silver again. The next morning the
"Daily Splash" runs a big front-page ... : "Gunman caught. Meterman the hero,"
it *reads*.

hostage	Geisel	... if the coast	... ob die Luft
plead	*hier*: inständig bitten,	is clear.	rein ist.
	flehen	rake	Rechen
ransom (money)	Lösegeld	fly up	*hier*: hochschnellen
bric-a-brac	Nippsachen	read	*hier*: lauten

II. What do you think of the ending to the story? Write down your opinion in a short paragraph.

III. Link these newspaper headlines (1-6) with their explanations (a-f).

1. STAR WEDS IN SECRET

2. PRESIDENT BACKS PEACE PLAN

3. KEY WITNESS DEATH THREAT

4. BOMB BLASTS KNIGHTSBRIDGE STORE

5. NEW TENNIS CLASH AT WIMBLEDON

6. **PRINCE'S BUTLER RIDDLE**

a. sporting stars play against each other in an important match
b. a person who saw a crime is in danger
c. there was an explosion in a big shop in central London
d. a famous person marries
e. a new person starts work in the royal household
f. leading stateman supports effort to end war

22E

Encounters

GENTLEMEN

TRAIN Spotter with nice new Anorak.....!!, Oh No!, fun loving, fit, forties, professional man only slightly mental, Sussex area, seeks seriously slim, sexy, sagacious soul mate thirties/early forties for sun, sea, sand holiday in the Greek Islands mid June. Photo plse & phone no Box 5826

VERY exceptional gentleman 28 seeks a very exceptional slim attractive lady 20-35 London area. Photo plse to Box No 5582

WARWICKSHIRE stylish, fit Co Director. Young 46, well travelled 5'11" considered good looking, GSOH. Romantic, almost unbelievable. Seeks younger, classy, tactile blonde?, who does not need to reply to adverts like this. Photo appreciated. Box 5885

WHERE & when shall we meet, wine, dine & travel? Unattached, unhindered, independent gent (smoker), aged 60 seeks much younger lady to indulge. Genuine replies only. Recent photo please. Please Reply to Box No 5830

57 YEAR OLD Bachelor, nr Genoa, youthful, cultured, communicative, well off, seriously motivated, seeks nice responsible dynamic English woman about 45 years old, knowledge of Italian, serious, well balanced, without children. About 5ft 6ins tall and slim. Reply to Box No 5720 with photo

YORKSHIRE/HUMBERSIDE. Why write to one man, reverse the odds in your favour, over 300 Elite men, call Elite Introductions now!! Open every day/evening, call on freephone 0500 525240

Zzzzz Wake up! Close Encounters is open Saturday and Sunday. Call free 0800 141 141.

GAY male 33, 6ft handsome N.West/W.Mids based seeks professional non scene for 1-2-1. Must be independent with many interests. Reply to Box No 5829

GAY MEN At last, an alternative to the scene! OUT&OUT is the dining club as featured on National TV/Radio (London) 0181 723 9245

KIND, sensitive, caring Gay man 31 WLTM similarly nice young gentleman to enjoy classical music, cinema, the Arts, & generally time together. London. Please Reply to Box No 5612

LADIES

AMERICAN in London and loving it! Slim, pretty, feminine and 40. Elegant, polished, but a jeans and boots girl at heart. Happy, with all of the ingredients for a perfect life but looking for that special someone to share it with. Please respond if you love to laugh and simply enjoy life. Wille exchange photos. Please Reply to Box No 5878

AMUSING single men 30-48 for mixed Italian holiday June 2. Call Christine already booked on holiday 0181 866 6875 fast.

ARE you caring, humorous, fun loving and interesting in sharing friendship and life to the full? I am 56 going on 36, attractive, sensitive, fun loving and keen to share the joys of life through love, growth and harmony. Photo plse. Lndn/ Home Counties. Box 5586

ARE you a warm, successful, fun-loving, Jewish guy, 42-48, n/s, looking for an attractive, romantic, Jewish, blue-eyed blonde for fun and love? I'm N.W. but not adverse to travel. Please Reply with photo to Box No 5837

ASIAN Muslim lawyer, 20's, very pretty, enjoys the Arts and good conversation. WLTM Muslim prof male 28-35. Photo please. Reply to Box No 5879

ATTRACTIVE, tall, slim, fun-loving lady, 34, with successful business career, WLTM attractive, intelligent, friendly man with GSOH. Enjoys good conversation, the outdooors, skiing, eating in and out. Reply with photo please. N. West/W. Yorks. Box No 5831.

ATTRACTIVE, professional lady, early 40's. Seeks similar male (40-50) for friendship /relationship & to enjoy the good things in life. Aberdeen based! Please Reply to Box No 5880

BEAUTIFUL brunette, tall, slender journalist with GSOH seeks tall professional gent 35-45 for true love. S/E. Photo please. Please Reply to Box No 5697

THE LATEST STYLE   UNIT 23

23A

Dealing with customers

A new assistant in a clothes shop is learning how to deal with customers. The shop
manageress has asked her to do a role play with another woman, who plays the customer. The customer doesn't know what she wants and the assistant is helping her.

5 *Shop assistant*:   Can I help you?
   Customer: I'm just looking really. Actually, I'm looking for something
                      for the evening. What I really want is a dress I can wear for
                      special occasions.
   Shop assistant: *What size are you?* About a 16?
10 Customer: 16 or I sometimes take an 18. It depends.
   Shop assistant: (showing her a dress:) We have this in a 16. It's a lovely style.
   Customer: Oh yes, that's nice. (She sees another dress:) This is nice, too.
                      Can I try these on?
   Shop assistant: Of course, the *fitting room*'s just over there.
15   Do call if you need any help.

(Some minutes later. The customer tries on a blue dress.)

Learning how to deal with customers

Customer:	This one's quite nice.
Shop assistant:	The colour is good. It's a very well cut dress. It suits you.
	What you need is a scarf, *draped* here, like that. Perhaps it's
20	a bit too full on the shoulders. We could *take it in* for you.
	(Turning to the manageress:) Sue, pass me the *pins*,
	will you?
	And the *waist*. We can *let it out* if it's too tight.
	If you could just turn round.
25 Customer:	Yes, the waist is too tight. (*Screams* loudly:) That's me!
Shop assistant:	I'm sorry, did I hurt you?
Customer:	Yes, you did.
Shop assistant:	I do apologize. There, that's better. How does that look?

(At this point the manageress interrupts them.)

30 Manageress:	That was very good, except that you stuck a pin into the
	customer. That is *unforgivable*. You must be more careful.
Shop assistant:	Yes, I'm sorry. I think I better practise on a *dummy*. (To the
	woman who played the customer:) I'm ever so sorry. I hope I
	didn't hurt you too much.
35 Woman:	I'll *survive*.
Manageress:	That will do for today. Here come some real customers.
	Make sure you don't stick pins into them!

deal with	umgehen mit, behandeln	pin	(Steck-)Nadel
shop assistant	Verkäufer(in)	waist	Taille
What size are you?	Welche Größe haben (tragen) Sie?	let sth out	auslassen (weiter machen)
fitting room	Umkleideraum, -kabine	scream	(auf)schreien, kreischen
drape	drapieren	unforgivable	unverzeihlich
take sth in	*hier*: abnehmen (enger machen)	dummy	*hier*: Kleiderpuppe
		survive	überleben

Understanding the text.

Which sentence (a–c) best completes the statement (1–3)?

1. The new shop assistant is practising how she can help customers ...
    a) to buy evening dresses.
    b) to choose which clothes to buy.
    c) to wear more scarves.

2. The only mistake the assistant makes is ...
    a) to be too polite to the customer.
    b) to sell a dress which is too big for the customer.
    c) to stick a pin into the customer.

3. At the end of the text the woman who plays the customer seems ...
    a) to be very angry with the assistant.
    b) to have almost forgotten what happened to her.
    c) to want to leave the shop.

Further questions. Answer them in complete sentences and use your own words as far as possible.

4. The customer says she wants a dress for "special occasions" (line 8). What do you think she means?
5. What does the manageress think of how her assistant managed the role play?

Choose the right ending for the sentence.

6. The expression "It suits you" (line 18) means ...
    a) the dress is the right size.
    b) the dress looks good on you.
    c) the dress looks like a suit.

7. The expression "That will do for today" (line 36) means ...
    a) the new assistant can go home.
    b) the assistant will not do any more role plays today.
    c) the shop will close now.

8. The expression "I'll survive" (line 35) means ...
    a) what you did hurt me a lot.
    b) what you did hurt me a bit.
    c) what you did didn't hurt me at all.

Find the English for the following.

9. Ich trage manchmal Größe 18.
10. Kann ich diese Kleider anprobieren?

And what about you?

11. Would you like to work as a shop assistant? Say why/why not.
12. Do you think it is necessary for shop assistants to learn how to deal with customers?

Multi-word verbs (II)
Zusammengesetzte Verben (II)

Could I **try** these **on**?	Könnte ich diese (hier) anprobieren?
We could **take** it **in** for you.	Wir könnten es für Sie enger machen.
We could **let** it **out**.	Wir könnten es weiter machen.

◆ Im Modul 15B (vgl. S. 32) wurde gezeigt, dass viele **Verben** im Englischen aus **zwei** oder **drei Teilen** bestehen. Die Bedeutung dieser Verben liegt in manchen Fällen auf der Hand, z.B.: *Can I try this dress on?* (*try on* = anprobieren). Die Bedeutung anderer zusammengesetzter Verben ist jedoch viel komplizierter. Hier **vier Beispiele** mit dem **Stammverb** *to look*:

1. She has always **looked up to** her father. (look up to = respect; *aufblicken*)

2. The police are **looking into** the burglary. (look into = investigate; *untersuchen*)

3. After last year's recession things are now **looking up**. (look up = improve; *besser werden*)

4. If you don't **look out**, she'll apply for your job. (look out = be careful; *aufpassen*)

◆ Und hier noch ein Hinweis zur **Grammatik** und **Wortstellung** der **zweiteiligen** *multi-word verbs*:

– Bei **intransitiven Verben** (d.h. Verben, auf die kein direktes Objekt folgen darf) sind **Stammverb und Partikel nicht trennbar** (z.B. ... *things are looking up.*).

– Bei **transitiven Verben** gibt es sowohl trennbare als auch nicht trennbare:

   • Bei **trennbaren transitiven Verben** kann das **direkte Objekt** in **zwei Positionen** stehen, z.B.:
   She tried on the dress.
   She tried the dress on.

   Wenn dieses **direkte Objekt** ein **Pronomen** ist (z.B. "*it*" statt "*dress*"), gibt es nur **eine Position,** und zwar **zwischen** dem **Verb** und der **Partikel**:
   She tried **it** on.

> • Bei **nicht trennbaren transitiven Verben** muss das **Objekt** (ob **Substantiv** oder **Pronomen**) **nach der Partikel** stehen, z.B.:
>
> The police are looking into **the burglary**.

Welche transitiven *multi-word verbs* trennbar sind und welche nicht, dafür gibt es keine Regeln. Hier hilft nur das Nachschlagen in einem guten einsprachigen Wörterbuch.

(Mehr zur Wortstellung der *multi-word verbs* im Modul 25B, S. 193)

Exercises

I. Match the multi-word verbs underlined in the sentences below with the more formal equivalents in the box. ●●

> to arrive • to manage (financially) • to recover from • to spend

1. He's <u>getting over</u> a bad cold.
2. They can't <u>get by</u> on one salary.
3. When does your train <u>get in</u>?
4. She <u>got through</u> all her pocket money in a week.

II. Replace the underlined expressions in the sentences below with the multi-word verb equivalents in the box. ●●

> to come across • to come up • to come round • to come off

1. Did the holiday you planned for Christmas <u>take place</u>?
2. You must <u>visit us</u> some time next week.
3. We <u>found by chance</u> this lovely pub last weekend.
4. Something important <u>was said</u> at the meeting yesterday.

III. Which answers (a-d) match the questions (1-4)? ●●

1. The car's broken down?
2. How many people turned up last night?
3. Can you guess who I ran into yesterday?
4. Shall we see them off at the airport?

a. No, who?
b. When is the flight?
c. I'm afraid so.
d. Fifty or so.

Now translate sentences 1–4 into German.

IV. Look at the verbs in exercise III and answer the questions below.

1. Which two verbs are intransitive?
2. Which two verbs are transitive?
3. Which transitive verb is separable (*trennbar*)?
4. Which transitive verb is inseparable (*nicht trennbar*)?

V. Which of these five situations would you NOT complain about?

1. You're in a fast food restaurant and your hamburger is cold.
2. You buy a CD and when you get home you find out that the last track is scratched.
3. The shoes you bought at the weekend are too small.
4. You order a book and when it arrives you discover that four pages in the middle are missing.
5. You buy an expensive jacket. Your friend buys the same jacket from a different shop but it costs half the price.

In a short paragraph (50-60 words) say why you would not complain.

VI. Look at the tables and work out what size you would ask for if you were shopping (for yourself or your girlfriend!) in Britain. The sentences may help you to form a dialogue. ●●

Shoes Ladies' Sizes		Dresses Ladies' Sizes	
G	GB	G	GB
36	3.5	36	10
37	4	38	12
38	5	40	14
39	6	42	16
40	6.5	44	18

(G = Germany; GB = Great Britain)

Can I help you?
Yes, I am looking for ... .
I see. What size are you?
Well, I ... .

23B

Preparing for a photo shoot ●●

We meet a group of students who are doing a *degree course in European fashion*. They are preparing for a photo shoot. As part of a team they each have their individual role to play in creating a *garment*. This is what they do.

5 1 Student: We are the designers. We're the people who create and develop the ideas for a new garment. I'm working on the *evening wear* collection at the moment. The styles which I like best are geometric and asymmetric and futuristic.

2 Student: I'm working on a *suit* collection. The *fabrics* which I like to work with 10 are transparent PVCs and *felted woollens*.

1 Student: We work with markers and only pencils to produce our sketches.

3 Student: We are the *pattern-cutters*. The pattern-cutter is the person who cuts the pattern in paper.

4 Student: After cutting the pattern in paper we then *adjust* it to fit the dummy.

15 3 Student: We work with pattern cutting paper, *pattern-master*, the *metre rule*, pencil and an *eraser*.

5 Student: I'm a *sample machinist*. The sample machinist is the person who makes the first sample of the garment in *calico*. I work with a sewing machine, an *overlocker* and a *steam iron*.

20 6 Student: I'm the model. The model is the person who wears the clothes which the designer and her team have created.

degree course in	*Studiengang für*	metre rule	Meterstab
European fashion	*europäisches Mode-*	eraser	Radiergummi
	design	sample	Muster, Probe
garment	Kleidungsstück	sample machinist	Musternäherin
evening wear	Abendkleid	calico	Nessel
suit	Kostüm; Anzug	overlocker	Overlockmaschine
fabrics	Stoffe, *hier*: Materia-		(*Nähmaschine, die*
	lien		*in einem Arbeits-*
felted woollens	Wollfilz		*gang Nähen,*
pattern	*hier*: Schnittmuster		*Versäubern und*
pattern-cutter	Schnittzeichnerin;		*Stoffabschneiden*
	Schnittdirektrice		*erledigt*)
adjust	anpassen	steam iron	Dampfbügeleisen
pattern-master	(Schnittmuster-)		
	Schablone		

One of the designers on the team

Understanding the text.

According to the text are these statements true or false?

	True	False
1. The first and second student do the same work.		
2. The third and fourth student have the most creative job.		
3. The fifth student designs and makes clothes.		
4. The sixth student tries the clothes on.		

1. The first and second student do the same work.
2. The third and fourth student have the most creative job.
3. The fifth student designs and makes clothes.
4. The sixth student tries the clothes on.

Further questions. Answer using your own words as far as possible.

5. Are these young women going to sell the clothes? Give a reason for your answer.
6. Which of the students seems to have a special role in the team? Why?

Say these words as the people in the Module do. ●●

7. clothes / kləʊðz /
8. machinist / məˈʃiːnɪst /
9. sewing machine / ˈsəʊɪŋ məˈʃiːn /
10. iron / ˈaɪən /

And what about you?

11. Are you fashion-conscious? Say why or why not.
12. Do you think it is easy to get a job as a fashion designer? Try and give some reasons for your opinion.

H   Defining relative clauses (II)

Bestimmende Relativsätze (II)

The pattern-cutter is the person **who** cuts the pattern.	Die Schnittzeichnerin ist diejenige, die das Schnittmuster erstellt.
The styles **which** I like best are geometric and futuristic.	Die Stile, die ich am liebsten mag, sind geometrisch und futuristisch.
The fabrics **which** I like to work **with** are transparent PVCs.	Die Materialien, mit denen ich gerne arbeite, sind aus durchsichtigem PVC.

◆ **Bestimmende Relativsätze** mit *which* (für Sachen, einschließlich Tieren) und *where* (zur Bezeichnung eines Ortes: *This is the room where all the fabrics are stored.*) wurden bereits im Modul 16A behandelt (vgl. S. 44).

◆ In diesem Modul kommt ein **weiteres Relativpronomen** hinzu: *who*, zur Bezeichnung von **Personen**. *Who* kann **Subjekt** (*We meet a group of students who are doing a degree course ...*) oder **Objekt** (*She is the person who I saw yesterday.*) des **Relativsatzes** sein. Die Objektform *whom* gehört mittlerweile weitgehend der formalen Schriftsprache an.

◆ Sind *who* und *which* **Objekt** eines bestimmenden Relativsatzes, werden sie – insbesondere in der gesprochenen Sprache – häufig **weggelassen** (*She is the person (who) I saw yesterday. We only create garments (which) we'd like to wear ourselves.*).

◆ *Who* und *which* können auch als **Objekt einer Präposition** stehen. Dabei bleibt die Präposition – wie in einem Hauptsatz – **hinter dem Verb** (*He is the person (who) we talked to yesterday.*).

Exercises

I. Match the two halves of the sentence. ●●

1. A customer is a person who ...	a. sells meat.
2. A butcher is someone who ...	b. flies planes.
3. An architect is a person who ...	c. buys things in shops.
4. A pilot is someone who ...	d. designs buildings.

II. Now explain what these words mean using the same structures as in exercise I and your own words.

1. a vegetarian   3. a fashion model
2. a burglar   4. a student

The sample machinist at work

III. Join the two sentences into one. The first words have been given. ●●

Example:

A child answered the phone. He said you were out shopping.

The child who answered the phone said you were out shopping.

1. A young assistant served us. She was very impolite. (The young assistant ... .)
2. A dog came out of the shop. It bit my leg. (The dog ... .)
3. A customer bought ten dresses. She was a film star. (The customer ... .)
4. A shop has closed. It sold lovely bread and cakes. (The shop ... .)

IV. Join the two sentences. ●●

Example:

She found the key.   (She had lost it.)

She found the key (which) she had lost.

1. The fish was delicious.   (We had it for breakfast.)
2. We stayed in a hotel.   (You recommended it.)
3. I liked the dress.   (You were wearing it yesterday.)
4. Where is the book?   (You gave me it this morning.)

V. Put in the appropriate relative clause to complete the sentences. ●●

- (which) she had applied for
- (which) I slept in
- (which) they went to
- (which) we wanted to travel on

1. The bed ... was very hard.
2. The party ... last night was really boring.
3. The ferry ... was booked up.
4. The job ... was not very well paid.

VI. There are many nouns which are really two nouns together (eg fashion designer, shop assistant, evening dress). These fixed expressions are called compound nouns. Read the sentences below and write down which compound nouns are being described or defined.

1. You wear them when it is very bright and sunny outside.
2. Young people like to stay in these places when they are on holiday because they are not as expensive as hotels.
3. This wakes you up in the morning at a specific time.
4. You can pay for things in shops with this if you have not got cash with you.
5. The first language you learnt when you were a child.
6. You stop at these when they are red.

Look at the key to exercises to see if you write these compound nouns as one word, two words or with a hyphen (Bindestrich).

23C

Joan Barrell – a fashion writer

Listen carefully to Joan Barrell talking about fashions and answer the questions on page 166.

I. What does Joan Barrell talk about in her interview? Tick two items.

- a. fashion magazines
- b. how much good clothes cost
- c. clothes for children
- d. what she herself wears
- e. what fashion is
- f. where to buy fashionable clothes in London

II. Answer these questions in full sentences.

1. Joan talks about accessories or "little nothings". Why does she think they are so important?
2. What message does Joan have for people who think they are the wrong shape and size for fashionable clothes?

III. Put the words in the boxes into the correct sentence.

1. A ... consists of a pair of trousers and a jacket.
2. A ... is a number of rooms in a hotel.

3. A ... is something you use to clean or cover something.
4. Shirts, jumpers, trousers, coats and dresses are examples of ... .

5. A ... has buttons at the front and a collar at the top. You wear it under a jacket or jumper.
6. A ... is usually worn by women instead of trousers.

7. A ... is a description of events, real or not, that is written down in a book or told.
8. Events that have happened in the past are ... .

IV. Joan talks about "street cred" which means "street credibility". What has this word got to do with fashion and the fashion business? Write down what you think in a short paragraph.

23D

Meterman the male model

I. Put these six paragraphs into the correct order to tell the story about Meterman at the fashion show. Start with paragraph d.

a. Meterman is still busy reading the meter in another room and doesn't realize what *is in store for* him. "These lights are using up an amazing amount of electricity," he explains to the viewers. "I must tell these ladies to turn them off. *Better safe than sorry.*"

b. Behind the stage the models are getting ready for the show. Two of them are talking. "Who's the *male* model for today?" one asks. "Jason," the other replies. "He's really gorgeous."

c. Meterman goes to the room where the models are getting ready. He wants to tell the organizer about the high electricity consumption. Everybody stares at him when he walks in. "*He'll have to do,*" says the show organizer. "Ladies! Get him. Come on, girls. The show must go on!"

d. Meterman finds himself watching the rehearsals for a *charity fashion show*. "I can't understand why people want to waste their time and money on fashion," he complains. "Still, it's none of my business."

e. At that moment another of the models comes in with bad news. "Jason can't get here. His car's broken down," she explains. The show organizer is worried. "Well, we'll have to find somebody. We've got to have a man. Well? Find one! Any man will do. Anyone!"

f. Soon Meterman is walking out onto the stage as a male model. He parades gracefully up and down the *catwalk* as the *compere* describes his outfit. "Yes, ladies," she announces, "with this top designer outfit *you can take the man in your marriage and put some sparkle in your spouse*. He *dazzles*, he *bedazzles*, he glitters and he shines. In this outfit your man is sure to be ... every woman's *desire*!"

be in store for sb	jmdm. bevorstehen, jmdn. erwarten	charity fashion show	Modenschau für wohltätige Zwecke
Better safe than sorry.	Vorsicht ist besser als Nachsicht.	catwalk	Laufsteg
male	männlich	compere	Moderator(in); Conférencier
He'll have to do.	Der muss genügen.	sparkle	Glanz, Funkeln
charity	Wohltätigkeit	spouse	Gemahl(in)

... you can take	... Sie können Ihren	dazzle	blenden
the man in your	Ehemann nehmen	bedazzle	verwirren
marriage and	und ihm etwas	desire	Wunsch,
put some sparkle	Glanz verleihen.		Wunschtraum
in your spouse.			

II. What nouns are formed from these verbs?

1. consume   –   ?   5. announce   –   ?
2. explain   –   ?   6. reply   –   ?
3. rehearse   –   ?   7. describe   –   ?
4. complain   –   ?   8. organize   –   ?

III. Safe or secure? Read the explanations and complete the sentences below using one of these words.

When something cannot cause physical harm you feel "safe".
If you are not worried that something terrible can hurt you, you feel "secure".

1. This house is very ... . Nobody can break into it.
2. Do you think nuclear power is ...?
3. They are financially very ... . They have had their own business for over thirty years.
4. It's not ... to let the dog out when there are children playing here.

23E

Shopping on Sunday

THERE MUST BE AN ANSWER   UNIT 24

24A

They should have done it before ●●

1 Woman (with child): The smell of *exhaust fumes* is really *disgusting*. The problem here is that the traffic moves so slowly. More and more children are getting asthma these days. I wish they would ban cars completely from the town centre. Well, they
5 have pedestrianized this high street and that's a great improvement. Cars are no longer allowed. They should have done it before, of course. But better late than never.

2 Woman: The noise is absolutely *appalling*. That's my house over there. The difficulty here is that we have the motorway just at the *bottom* of the garden – and it's getting *busier* and busier all the time. I wish we could move house, but we can't,
10 so we just have to *put up with* it.

Man: The trouble is everyone is in such a hurry and they want to go faster and faster. I just wish they would keep to the speed limit here. Now this is a busy road. But they have *introduced* the *traffic calming system* and it's much better. They should have introduced it ten years ago.

exhaust fumes	Abgase	busy	*hier*: viel befahren
disgusting	abstoßend, Abscheu erweckend	put up with	sich abfinden mit
		introduce	*hier*: einführen
appalling	entsetzlich, erschreckend	traffic calming system	System zur Verkehrsberuhigung
bottom	unterer Teil; *hier*: Ende		

Understanding the text.

Which sentence (a–c) best completes the statement (1–3)? Tick it.

1. The woman with the child wants cars ...
   a) to be banned completely.
   b) to be banned from the middle of towns.
   c) to be driven more quickly.

2. The other woman would like to live somewhere where ...
   a) there is less space.
   b) there is less garden.
   c) there is less traffic.

3. The man wants car drivers to ...
   a) drive more slowly.
   b) drive more quickly.
   c) drive more carefully.

Further questions. Answer them in complete sentences using your own words as far as possible.

4. Why doesn't the woman with the child like cars?
5. Why has the other woman's problem got worse over the years?
6. Why is the man happy about one thing and disappointed about another?

Find the words in the text which are defined or explained below.

7. the bad substances which come out of a car engine
8. a restriction on how fast you can drive

Find the English equivalent for these German expressions.

9. Sie hätten es früher machen sollen.
10. Wir müssen damit zurechtkommen.

And what about you?

11. Which of these people's problems – the smell of fumes, the noise, the danger of driving too fast – do you think is the most serious? Why?
12. How do you feel about cars? Are they a danger to the environment? Write down your own opinion in a few sentences.

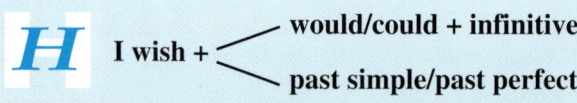

I wish + would/could + infinitive / past simple/past perfect

I wish they **would keep** to the speed limit.	Ich wünschte, sie würden sich an die Geschwindigkeitsbegrenzung halten.
I wish we **could move** house.	Ich wünschte, wir könnten umziehen.

◆ Auf den Ausdruck *"I wish"* folgen oft *would/could* + **Infinitiv**. Mit dieser Form bringen wir unsere **Unzufriedenheit mit einer gegenwärtigen Situation** zum Ausdruck, verbunden mit der **Bitte um Abhilfe**. Wir möchten, dass etwas geschieht oder dass jemand etwas unternimmt, damit wir uns nicht länger beschweren müssen.

I wish I **had** more money.	Ich wünschte, ich hätte mehr Geld.
I wish I **had not eaten** so much.	Ich wünschte, ich hätte nicht so viel gegessen.

◆ Der Ausdruck *"I wish"* wird häufig auch im Zusammenhang mit dem *Past Simple* oder dem *Past Perfect* verwendet.
Ein mit dem *Past Simple* formulierter Satz, wie z.B. *"I wish I had more money."*, beschreibt eine **Situation in der Gegenwart**. Der geäußerte **Wunsch** ist zwar **theoretisch erfüllbar**, dem Sprecher erscheint dies jedoch **unwahrscheinlich** (vgl. dazu auch Modul 15B, S. 34). Im Gegensatz dazu bezieht sich ein Satz wie z.B. *"I wish I had not eaten so much."* auf eine **Situation der Vergangenheit**, ausgedrückt durch das *Past Perfect*. Der **Wunsch** des Sprechers lässt sich mittlerweile **nicht mehr erfüllen** (vgl. dazu auch Modul 24B, S. 177).

Exercises

I. Read the situation and write a sentence beginning with "I wish ..." and "would". ●●

1. A lot of people drive too fast. I don't like this.
2. I want a job. Can't somebody offer me one?
3. There's been snow outside for two months. I want the spring to come.
4. The person in the flat next to me always plays his music too loudly.

II. Read the situation and write a sentence beginning with the words "I wish ..." and a past tense form of the verb. ●●

1. I'm not fit but I'd like to be.
2. I don't have enough money for a holiday.
3. My friend is not here and I need her.
4. I can't give up eating chocolate but I'd like to.
5. I don't know how to type properly but it would be helpful.
6. I live in a small flat and I don't like it.

III. Read the situation and write a sentence which begins with "I wish ..." and a past perfect form of the verb. ●●

1. Yesterday you talked to a friend about your new boss. Today you think it was a mistake to tell him. What do you say?
2. You are cycling and want to take some photographs but you have forgotten to take your camera. What do you say?
3. You come back from a holiday where everything was lovely except for the hotel you stayed in. What do you say?
4. You find out that a friend had a bad car accident and was in hospital. He's at home now and feeling much better but you did not visit him in hospital. What do you say?
5. Last weekend you visited your parents. Now you decide it was not a good idea. What do you say?
6. You left school when you were sixteen. Looking back you think it would have been good for you to stay at school longer. What do you say?

Helping verbs + "have" + past participle

Hilfsverben + "have" + Partizip Perfekt

She **could have asked** me before she borrowed my car.	Sie hätte mich fragen können, bevor sie sich mein Auto auslieh.
You **should have called** me.	Du hättest mich anrufen sollen (müssen).
They **must have missed** the plane.	Sie müssen das Flugzeug verpasst haben.

Mit der Konstruktion *could/should + have* + **Partizip Perfekt** drücken wir aus, was geschehen hätte **können, sollen** bzw. **müssen**. Mit *must* als Hilfsverb äußern wir eine **Vermutung** oder **Gewissheit** über etwas, das sich in der Vergangenheit zugetragen hat.

IV. Complete the sentences using the correct form of the words in brackets. ●●

1. Why did you take the train? You ... (could/fly). It's not more expensive.
2. Have you lost your purse? You ... (could/leave/it) on the bus.
3. Didn't you go out? You ... (could/go) to the cinema with me.
4. Did you stay in a hotel? You ... (could/spend) the night with my uncle and aunt.

V. Complete the mini-dialogues by using the correct forms of the words in brackets.
You may have to add some small words (eg prepositions). ●●

1. Where's Fiona? I haven't seen her for ages.
   (she/must/go away)
2. Why didn't you hear the doorbell when I rang?
   (I/must/be listening/music/headphones)
3. How did Kevin know where we were?
   (someone/must/tell/him)
4. How come Samantha did so well in her exam?
   (she/must/work/hard)

VI. Read the situation and write a sentence which begins with
   "I should (not) ..."/"It should (not) ...". ●●

1. You get on the train and all the seats are occupied.
2. The party you did not go to turned out to be a great success.
3. The post office opens at 9.00. It's now 9.30 and it's still not open.
4. You feel tired because you drank too much wine last night.

24B

And if they hadn't done it?

In the south-east of England there are not many green spaces left. What do people think about more housing developments, more roads and more motorways?

Were the two ladies against the new motorway?

5 1 Woman: Well, yes frankly, I wish they hadn't built the motorway. I used to walk along here when there was *nothing but* fields and woods and open countryside. And now everywhere you look you see that awful motorway and everywhere you go you hear the noise of the traffic. I wish they had left it as it was.

"The village is much quieter now."

2 Woman: There was no alternative. They had to build the motorway. The roads
10 were too crowded. If they hadn't built the motorway, all that traffic would have gone
through the towns and villages.

A man talks about the *by-pass* which goes around the village where he lives. Is he
happy with it?

1 Man: The by-pass is a good thing for this village. If they hadn't built it, all that
15 traffic would still come through the village today. Can you imagine that? Frankly,
I wish they had built it years earlier.

Next, a man talks about a *proposal* to build a *high-speed railway* which was
refused. Is he pleased that the proposal was *turned down*?

2 Man: I campaigned against the railway and I'm very happy that we won. If they
20 had built the railway here, they would have destroyed the peace and beauty of
this *valley* for ever. I think if they had built the railway, we would have moved to
Scotland or somewhere far away.

Not everyone is against *development*, however. Let's see what two young people
say.

25 1 Young person: People have got to live somewhere. (Pointing to some new houses
behind her:) In ten years' time this will look fine. The trees will have grown, the
bricks will have *mellowed*, the gardens will have *matured*.

2 Young person: Science is moving forward all the time. In 20 years from now
hopefully people will be driving electric cars, which will be clean and quiet. We will
30 be heating our houses by solar energy or wind power. We will be using *resources*
more economically. You'll see – where there is a problem, there must be an answer.

nothing but	nichts als, nur	brick	Ziegel-, Backstein
by-pass	Umgehungsstraße	mellow	*hier: durch äußere Einflüsse*
proposal	Antrag, Vorhaben		(*Verwitterung*)
high-speed	*hier:* Schnelltrasse		warme Farben annehmen
railway	(*für Hochgeschwindig-*	mature	reifen, *hier:* richtig
	keitszüge)		einwachsen, sich voll
refuse	*hier:* ablehnen		entwickeln
turn down	ablehnen	resources	Rohstoffquellen,
valley	Tal		Ressourcen
development	Erschließung, Umgestal-		
	tung, Veränderung		

Understanding the text.

Are these statements true or false according to the text?
Tick the appropriate column.

	T	F
1. The first and second woman were both against the new motorway.		
2. The first and second man did not want any changes to take place in the area where they live.		
3. Both young people seem optimistic about the future.		

Further questions. Answer them in full sentences using your
own words as far as possible.

4. The first man is happy with the by-pass around his village. What is he less happy
about, however?
5. We can see that the second man likes the peace and quiet of the countryside.
How?
6. Do both young people think better and different technology will improve life
in the future? Explain.

Give a synonym or similar expression for the following words.

7. crowded (line 10)
The roads were too ... .

8. happy (line 19)
I'm very ... that we won.

9. moving forward (line 28)
Science is ... all the time.

10. an answer (line 31)
There must be ... .

And what about you?

11. What sort of things do you do on a day-to-day basis (*im Alltag*) to help look after the environment?

12. Do you think, as the second young person in the text says, that in 20 years' time we will have electric cars and alternative energies to heat our houses? Give some reasons for your opinion.

 ## If-pattern 3

Bedingungssätze, Typ 3

If they **had built** the railway here, they **would have destroyed** the peace of this valley.	Wenn sie die Eisenbahntrasse hier gelegt hätten, hätten sie den Frieden dieses Tals zerstört.

◆ Bei **Typ 3** geht es um **Bedingungen**, die sich **nicht mehr erfüllen lassen**, da sie auf etwas Bezug nehmen, das in der **Vergangenheit** bereits geschehen (bzw. nicht geschehen) ist und folglich nicht mehr geändert werden kann. (Vgl. im Gegensatz dazu: Typ 1 = erfüllbare Bedingung, Typ 2 = theoretisch erfüllbare Bedingung/Hypothese; siehe Module 12A, S. 189 und 15B, S. 34.)

◆ Im Satzteil nach *if* steht das ***Past Perfect*** (*If they had built the motorway ...*). Im **Hauptsatz** stehen *would* (oder ein anderes Hilfsverb, wie z.B. *could* oder *might*) **+ have + Partizip Perfekt** (*... I would have moved to Scotland.*). In der **gesprochenen Sprache** steht die **Kurzform** *'d* für zwei unterschiedliche Langformen: *had* und *would* (*If they'd built a motorway, I'd have moved to Scotland.*).

◆ Wie das folgende Beispiel zeigt, gibt es auch die Möglichkeit, **Typ 3** und **Typ 2** miteinander zu **kombinieren** (im *if*-Satz: *Past Perfect*, im **Hauptsatz**: *would + infinitive*): *If they hadn't built the motorway, the traffic would still come through the village.* (Wenn sie die Autobahn nicht gebaut hätten, würde der Verkehr immer noch durch das Dorf fließen.)

Exercises

I. Link the two halves of the sentence together. ●●

1. I would have told you the number
2. He would have helped you
3. She would have got up earlier
4. She would have waved

a. if you had asked him.
b. if she had seen him.
c. if I had known it.
d. if she had set her alarm clock.

II. Complete these sentences using the correct form of the words in brackets (if-pattern 3). ●●

1. If I ... (miss) the train, I ... (miss) the bus but fortunately the train was late.
2. We ... (not, go) to that restaurant if you ... (not, recommend) it to us.
3. If you ... (give) me your address, I ... (send) you a postcard. Sorry.
4. If she ... (remind) him about her birthday, he ... (buy) her a present.

III. Read the situation and write a sentence which begins with "if". ●●

1. I bought the motorbike with the money my father lent me.
2. I was tired yesterday. I went to bed too late.
3. I didn't buy any bread because you didn't say we needed some.
4. I came late. Nobody had told me the lesson began at 9.00.

IV. Read the text and complete the sentences below. ●●

Clare went to London for the day. When she caught the train, there was not a cloud in the sky so she did not take a coat or umbrella. The weather changed at lunchtime. It rained all afternoon and she got very wet. From that point on everything went wrong. She fell over on the street and hurt her hand. Somebody stole her credit cards while she was having lunch in a café and the train back home was an hour late because of important engineering work. When she eventually got home, her son was waiting for her outside the front door. He had forgotten to take his key with him to school and couldn't get in.

1. If Clare had taken her umbrella, ...
2. If she had not had lunch in that café, ...
3. If they had not carried out work on the line, ...
4. If she had arrived home earlier, ...

H The future perfect (simple and continuous form)
Futur II (einfache Form und Verlaufsform)

In ten years' time the trees **will have grown**.	In zehn Jahren werden die Bäume gewachsen sein.
By October they **will have been working** on this motorway for two years.	Im Oktober werden sie bereits zwei Jahre an dieser Autobahn gearbeitet haben.

◆ In *Part One* haben wir gesehen, dass es im Englischen **verschiedene Möglichkeiten** gibt, um über ein **zukünftiges Geschehen** zu sprechen: *to be going to* + Infinitiv, die Verlaufsform und die einfache Form der Gegenwart, das Hilfsverb *will* + Infinitiv ohne *to* und das Hilfsverb *will* + *be* + -ing Form (siehe dazu die Module 11B, S. 178, 6A, S. 89, 13B, S. 208 und 12B, S. 193). In diesem Modul treffen wir auf **zwei weitere Formen**: das *Future Perfect*, sowohl in der einfachen Form als auch in der Verlaufsform.

Mit dem *Future Perfect* beschreibt man eine zu einem **bestimmten Zeitpunkt in der Zukunft abgeschlossene Handlung** (**einfache Form**) oder eine zu einem bestimmten Zeitpunkt in der Zukunft noch **andauernde Handlung** (**Verlaufsform**). Häufig wird eine Zeitbestimmung mit *by* (*by the year 2020*) oder *in* (*in thirty years' time*) ergänzt. Die Verlaufsform wird jedoch eher selten verwendet.

◆ Die **einfache Form** des *Future Perfect* wird mit *will have* + **Partizip Perfekt** gebildet (*In twenty years' time the trees will have grown.*). Zur Bildung der **Verlaufsform** verwendet man *will* + *have been* + -ing **Form** des Verbs (*By October they will have been working on this motorway for two years.*).

V. Use the future perfect simple form of the verb in brackets to complete these sentences. ●●

1. Hurry up. When we get to the cinema, the film ... (already, start).
2. We mustn't buy anything else. In two days we ... (use up) all our money.
3. She came to England in June so in two weeks' time she ... (live) here for exactly a year.
4. My parents married in the 1970s. In fact soon they ... (be married) for 25 years.

VI. Complete the sentences using the future perfect continuous form of the verb in brackets. (Be careful, however. One verb cannot be used in the continuous form!)

By the end of next month ...

1. I (live) in my own flat for five years.
2. I (use) this book for one semester.
3. I (have) my own car for half a year.
4. I (do) my present job for over two years.
5. I (run) marathons every year for ten years.

VII. Make some environmental predictions for the year 2020. What will people be doing? Will they be driving around in electric cars? What will people have done? Will they have built more railway lines? Use some of the ideas in this Module. Write down your ideas in a short paragraph (50–60 words).

24C

Duncan Brown and Michael Winter – looking for alternatives

Listen carefully to Duncan Brown, horticulturalist, and Michael Winter, architect, talking about environmental alternatives and answer the questions below.

Duncan Brown

I. What does Duncan talk about in his interview? Tick three items.

a. using trees as a noise barrier
b. the traffic problems in London
c. the population explosion in India
d. fast grass
e. new ways of growing apples
f. fast-built houses

Michael Winter

II. Answer these questions about Duncan using full sentences.

1. Duncan talks about using fast grass "to develop rural areas in India" and help the government. What is the connection between fast grass and the Indian government?
2. Why are fast-built houses so useful in a country like India?

III. Michael Winter talks about his own house in Britain. What is special about it? Put a cross against the <u>one</u> item which does <u>not</u> apply to his house.

a. It is mainly made of wood.
b. It uses recycled rainwater.
c. It has special windows.
d. It is situated on the top of a hill.
e. It has solar panels on the roof.
f. It uses a special heat pump.

IV. Answer these questions about Michael using full sentences.

1. Why has Michael built his house in the way he has?
2. Does Michael think his house is the answer to future living? Explain.

V. Complete the sentences by supplying the missing word. The first letter is given.

1. A person who grows flowers, fruit and vegetables is called a h... .
2. An i... is a new idea or method of doing something.
3. Wood that is used for building or making furniture is called t... .
4. The f... is what you walk on in a house.
5. You can keep food and drink cool in a f... .

24D

Meterman the environmentalist

I. As you read the text choose one of the three expressions in the brackets. There are two sets of brackets in each paragraph.

Meterman is making fun of some conservation *volunteers* at work in a (post office/wood/pub). He talks to them: "You*'re* always *on about* helping the environment, recycling, saving the earth. Well, if you ask me, it's all *a load of rubbish*! If I had wanted an (difficult/easy/hectic) life, I would have become a conservation volunteer."

He drives past a recycling centre and sees a lady putting bottles in the wrong bottle *bank*. He (stops/cleans/strokes) his car and walks up to her. "That was a green bottle," he says. "You've put it in the wrong *bin*. You've put it in the brown bin. It (could/must/should) have gone in the green bin."

Meterman uses his long arms to (throw/fish/move) the bottle out of the bin. Suddenly he is held tight by his environmentally-friendly "alter ego". "Meterman. Oh, Meterman. You stand accused of (helping/disturbing/polluting) the environment. How do you plead? Guilty or not guilty?" "Guilty," Meterman admits.

Meterman *swaps Molly his van for* Milly his bicycle and returns to the wood to see what the conservation volunteers are doing. He opens the (box/wallet/envelope) on the back of his bicycle and pulls out an *"Omniometer"*, a *device* which (sees/measures/writes down) everything: how much noise, how much energy and how much smell there is in the environment.

The "Omniometer" is obviously a very (powerful/interesting/expensive) piece of equipment. It can *immobilize* anything which is wasting energy: cars, *bonfires* and even conservation volunteers. Suddenly Meterman realizes that the viewers' television sets are also using up energy. "Don't worry," he warns. "The Omniometer will deal with it." He aims the device at the camera and the picture (goes red/turns over/disappears). "Hello. Hello?" Meterman shouts. "Is anybody there? Can you see me? Use your eyes!"

volunteer	Freiwillige(r)	swap sth for	etw. eintauschen für
be on about sth	ständig über etw. sprechen	"Omniometer"	*etwa*: „Allesmesser"
a load of	ein Haufen, eine Menge (von)	device	*hier*: Gerät
		immobilize	außer Gefecht setzen
rubbish	Abfall, *hier*: Unsinn	bonfire	Freudenfeuer, *hier*:
bank	*hier*: Behälter		Feuer im Freien (*zur*
bin	Abfallbehälter, *hier*: Glastonne		*Unkrautvernichtung*)

II. Which one of the items below can you not normally save? Put a cross against it.

- a life
- costs
- paper
- money
- time
- energy
- a wish
- a shot (football)

What does the verb "save" mean in German in combination with these items?

24E

Windpower

THE OFFICE AT HOME   UNIT 25

25A

On the phone

Maggie and her daughter Sophie run a *holiday homes letting agency* from their home. One morning Maggie goes into the office to take the messages from the *answerphone*.

5 (First call on answerphone: Maggie. Hi. This is Jane. Just to let you know that the new *tenants* of Stone Cottage arrived and everything is OK. Talk to you soon. Bye.)

Maggie: (to herself:) That's good.

(Second call on answerphone: Hello. My name is Carol Lane. Please send your brochure to me at this address: Mrs C. Lane, PO Box 174, Dubai, United Arab
10 Emirates. Thank you.)

Sophie: Any messages on the answerphone about Stone Cottage? Have the new tenants arrived?
Maggie: Yes. Jane rang. Everything's fine.
Sophie: Brilliant. *What a relief!*
15 Maggie: (handing her daughter Mrs Lane's address:) Someone here wants a brochure. Will you *see to that*? And there may be more *enquiries* on the e-mail. *Search* the post box, will you?

Sophie: OK. And I'll see to the brochures.

Maggie: (answering the phone:) Freedom Holidays. What? Rose Farm Cottage?
20   A *leaking radiator*? Oh no! And there's water everywhere?
          What a nuisance! How annoying! I'll call the *plumber* right away!
          Thank you. Bye-bye.

Later on Bob, the plumber, phones Maggie.

Bob: Maggie. It's Bob here. You were trying to *get me*.
25 Maggie: Oh, *at last*. I've been trying to get you all morning.
Bob: Sorry. I forgot to take my mobile with me. I've been out all morning.
          Anyway, what can I do for you?
Maggie: Bob. I've got a problem at Rose Farm Cottage. A leaking radiator.
          Water all over the place. New people coming in tomorrow.
30   It's a terrible mess. Any chance you can ...
Bob: ... ah ... I'll see if I can *fit it in* this afternoon. Well, I've got to *have a
          bite to eat* first.
Maggie: Thanks, Bob. Will you *pop round* here for the key?
Bob: Will do.
35 Maggie: Thanks, Bob. Bye.

let	*hier*: vermieten	radiator	Heizkörper, Radiator
holiday homes	Agentur zur Ver-	What a nuisance!	Wie unangenehm!
letting agency	mietung von Ferien-	How annoying!	Wie ärgerlich!
	wohnungen	plumber	Klempner, Installateur
answerphone	Anrufbeantworter	get sb	*hier*: jmdn. erreichen
tenant	Mieter(in)	at last	endlich, schließlich
relief	Erleichterung	fit sth/sb in	etw./jmdn. einschie-
What a relief!	Na, endlich!		ben, dazwischen-
see to sth	sich um etw. kümmern,		schieben
	etw. erledigen	have a bite to eat	schnell einen Happen
enquiry	*hier*: Anfrage		essen
search	*hier*: durchgehen,	pop round (*coll*)	vorbeischauen,
	durchsehen		reinschauen
leak	leck, undicht sein		

Understanding the text.

Which sentence (a–c) best completes the statement? Tick it.

1. Maggie and Sophie ...
   a) run their own business.
   b) buy and sell holiday homes.
   c) organize computer courses.

Sophie explains what equipment they use in the office

2. Mrs Lane ...
    a) wants to work with Maggie.
    b) might rent a cottage from Maggie.
    c) would like to stay a few nights with Maggie.
3. Maggie rings Bob because he ...
    a) can repair her phone and fax.
    b) is cooking lunch for her and Sophie.
    c) could help her with a problem in one of the holiday homes.

Further questions. Answer them in full sentences and in your own words as far as possible.

4. Why is Maggie pleased that Jane rang her?
5. Why is the problem with Rose Farm Cottage so annoying for Maggie?
6. Why does Bob go around to see Maggie later in the day?

What word from the text is being described or explained?

7. a person who pays money to somebody else so that they can live in their house
8. a device which is filled with hot water and which keeps a room warm
9. a person whose job is to fit and repair water pipes
10. a type of telephone that you can take with you from one place to another

And what about you?

11. Can you imagine that letting holiday homes is a good business in Britain? Give some reasons for your opinion.
12. Would you like to work from home? Say why/why not.

The small word "will"

Das kleine Wort "will"

The prime minister **will visit** Japan tomorrow for talks with the Japanese government.	Der Premierminister wird morgen Japan besuchen, um Gespräche mit der japanischen Regierung zu führen.
I'll see to the brochures.	Ich kümmere mich um die Broschüren. (Ich werde mich ... kümmern.)

Das kleine Wort *"will"* zählt zu den schwierigsten Wörtern in der englischen Grammatik. Man muss zwischen **zwei „Arten"** von *"will"* unterscheiden:

◆ Wie bereits in *Part One*, Modul 12B erläutert, wird die Form **will + infinitive** oft als **„neutrale Zukunft"** bezeichnet. Mit *will* kann man sachlich und objektiv über zukünftige Ereignisse sprechen. So soll z.B. mit einem Satz wie *"The prime minister will visit Japan tomorrow for talks with the Japanese government."* einfach nur signalisiert werden, dass das betreffende Geschehen in der Zukunft stattfindet.
Obwohl *will + infinitive* nur eine von vielen Zukunftsformen im Englischen ist, wird sie von Lernenden häufig überbeansprucht.

◆ *Will* ist aber auch ein **modales Hilfsverb** und wird als solches dazu verwendet, die **Meinung** bzw. **Einstellung** des Sprechers zum **Zeitpunkt des Sprechens** auszudrücken (vgl. dazu Modul 20B, S. 116). So bringt z.B. der Satz *"I'll see to the brochures."* ein Angebot oder ein Versprechen zum Ausdruck. Wie die nachfolgenden Übungen zeigen werden, gibt es für *will* eine **breite Palette von Bedeutungen**, die vom **Angebot** über die **Weigerung** bis zur **Drohung** reichen. Im **Deutschen** stehen solche zumeist als **spontane Reaktion** auf eine bestimmte Situation **erfolgenden Äußerungen** häufig in der **Gegenwartsform**. Daher setzen Lernende, die Deutsch als Muttersprache haben, *will* in vergleichbaren englischen Sätzen meist zu selten ein.

Exercises

I. Match each sentence to a function. Choose one word from the box below.

> intention (*Absicht*) ● offer (*Angebot*) ● promise (*Versprechen*) ● refusal (*Weigerung*) ● ·request (*Bitte*) ● threat (*Drohung*)

1. I'll ring you next week.
2. Look! I'll get really angry if you do that again.
3. Don't worry. I'll take you to the station.
4. Me? I'll have a coffee, please.
5. No, I won't tell you. Sorry.
6. I think I'll go to bed. I'm tired.

II. Complete the responses below by using the words in brackets.

1. The phone rings.   "I ... (answer) it."
2. There's a knock on the door.   "I ... (go)!"
3. A friend wants a lift.   "I ... (take) you."
4. A colleague feels sick.   "I ... (get) some water."
5. You can't speak on the phone.   "I ... (call) you back."
6. It's hot in here.   "I ... (open) a window."

III. Link the sentences and then complete the second sentence by using the correct form of the words in brackets. ●●

1. "If you do that again,   a. and I ... (have) a beer."
2. "Hold on a second.   b. I ... (fetch) a sweater."
3. "I'm going now.   c. I ... (open) the door for you."
4. "The battery's flat.   d. I ... (scream)!"
5. "It's cold.   e. I ... (see) you next week."
6. "I'd like a pizza and salad   f. It ... (not, start)."

IV. The form "will" + infinitive is used for spontaneous reactions. The verb "to be going to" is used when the speaker has already thought about the future action or situation. Complete these mini-dialogues with "will" or "be going to" and the correct form of the words in brackets. ●●

1. Did you buy those stamps for me?
   Oh no. I completely forgot. I ... (do) it now.

2. Are you going out?
   Yes, I ... (buy) something for dinner.

3. We've decided to paint this room.
   Really? What colour ... (you/paint) it?

4. I can't operate this video camera.
   It's quite easy. I ... (show) you.

5. Thanks for all your help.
   You're welcome. I ... (see) you tomorrow.

6. You look awful.
   I feel terrible. I think I ... (be sick).

*V. Look at the short answers in the box below and translate the four
mini-dialogues.* ●●

> - I hope so.   ● I hope not.
> - I think so.   ● I don't think so.
> - I suppose so.   ● I suppose not.

1. Sind die neuen Broschüren angekommen?   Ich denke schon.
2. Hat der Klempner schon angerufen?   Ich glaube nicht.
3. Ist die Post schon da?   Ich nehme es an.
4. Haben Sie den Schlüssel verloren?   Ich hoffe nicht.

*VI. Put the eight sentences in the correct order to form
a telephone conversation.* ●●

a. OK, I'll tell her. Bye now.
b. Hello. This is John speaking. Is Jessica there, please?
c. No, I'm afraid she isn't.
d. No, it's OK. I'll try again later.
e. Oh, I see. Do you know when she'll be back?
f. Sevenoaks 712789.
g. She didn't say. Can I take a message?
h. Thanks very much. Bye.

VII. How good is your telephone English? Do this quiz and find out.

What would you say in these situations? Tick the correct answer. ●●

Someone says: You say:

1. Sorry, what's your name?   a. It's John Dunne.
                                       b. Dunne.

2. Could I speak to Mary, please?   a. Wait.
                                       b. One moment, please.

3. This is Neil Davies speaking.   a. Again.
                                       b. Sorry?

4. Can I leave a message?   a. If you want.
                                       b. Certainly.

5. Thanks for calling.   a. You're welcome.
                                       b. It doesn't matter.

Which sentence (a or b) on the right is another way of saying the sentence on the left? Tick it.

6. I'll connect you.   a. I'll put you through.
                                       b. I'll join you.

7. The line's busy.   a. Somebody's speaking.
                                       b. It's occupied.

8. Could you speak up a bit?   a. Could you speak a bit louder?
                                       b. Louder! OK?

9. How are you doing?   a. How are you?
                                       b. How do you do.

10. I'll ring you later.   a. I'll call you later.
                                       b. I'll shout later.

Identify the right endings (a–e) for the half-sentences (11–15). ●●

11. My extension is ...   a. 0171.
12. The code for central London is.   b. telephone directory?
13. Can I take a ...   c. is not answering.
14. Is your number in the ...   d. 319.
15. I'm afraid she ...   e. message?

25B

Office equipment ●●

Maggie and Sophie talk about the office equipment they use in their business.

Maggie begins: "I always put the answerphone on at night. Then *first thing in the morning* I check it for messages." Sophie continues: "We also check the fax machine
5 because a lot of faxes come in over night."
Maggie goes on to say that they have recently *acquired* e-mail, which is electronic mail. Each morning one of them searches the postbag. Sophie explains how she does it. "First you *boot up*, then with the mouse you click on this *icon* to get your mail." Maggie holds up a brochure. "We print a new one each year to keep it up-to-date.
10 We are planning to *advertise* on the European Internet soon. We have ordered the software for it already."
The PC, or personal computer, is in use all the time. Sophie thinks the software *package* for the PC is excellent. "A large number of *fonts*, any size you want, and a choice of layout." Maggie says that they have a database of the properties that they
15 *handle*. "We update it with new information all the time." Nevertheless they find it useful to have a good old-fashioned *visual display* on the wall as well. Finally Sophie mentions the fax machine, which *doubles as* a photocopier and a printer.
Maggie has the last word: "We may look like an old-fashioned country cottage from the outside," she remarks. "But we are quite up-to-date on the inside."

first thing in the	als Erstes in der Frühe	fonts	*hier*: verschiedene
morning			Schriftarten
acquire	erwerben, anschaffen	handle	*hier*: betreuen
boot up	hochfahren, laden	visual display	Schautafel
icon	Symbol	double as	*hier*: sowohl als ...
advertise	werben		als auch als …
package	*hier*: Paket, Programm		dienen

Understanding the text.

Are the following statements true or false according to the text?
Or does the text not say?

1. Maggie and Sophie do not need a fax machine because they have e-mail.
2. They would like to advertise their properties on the Internet soon.
3. The PC database of holiday homes is more useful to them than the visual display.
4. They do not have a photocopier because they have a fax machine.

The office of "Freedom Holidays"

Further questions. Answer them using your own words as far as possible.

5. Why do you think Maggie and Sophie receive a lot of faxes over night (line 5)?
6. What does it mean exactly to "search the postbag" (line 7)?

Which word in the text is being defined?

7. a type of book with pictures which gives you information about a product or company
8. a formal word which means the same as "house"

Which word/expression (a–c) can best replace the word/expression underlined in the sentence?

9. "I always put the answerphone on at night." (line 3)
   a) take the answerphone with me
   b) switch the answerphone on
   c) place the answerphone on the desk
10. Maggie goes on to say that they have recently acquired e-mail. (line 6)
    a) stole   b) borrowed   c) bought

And what about you?

11. Why can a visual display on the wall sometimes be as useful as a computer database? Explain your answer.

12. Could you imagine running a family business yourself?

 ### Multi-word verbs (III)

Zusammengesetzte Verben (III)

I always **put** the answerphone **on** at night. (**put sth on**)	Ich schalte nachts immer den Anrufbeantworter ein.
You **boot up** the computer. (**boot sth up**)	Sie fahren den Computer hoch.
You **click on** this icon to get your mail. (**click sth on**)	Sie klicken dieses Symbol an, um Ihre Post zu bekommen.

Im Modul 23A (S. 158) wurde gezeigt, dass die **Wortstellung** der *multi-word verbs* von ihrer **Grammatik** abhängt. Diese entnimmt man am besten einem guten **einsprachigen** Wörterbuch.

◆ Die **intransitiven** *multi-word verbs*, d.h. Verb+Partikel-Verbindungen **ohne direktes Objekt**, sind die einfachsten ihrer Art, weil **Verb** und **Partikel nicht trennbar** sind. In einem einsprachigen Wörterbuch werden solche Verben in der Regel **ohne** *"sb"* (= *somebody*) oder *"sth"* (= *something*) geschrieben, z.B. *set off* (*We set off for England at seven o'clock.*).

◆ Die **transitiven** *multi-word verbs*, d.h. Verb+Partikel-Verbindungen **mit einem direkten Objekt**, sind für Lernende etwas schwieriger, weil man nicht weiß, in welcher Reihenfolge die einzelnen Teile vorkommen können. **Manche** dieser Verben sind sogenannte **trennbare** *multi-word verbs*, bei denen das **Objekt sowohl zwischen Verb und Partikel als auch nach der Partikel** stehen kann. In einem einsprachigen Wörterbuch werden solche Verben mit *"sb"* oder *"sth"* **zwischen** Verb und Partikel geschrieben, z.B. *put sth on* (*We put the answerphone on every night.* Oder: *We put on the answerphone every night.*). Wenn das **Objekt** des Verbs die Form eines **Pronomens** hat, **muss** es jedoch **zwischen** Verb und Partikel stehen (*We put it on every night.*). **Andere transitive** *multi-word verbs* sind **nicht trennbar**. Das **Objekt folgt** immer **auf die Partikel**. In einem einsprachigen Wörterbuch werden solche Verben mit *"sb"* oder *"sth"* **nach** der Partikel geschrieben, z.B. *look after sb* (*We looked after grandfather/him while our parents were away.*).

Exercises

I. Match the meanings of the underlined multi-word verbs to their more formal equivalents in the box below. ●●

> destroy ● re-introduce ● lower ● raise

1. He was <u>brought up</u> in Germany but lives in Canada.
2. Rising unemployment will <u>bring down</u> the government.
3. Are they going to <u>bring back</u> school on Saturday?
4. Is it true that they are <u>bringing down</u> taxes in April?

II. Replace the underlined verb with a multi-word verb equivalent from the box below. ●●

> set sth aside ● set off ● set out (to do sth) ● set sth up

1. Don't forget to <u>keep</u> some money for later.
2. She <u>intended</u> to windsurf around Britain.
3. Is it easy for young people to <u>start</u> a business?
4. If we <u>leave</u> before 5, we'll be there at 12.

III. Rewrite these sentences using a pronoun instead of the noun underlined. Be careful with the word order. ●●

1. Should I press this button to boot up <u>the computer</u>?
2. You must set aside <u>money</u> for later.
3. She set up <u>her business</u> last year.
4. Must I click on <u>an icon</u> to get page preview?

IV. Perhaps the most common verb in English – after "be", "do" and "have" – is "get". Which verb from the box can replace the verb "get" in the sentences below? ●●

> annoy ● arrive ● grow ● buy ● catch ●
> prepare ● receive ● understand

1. Which train shall we <u>get</u>? The one at 8.20?
2. Can you <u>get</u> some bread for me on the way back from the shops?
3. Sorry. I didn't <u>get</u> the joke. Say it again, will you?

4. We <u>got to</u> the airport just as the plane was leaving.
5. His stupid remarks really <u>get</u> me sometimes!
6. Did you really <u>get</u> the best mark in the test?
7. We're <u>getting</u> older. But are we <u>getting</u> wiser?
8. I'll <u>get</u> dinner tonight if you wash up afterwards.

(Don't forget to change the preposition in sentence 4.)

V. Look at these symbols. Which explanation goes with which symbol?

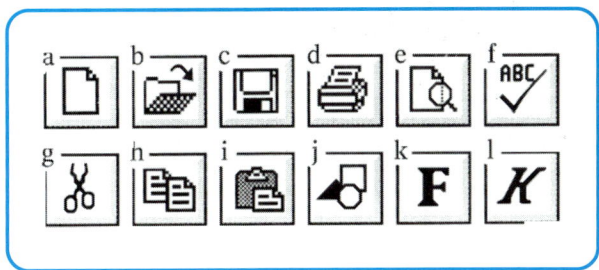

1. starting a new document
2. printing
3. cutting a piece of text
4. checking the spelling
5. saving a document
6. inserting ("pasting") the part of the text you have copied
   into a different place
7. inserting graphics
8. copying a part of a text
9. opening a document
10. using **bold** letters
11. using *italics*
12. seeing what the printed page will look like

VI. Which two words are missing from these questions?
Write down the complete questions.

1. Like a cigarette?   4. Tired?
2. Want a coffee?   5. Finished?
3. Get what you were looking for?   6. Have a good flight?

25C

David Fitzpatrick – on line at home

Listen carefully to what David Fitzpatrick says about his work and answer the questions below.

I. Choose the correct ending (a–c) to the sentence (1–3).

1. David Fitzpatrick is ...
   a) a computer programmer.   b) a consultant engineer.
   c) a furniture designer.

2. David Fitzpatrick's office is in his ...
   a) garage.   b) kitchen.   c) cellar.

3. In order for David Fitzpatrick to work efficiently he needs to ...
   a) live near his home.
   b) sit at his desk during the night.
   c) have access to modern office equipment.

II. Answer these questions in full sentences.

1. What sort of software does David Fitzpatrick need in order to do his job properly?
2. What, in David Fitzpatrick's view, are the advantages and disadvantages of working from home?

III. Which words from the interview are being defined? (The first and last letters have been given.)

1. a formal word which means "next to"   a...t
2. a common word which means "perfect"   i...l
3. another word for "send" (sound, data)   t...t
4. a word which means "customer"   c...t
5. a word which means "at the moment"   c...ly
6. to stop somebody speaking when they
   are in the middle of a sentence   i...t

25D

Meterman the computer specialist

I. What happens to Meterman in this story? Read the text and choose the most appropriate summary (a-c) below.

a) While he is reading the meter in Mr Fleming's house, Meterman dreams that his family and friends are calling him from all over the world on his new mobile phone.

b) While he is reading the meter in Mr Fleming's house, Meterman dreams that he is a special agent with access to the country's best-kept secrets.

c) While he is reading the meter in Mr Fleming's house, Meterman dreams that he is working for his cousin Bruce, a well-known Internet specialist in Australia.

Meterman arrives at Mr Fleming's house to read the meter. There's a problem. Mr Fleming's dog does not *allow* Meterman *past* the front gate. Meterman rings Mr Fleming on his mobile phone and asks for assistance.

Mr Fleming deals with his dog and lets Meterman into his house. "I'm just off to buy another roll of paper for the fax machine," he says. "You know where the meter is? Shut the door behind you when you leave."

Meterman is alone in Mr Fleming's house. He goes into the study and sees computer equipment everywhere. "Look at all this," Meterman says to the viewer. "No wonder he's using up so much electricity." Suddenly his mobile phone rings. It's Bruce, his Australian cousin. "Look," says Bruce, "I've been surfing the Internet and I've come across your name. It looks as if you're in a spot of trouble. So I thought I'd better give you a bell. Now, if you want to get out of trouble, you're going to need a password."

Suddenly Meterman finds himself wearing a black cap and dark *moustache*. He's dressed as secret agent MM7. Mr Fleming is standing behind him as M. "I have a fax from upstairs," M says to MM7. "I think you should see it." MM7 reads it out loud: "MM7, HM to PM, 5am. OK." MM7 turns to M. "What's the code?" he asks. "101, MM7," M replies. "The country depends on you."

MM7 works feverishly on the computer. Suddenly he stops and looks at the screen. He can't believe it. "10 Downing Street!" he says. "I *have access to* the crown jewels!" At that moment M pulls out a roll of fax paper and hits MM7 on the head. MM7 falls to the ground unconscious. "He means I've accessed the crown jewels," says M looking into the camera.

Meterman is on the floor of Mr Fleming's office. His mobile phone is ringing. It's his mother. "You get back here at once," she shouts. "At once. It's Thursday night and I've made your special dinner for you."

At that moment Mr Fleming comes back from buying his fax paper. "What on earth are you doing?" he asks, seeing Meterman on the floor. Meterman is slightly embarrassed. "My dear sir, I was just checking your wiring," he explains. "I know how you can save electricity. Switch off the machine."

Meterman goes to the computer and presses the on/off button. The button is very hot and burns Meterman's finger. "Now, remember, sir," says Meterman looking at Mr Fleming. "If things get too hot to handle, dial M for Meterman! Good day!"

allow (sb) past	(jmdn.) an ... vorbeilassen
moustache	Schnurrbart
have access to	Zugang haben zu (*Daten*)

II. Words which look the same in English and German and have different meanings are called "false friends". Complete the table below by putting in the correct equivalents of the German and English words. (Use a dictionary if you want.)

	German ← English		German → English	
1.	...	handy	Handy	...
2.	...	floor	Flur	...
3.	...	study	Studium	...
4.	...	personal	Personal	...
5.	...	spare	sparen	...
6.	...	control	kontrollieren	...
7.	...	sympathetic	sympathisch	...

III. Match the idiomatic expressions (1–6) with their "meanings" (a–f).

1. "I think it's too hot to handle."
2. "They are blowing hot and cold about it."
3. "We got into hot water."
4. "The whole thing leaves me cold."
5. "I got cold feet."
6. "They threw cold water on it."

a. It doesn't interest or excite me.
b. It frightened me.
c. They thought it wasn't good.
d. It's too difficult for me to deal with.
e. We got into trouble for doing something wrong.
f. They are changing their minds about it.

Now use four of these expressions (in the correct form) to complete the sentences below.

7. You ... if your boss finds out that you have been using the computer for private correspondence.
8. I enjoyed the play as a whole but the music ... . It was too loud and monotonous.
9. He asked me to marry him and at first I said yes. Then I ... and said I had changed my mind.
10. The management ... about the company's flexible working hours. First they said they liked the idea. Now they are saying they don't like it.

25E

Computer technology

"This one frankly admits it's overpriced."

A SECOND CHANCE   UNIT 26

26A

Getting more qualifications ●●

Cathy returned to college and worked hard to become a *classroom assistant* in a *nursery school*.

"I left school at the age of 16 with three *GCSEs*. A year ago I returned to college
5 because I wanted to become a qualified classroom assistant. As a parent I had been helping out in a classroom for several years on a voluntary basis. I'd also worked as a *lollipop lady*. I'd always enjoyed working with children and I decided that I wanted to *do this work as a career*. I passed my exams and I'm now doing the work I love and I'm getting paid for doing it."

10 Bob Bage got his *A levels* last year and is now going to study law at Sussex University.

"I'm afraid that school just didn't work for me. I left when I was 15 with no qualifications at all. I got a job and *worked my way up through* the *travel industry*. I'm 47 now and last year I returned to college because I wanted to study for A levels.
15 I had been running my own shop for several years, selling antique toys. I found that being in business was very stressful. I had always enjoyed reading a lot and I decided that I wanted to study law."

classroom	eine Art Assistentin	lollipop lady,	Schülerlotse
assistant	der Kindergärtnerin	lollipop man	
	bzw. Lehrerin	do sth as a career	etw. beruflich machen
nursery school	Kindergarten, Vorschule	A levels	etwa: Abitur
GCSE	etwa: mittlere Reife	("A" short for	
(= General		Advanced)	
Certificate of		work one's way	sich durch ... hindurch
Secondary		up through ...	hocharbeiten
Education)		travel industry	Tourismusgeschäft

Understanding the text.
Are these statements true or false according to the text? Explain what part of the text gave you the answer. Begin your answers as follows: "This is true/false because the text says ... ".

1. Cathy decided to become a classroom assistant because the job pays so well.
2. She has had a lot of experience of working with children.
3. She is a mother herself.
4. When he was a child Bob worked hard at school.
5. He has had a lot of experience of working in business.
6. He is waiting to see if he has got a place at university.

Find words in the text which have the same meaning as the following.

7. to go back to
8. unfortunately
9. a number of
10. to realize

And what about you?

11. Which would you prefer to do - the job of a teacher or the job of a lawyer? Say why.

12. How important in your opinion are academic and/or professional qualifications for getting a job in Germany?

Overview of tenses

Die Zeiten im Überblick

Zu den acht Formen des Verbs aus *Part One* (vgl. auch Übersicht in 14A, S. 13) sind in *Part Two* mit dem *Past Perfect* und dem *Future Perfect* vier weitere hinzugekommen. Daraus ergibt sich folgende abschließende Zusammenschau:

	simple	continuous
present	I work	I am working
past	I worked	I was working
present perfect	I have worked	I have been working
past perfect	I had worked	I had been working
future	I will work	I will be working
future perfect	I will have worked	I will have been working

Exercises

I. Remember that "be" does a lot of work in the English grammar system. For example, it helps to build all continuous forms. Complete these sentences using the correct form of the words in brackets. ●●

1. Where ... (you, go) when I saw you in your car yesterday?
2. ... (you, still live) with your parents or have you got a place of your own?
3. We ... (drive) along the motorway for an hour when it started to rain so heavily that we had to stop.
4. I'm sorry I couldn't make it earlier. How long ... (you, wait)? Not more than fifteen minutes surely?
5. I ... (try) to reach you all morning but the phone was always engaged. Who ... (you, talk) to all the time?
6. No, I can't go out tonight. I'm ill. I ... (lie) in bed!

II. Remember that the word "do" has an important grammatical function in English. It helps, for example, to build questions in present and past simple tenses. Ask the questions to get the information which is missing in the sentences below.

1. We met .?. yesterday on the train.
2. She lives in .?., which is near London.
3. The performance finished at .?., I think.
4. The course lasts .?. years in total.
5. He doesn't come to work by car. He comes by .?. .
6. They saw a .?. as they were driving to France.

III. Remember that the word "have" has an important role in English grammar. It helps to build all perfect forms (present perfect, past perfect and future perfect). Complete these sentences using the correct form of the words in brackets. ●●

1. How long ... (you, have) your present job?
2. The shop ... (already, close) when we arrived.
3. In two months we ... (live) in this house for twenty years.
4. My sister ... (be) in the US for the last five years.
5. ... (anybody, know) about the decision before it was officially announced?
6. This time tomorrow I ... (do) this exercise.

IV. Remember that using English grammar correctly means not only choosing between what is right and wrong: it also means choosing the appropriate form for the meaning you want to express. Both the sentences in each pair below are grammatically correct. Which sentence is more likely? Tick it.

1a. The driver slowed down when he saw the police car.
1b. The driver was slowing down when he saw the police car.

2a. We will close this shop from December 24 - January 1.
2b. This shop will be closed from December 24 - January 1.

3a. It was nice meeting you. You must come and visit us some time.
3b. It was nice meeting you. You have to come and visit us some time.

4a. I was calling you all evening. Were you out?
4b. I called you all evening. Were you out?

5a. I suppose you haven't been to England before, have you?
5b. I suppose you've been to England before, haven't you?

6a. I'll see you later. Bye.
6b. I'm going to see you later. Bye.

V. Remember that there are a special group of verbs in English which speakers use to express their own feelings or attitudes towards actions and situations. Which helping verbs are missing from the sentences below? Choose one from the brackets. ●●

1. The woman waiting at the bus stop over there (should/must/could) be my aunt but I'm not absolutely sure.
2. (Shall/May/Must) I borrow your pen for a minute? I'm afraid I've forgotten mine.
3. You (will/can/might) catch the train if you leave now. You've got over half an hour to get to the station.
4. You (wouldn't/shouldn't/couldn't) go out without a coat. You'll freeze!
5. We're going to the shops. (Must/Will/Shall) we get something for you?
6. (To a small child:) You (shouldn't/mustn't/couldn't) do that! You'll really hurt yourself.

VI. Remember that verbs often combine with other verbs in the form of an infinitive or a gerund. Complete the sentences below using the correct form of the word in brackets. ●●

1. She promised ... (ring) this evening.
2. Does he really admit ... (be) lazy?
3. They don't mind ... (work) at the weekend.
4. I hope ... (get) a job by the end of the year.
5. Does she enjoy ... (go) to college in the evenings?
6. We agreed ... (reach) a compromise.

26B

Back to college ●●

Jane, Michael and Jo decided to take a second chance when they returned to college. What are they studying? Why are they doing the course? Are they enjoying it?

Jane: I'm doing a course in Tourism - or *Service Industries Management*
5   *Tourism* to give it its full name. I'm doing the course so as to be able to
             work in tourism in this part of the country. I left school with GCSEs
             and A levels and then trained as a textile designer and worked in an art
             college for several years. I married and had children. Before returning
             to college I had been looking after the family but I had to continue
10   *part-time* as well. I'm hoping to get my HND - that's the Higher

National Diploma – in Tourism this year. I may go on to do an extra
year, which will give me a university degree at a later date. On this
course we learn about the business side of tourism as well as the other
aspects. We learn *computing skills*, we *practise giving presentations*
15   and we learn how to *dress for the part*, how to present ourselves.
We also have the opportunity to study foreign languages. I enjoy the
course because it is so completely different from what I've done before.
For me it really is a second chance – and I love it!

Michael: I'm doing a course in *Business Studies* and this is my second year.
20   I'm doing the course firstly in order to improve my knowledge of
business and, secondly, so as to learn the vocabulary of modern
business and information technology. I'm hoping to do a TEFL
course – that's teaching English as a foreign language – so that I can
teach English to students of business. I left school with five GCSEs and
25   then went to art school and studied Art. Before I started this course in
Business Studies, I had been teaching English in Spain. I'm hoping to
get my HND in Business Studies next summer. Then I'm planning to do
a teaching diploma. Eventually I would like to teach business English
to students in a developing country. On this course we learn how to
30   develop our skills as part of a group. We practise doing individual
project work. I find it useful because I'm learning modern teaching
methods and I'm enjoying it because I've gained a lot more confidence
in my own abilities.

Jo: I'm doing a *university degree course* in *Media Studies*. I had started a
35   degree some years ago but had to leave when I had my son. I'm doing
this course in order to complete my degree. I left school with six
GCSEs and went to college. As I said before, I had to leave college to

Jane is studying
Tourism

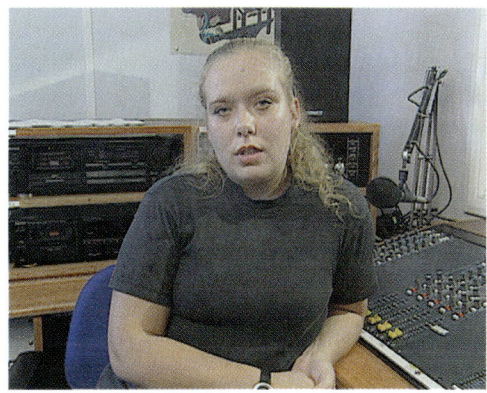

Jo is doing
Media Studies

have my son. Before starting back in education, I had been working for
a *publishing company* in London. I'm now in the second year of my
40 course. I hope to get my degree at the end of my third year. On this
course we learn all about journalism and the media. We learn how to
write newspaper articles and we practise making radio programmes and
short films. I find it very useful because we learn both academic and
practical skills. I'm enjoying the course because I have made new
45 friends and it's such fun!

Service Industries	*etwa*: Management	dress for the part	*hier*: sich (beruflich)
Management	im Dienstleistungs-		passend kleiden
Tourism	sektor Tourismus	Business Studies	Betriebswirtschafts-
part-time	Teilzeit, *hier*:		lehre
	Teilzeitarbeit	university degree	Universitätsstudium
computing skills	PC-Kenntnisse	course	
practise giving	*hier*: freies	Media Studies	Medienwissenschaften
presentations	Sprechen üben	publishing company	Verlag

Understanding the text.

Which ending (a–c) best completes the statement (1–6)? Tick it.

1. Jane has gone back to college in order to ...
   a) practise her computing skills.
   b) get the sort of job she wants.
   c) learn some more foreign languages.

2. Jane has already ...
   a) got higher qualifications and work experience.
   b) received an offer of a job in tourism.
   c) finished her course at college.

3. Before Michael started his course he ...
   a) was a teacher.   b) was a painter.   c) was a singer.

4. After his course Michael hopes to ...
   a) start his own company.
   b) get a teaching qualification.
   c) study Art.

5. Jo probably would have finished her course earlier if she ...
   a) had worked harder.
   b) had not had a child.
   c) had not taken a job with a publishing company.

6. Jo finds her university course ...
   a) a bit difficult.   b) very enjoyable.   c) slightly frustrating.

Further question. Answer it using complete sentences.

7. The three people in this Module are studying different subjects but they all have something in common. What is it?

Replace the words in brackets with words of the same meaning.

8. We have the (opportunity) ... to study foreign languages. (line 16)
9. Then I'm (planning) ... to do a teaching diploma. (line 27)
10. I'm doing this course in order to (complete) ... my degree. (line 36)

And what about you?

11. What do you think makes studying difficult for people who are in their 30s or 40s?
12. Do you think retraining (*Umschulung*) will become more or less important for working people in the future? Give some reasons for your opinion.

H   Connecting words

Verbindungswörter (Konjunktionen)

I'm doing the course **so as to** be able to work in tourism.	Ich nehme an dem Studiengang teil, um auf dem Gebiet des Tourismus arbeiten zu können.
I'm doing the course **in order to** improve my knowledge of Business Studies.	Ich nehme an dem Studiengang teil, um meine Kenntnisse in Betriebswirtschaftslehre zu verbessern.
I'm enjoying this course **because** I've made new friends.	Mir macht dieses Studium Spaß, weil ich neue Freundschaften geschlossen habe.
I had started a degree **but** had to leave **when** I had my son.	Ich hatte mit dem Studium begonnen, musste jedoch von der Universität abgehen, als ich meinen Sohn bekam.

Satzverbindungen machen einen großen Teil der geschriebenen und gesprochenen Sprache aus. Die Verbindung zwischen Sätzen wird durch **Konjunktionen** (*connecting words* oder *connectors*) hergestellt. Im Folgenden eine **kleine Auswahl** von geläufigen Verbindungswörtern:

and (und), **after** (nachdem), **although** (obwohl), **as** (da), **as if** (als ob), **because** (weil), **before** (bevor, ehe), **but** (aber, jedoch), **if** (wenn), **in order that** (damit), **in order to** (um ... zu), **since** (da), **so** (daher), **so as to** (um ... zu), **to** (um ... zu), **when** (als, wenn), **while** (während).

Exercises

I. Put in the right connector to form appropriate sentences. Use the expressions in the box below. ●●

> although ● but ● in order to ● when

1. There was a lot to eat ... I wasn't really hungry.
2. ... she didn't have much experience she was offered the job.
3. ... she had finished her course, she started applying for jobs.
4. He went swimming every day ... lose weight.

II. Put in the right connector to form appropriate sentences.
Use the expressions in the box below. (Be careful, though.
There are four sentences but six expressions!) ●●

although ● because ● but ● if ● so as to ● while

1. We had to sit in the front row ... all the other seats were full.
2. He works at the weekend ... be able to afford his studies.
3. ... you want to get a ticket, make sure you're at the ticket box an hour before it opens.
4. ... we were waiting for the train, we ate some fish and chips.

III. Now think of a connector yourself to form appropriate sentences.
(There may be more than one answer possible.) ●●

1. It was warm and sunny ... it was still the beginning of February.
2. She speaks English ... she really was English. Her pronunciation is perfect.
3. It was getting cold and dark ... we decided to go home.
4. ... I was feeling tired, I went to bed early.

IV. Finish these sentences in a logical way. Use your own words. ●●

1. We got up early in order to ... .
2. She likes to go jogging at the weekend because ... .
3. I wanted to get a better job so ... .
4. Although he had worked very hard for his exam, ...

V. Common abbreviations. What are they? Write them out in full.

1. MP	3. CD	5. VIP	7. CD-ROM
2. UK	4. USA	6. UFO	8. VAT

VI. Write a short text about your educational background and your work experience.
Write about 70–80 words. These questions may give you some ideas:

● What school did you go to?
● What were you good/bad at?
● How old were you when you left school?
● Did you train for a job afterwards?
● What academic or professional qualifications did you get?
● Where have you worked?
● What are your career aims?

26C

Margaret McIntyre – a mature student

Listen carefully to Margaret McIntyre talking about her life. Then answer the questions below.

Margaret (middle) with her colleagues

I. What does Margaret McIntyre talk about in the interview?
Choose one of the alternatives (a-c) below. She talks about ...

a. how she has become a successful businesswoman.
b. how she has learnt to enjoy life more.
c. how she has found out more about her own childhood.

II. Put these nine events into the correct order to tell the story of
Margaret McIntyre's life. Start with event b.

a. she brought up her two children alone
b. she did badly at school
c. she found the course difficult at first
d. she had an unhappy marriage
e. she saw her children do well at school
f. she sees a purpose in her life
g. she slowly began to enjoy the course
h. she started her own voluntary group
i. she decided to go back to college

Angela Sparke,
Adult Education
Tutor

III. Answer these questions in full.

1. Margaret McIntyre started a group called "Community Link". What does this group do exactly?
2. At the end of the interview Margaret McIntyre says that people "deserve a second chance". What does she mean? Do you agree with her?

IV. Put the six expressions below into a logical order.

a. to pass an exam
b. to receive a certificate showing how well you did in an exam
c. to sit (= do) an exam
d. to study for an exam
e. to wait for the results of an exam

26D

Meterman looks to the future

I. Complete the first four paragraphs of this text using the correct forms of the words in brackets.

Meterman ... (drive) up to a college of further education. He notices a group of young people sitting outside and asks one of them what he would like to do when he ... (be) older. The young man hesitates. He ... (not, seem) to have any career plans. Meterman turns to the camera. "I don't know. Young people these days. They just ... (not, take) life seriously. Most of them don't even know what they want to do with their ... (life). When I *was knee high to a grasshopper* ... ." Meterman begins to recall his childhood days.

He remembers that his electrical experiments ... (be) quite shocking, especially to his mother. He remembers playing *hopscotch* along the pavement and one day finding inspiration when he ... (see) the word "meter". From that moment on Meterman ... (know) what he would *grow up to be*.

He ... (leave) school at sixteen with few qualifications, trained for a year and ... (become) a fully qualified meterman. Finally he remembers another milestone in his life; the day he ... (take) possession of Molly, his van. "As with any intimate relationship," Meterman remarks, "Molly and I have had our ups and downs, but on the whole it's been a *smooth* ride."

Meterman ... (go) into the college. He walks into a class on information technology and asks where to find the meter. He listens ... (careful) as the teacher talks about jobs in the future. She points at Meterman: "In two years he ... (be) like the *dinosaur - extinct*," she explains. "Electricity consumption will be registered by advanced computer technology. And what ... (that, mean)? For one thing, it means that poor chap will have to retrain." Meterman begins to think whether there is a future for him in reading meters.

In the end Meterman decides he has to be practical so he *enrols* for a course at a college for adult education. Wearing jeans and a T-shirt he stops at the bottom of the steps to the college and turns to the camera. "This is where I begin," he announces throwing his meterman cap aside. "Today, Meterman. Tomorrow, who knows?"

be knee high to a grasshopper	ein Dreikäsehoch sein	smooth	ruhig, angenehm, glatt (*Fahrt, Flug*)
hopscotch	„Himmel und Hölle" (*Kinderspiel*)	dinosaur (be) extinct	Dinosaurier ausgestorben (sein)
grow up to be sth	etw. später (als Erwachsener) machen, werden	enrol	einschreiben, sich anmelden

II. Complete the sentences below by adding the missing word. The first letter is given.

1. A metre, a mile and an inch are all types of m... .
2. Chair, table and wardrobe are items of f... .
3. Lorry, van and car are different kinds of v... .
4. Hammer, drill, pliers are examples of t... .
5. Beef, lamb and p... are types of meat.
6. The sun, the water and the w... are alternative energy sources.
7. Spring, summer, a... and winter are the four seasons.
8. Radio, television and the printed p... make up the media.

III. Two different words with two different meanings can be pronounced in the same way. Complete the table with another word with the same pronunciation. (The first one has been done for you.)

1.	source	sauce	sɔːs
2.	blew	...	bluː
3.	weigh	...	weɪ
4.	roll	...	rəʊl
5.	wore	...	wɔː
6.	sale	...	seɪl
7.	check	...	tʃek
8.	piece	...	piːs

IV. What course do you think Meterman is doing at the college for adult education? What sort of job will he be doing in the future?

26E

It's never too late!

Woman of 77 lands job at supermarket

By Sean O'Neill

A GREAT-grandmother has beaten 1,000 other job applicants to become a fishmonger for a supermarket.

Doris Morse, 77, will start part-time work in March on the fish counter at a new Asda branch in Cardiff bay.

Mrs Morse, who first worked as a fishmonger in 1938, will earn £53 a week but will make a net gain of only a few pence after losing social security benefits.

"I dc not want to sit around twiddling my thumbs all day. I want to work and meet people," said Mrs Morse, from Penarth, South Wales. "So many employers take the attitude that you should not work after a certain age, but they forget there are so many people out there with valuable experience and a lot to offer."

Alicia Woodhouse, personnel manager with Asda, said: "We do not see why Doris's age should stand in the way of her getting a job. We all think she's marvellous."

MODULE C TAPESCRIPTS

UNIT 14C

Howard and Christine Smith are landlord and landlady of a pub called "The Flying Horse". Who are the customers of "The Flying Horse"? Is it popular with tourists visiting the area or with the people who live nearby? They call them "the locals".

Howard: "We have a very, very active local *trade*, brought from people who live directly in the
5   village, *associated with* the village, with the cricket club, which plays on the green opposite the pub. And these people become *regulars*, or we call them locals in our pub. The pub is not just a place for selling drinks, it becomes a part of the community. We have an increasingly large amount of *custom* coming from the continent, with the *advent* of the Channel Tunnel, which is only about 8 miles away, so we ... we get an increased trade from the continent."

10   Howard and Christine work hard to give all their guests, locals and visitors, a warm welcome.

Christine: "Our customers are our friends. They're there to enjoy your company, and we to enjoy their company. It's ... it's great fun, it's good fun."

As well as being good fun, managing "The Flying Horse" is also very hard work, with long working hours.

15   Howard: "We have a very busy, hectic *schedule* in this business. Seven days a week, seven ... from early hours in the morning to late hours in the evening. And it's not only beer, it's coffees, *soft drinks*, ice-creams, sandwiches when they want them, cooked meals when they want them."

The working day begins early in the morning.

Christine: "Our alarm goes off about half-past six, quarter to seven. Howard's the first one to get up,
20   *bless* him. He comes down and makes me a cup of tea. Howard starts the breakfast and I *get the toast on* and *the boiler on* and the first guests come down."

Not many pubs offer rooms for the night but "The Flying Horse" is different.

Christine: "We offer bed and breakfast accommodation, and also because we do evening meals then anyone who stays with us is likely to have an evening meal with us as well. They like to ... to stay
25   in a *homely* atmosphere, which is what we hope to offer. Once a year we have a *health inspector* come round, just *on spec*, he won't make an *appointment* or anything, and he has *stringent* rules that we have to *abide by* as far as hygiene is concerned in the kitchen. We could get our licence taken away, *revoked*, just like that, if they found that it *wasn't up to scratch*, up to standard."

"The Flying Horse" is a traditional English pub and it sells traditional English beer, or real ales.

30   Howard: "The real ales that we supply really do need a lot of attention. We have to put the barrels onto a *stillage*. They have to be kept there for about twenty-four hours. They have to be *vented*. They then have to be *tapped* without *upsetting the consistency* of the beers too much. And then twenty-four hours later the beers are usually ready for sale. The beer has to be tasted before the beer is ready to go on. We have to make sure that the ... the temperature is right and the clarity of the beer is right
35   because if the beer was served when it first came in it would be very cloudy, but once it's left to stand for 24 hours it should clear. And once that the beer looks clear and it tastes right, then we're ready for action."

"The Flying Horse" also has a restaurant, with a *tempting menu* offering food from the local area.

Christine: "Howard and I both work together as far as the food is concerned."

40 Howard: "We will find out what local *produce* is available, as we always try to use local produce. And then we work our menu through together. The pub closes at 11.00, by the time we finish and everybody is gone, it's generally around half-past eleven, quarter to twelve. I *guess* we tend to get to bed about 1.00."

Going to bed at one o'clock in the morning, and getting up again at 6.30, can they possibly enjoy
45 such a busy life?

Christine: "I like to be busy and I like to have my family around me and I love people. And this ... this sort of business has that to offer, and if we love people then we're in the right business."

trade	Handel, *hier*: Umsatz	stringent	streng, hart
associated with	verbunden mit	abide by	sich halten an
regular	*hier*: Stammgast	revoke	entziehen, widerrufen
custom	Kundschaft	be up to scratch	den Anforderungen
advent	Aufkommen, *hier*:		entsprechen
	Eröffnung		(*scratch* = Kratzer)
schedule	(Stunden-)Plan, *hier*:	stillage	Gestell
	Tagesablauf	vent	*hier*: das Spundloch
soft drink	alkoholfreies Getränk		(*des Fasses*) öffnen,
bless	segnen		(*Fass*) belüften
get the toast on	den Toast auflegen,	tap	anzapfen
	vorbereiten	upset the	*hier im Sinne von*: die
get the boiler on	den Wasserkocher	consistency	„Beschaffenheit"
	anschalten		(*des Bieres*) stören
homely	heimelig, gemütlich	tempting	verführerisch,
health inspector	Vertreter(in) des		verlockend
	Gesundheitsamtes	menu	Speisekarte
on spec	auf Verdacht, unange-	produce	(landwirtschaftliche)
	meldet		Produkte, Erzeugnisse
appointment	Termin(vereinbarung)	guess	schätzen, vermuten

UNIT 15C

An unusual way of buying and selling houses is by auction. Sophie Duncker, a teacher from Hamburg in Germany, has gone along to the auction just to see what happens there. Sophie has been living in England for five years but she plans to return to Germany in the future so she is not certain if she wants to buy a house in England.

5 "I've never been to a property auction at all. They're quite unusual in Germany and when I heard about this one I was quite interested in it. I think I would always try and rent a house but I think if I knew that I was staying in England, I would try and start thinking about buying something because the renting ... the places you can rent are quite of ... of quite a low quality, they are not very attractive."

10 She finds the British *habit* of buying a house a big contrast to what most people in Germany like to do. There are many sayings in English which reflect the tradition, like "an Englishman's home is his castle".

"This part of the tradition in England to own your ... your ... your own property ... 'my home is my castle' I think is ... is one of those sayings in the English language where ... which shows how 15 important it is for an Englishman to have a house."

"To have a *roof* over your head" is another saying.

"A 'roof over your head' is important but for me it is not linked to buying a house. It would be linked to finding an attractive flat which *is within my means*, which is within my walking or short driving distance from my job, that sort of thing."

20 And if you say that something is "as safe as houses", you mean it is very safe indeed, especially from a financial point of view.

"'As safe as houses' is another one. I don't think houses are particularly safe. There's *subsidence* and there's inflation, there's storms, hurricanes, and I don't know what. I would always try and open a *savings account* rather than buy a house. If I had the choice."

25 If you rent a house or a flat in Britain, you do not have as much security as you might wish for. One of the reasons could be that the contract, or *lease*, is often for a short period of time.

"The rented flats I've come across now, here in England, are always *short-term* contracts which means that you can, you have to renew the contract every year, or every two years, or something like that. So you never get that feeling of security. There doesn't seem to be much *point* in buying 30 furniture, for example, for a rented flat you're living in because you may expect to have to move in two or three years' time and you would then have to pay quite a high price for moving the furniture again, it may not fit into your new flat or house. So it's very risky, and you would always try and look at ... a rented flat as a short-term *solution* before you *get round to* buying something."

Sophie thinks that *tenants* in rented property in Germany are more secure.

35 "You *are covered by* the law to quite a high *degree* in Germany. If you have lived in a rented flat for a period of time, five years or more, it's very difficult for the owner of the flat to *get rid of* you."

Walk down any high street in England, and you will see the large number of *estate agents* with all kinds of properties for sale.

"It's very unusual in Germany to have that *density of* estate agents, first of all, in the high street, and
40 it's also unusual to have estate agents which are open to the public like shops are. An estate agent
in Germany would have a 'closed' office and you would have to ring up in advance and they would
probably give you an appointment. The reason for that is probably that there isn't such a mobile
market for buying houses as there is in England."

Let's hope that if she does decide to buy, Sophie finds her "dream house".

habit	(An-)Gewohnheit	point	*hier:* Sinn, Zweck
roof	Dach	solution	Lösung
be within one's	*hier:* im Rahmen der	get round to	*hier:* sich endlich
means	eigenen finanziellen		entschließen
	Möglichkeiten	tenant	Mieter(in)
	sein	be covered by	geschützt sein durch
subsidence	Senkung, Absacken	degree	Grad
	(*eines Geländes,*	get rid of	loswerden
	Gebäudes)	estate agent	Grundstücks-, Immo-
savings account	Sparkonto		bilienmakler(in)
lease	Mietvertrag	density of	Dichte an, Konzen-
short-term	von kurzer Laufzeit,		tration von
	kurzfristig		

UNIT 16C

Edward Jackson is the Director of the *Field Studies Centre* at Flatford Mill. The Field Studies Centre is part of the Field Studies *Council*. What is the Field Studies Council and what does it do?

"The Field Studies Council is a *charity*. We'*re involved in environmental* education. We *run* short courses for people of all ages, and they come from their homes or from their schools, or from their
5   colleges, and they stay with us for a few days, and the courses we run *are based around the arts*, and also the local environment."

In the eighteenth and nineteenth century, Flatford Mill was owned by the Constable family but later it *changed hands*.

"Back in 1946 the National Trust took over Flatford Mill and all the buildings here and very soon
10   afterwards they invited the Field Studies Council to come to Flatford Mill and take a lease. So the Field Studies Council became tenants of the National Trust, and we run our business here, and the Field Centre has grown since then."

Edward Jackson has worked for the Field Studies Council since leaving university.

"I came in 1986. I've worked for the Field Studies Council for all my career, for 20 years. And I
15   used to work in Yorkshire, at one of our other Centres, and I worked my way up there and then one of the top jobs *came up* and they asked me whether I would like to come to Flatford Mill and I said, yes, very much so."

The Field Studies Centre at Flatford Mill has grown a lot over the past 50 years. It runs courses for individuals and for families. The old buildings have been *adapted* to provide accommodation for
20   70 people.

"The Field Centre is very much a living-working community. It could have been turned into a museum but we feel that it would've made the place very ... very *dull* and ... and boring to have people coming in ... in and out of the building. So when people come to Flatford we have maybe 70 people at any one time, and ... and twenty staff. So there are lots of people here doing all sorts of different
25   activities.

I personally am responsible for teaching with young people. I ... I teach environmental studies, I teach geography to older students and I also do many courses for adults and families. My own particular interest is in bird watching and within that I have a special interest in bird song. So people come and spend a weekend with me in the springtime and they learn how to *appreciate* and
30   how to listen to and how to identify all the bird songs and calls."

Flatford Mill is most famous today because of the work of the artist John Constable.

"John Constable's father owned Flatford Mill and John was born in 1776 and Flatford Mill was his father's main workplace. And John Constable knew this place extremely well. He would come down and be with his father when he was a young boy. But in walking and *exploring* around Flatford,
35   he became fascinated by the place. Constable was a person who *was* very *aware of* his own environment. From the age of 7 or 8 he *was* very ... very *wrapped up* in the local environment here. And the way that he *responded to* it was through his painting and drawing. And so we ... we respond to our environment in ... in all sorts of ways, some of them - the ways we respond - are through painting and drawing, but also in many other ways as well. People often see Constable's paintings,
40   and ... and say, 'Oh isn't that wonderful, it's ... it's ... it hasn't changed since then. It was ... he was painting things that were constant.' Now, in fact, *that's the wrong way round*. Constable was

painting a *tremendous* amount of change *in effect*, because he lived at the beginning of the Industrial Revolution and saw changes going on around him. His paintings are simply snapshots, they are little views of all the changes that were going on in his time, so he would *be very tuned in*
45 to the changes that we *experience* today."

But like many artists in the past John Constable was not *admired* or appreciated in his own lifetime.

"Well, strangely, in Constable's own lifetime he was not *recognized* because he *was* actually *way outside* the experience of most people at the time. The sort of paintings he was doing was ... was ... we would say now is *avant-garde*. But now *with the benefit of hindsight*, looking back to
50 Constable's time, we realize that he was a very revolutionary painter."

Edward Jackson's job brings together two aspects. On the one hand, the creativity of a great artist; on the other hand, our care and concern for the environment today.

"Environmental *issues* are increasingly important to us nowadays. The way that we live in and use the environment is ... is quite critical to ... to our future, and we have recognized this over the last
55 10, 20 years. And so our job is to *encourage* young people to have an awareness and understanding, and hopefully an *empathy*, for the environments in which they live and also the environments in which other people live so that they can appreciate it and learn to *cherish* it and look after it for future generations."

Field Studies	Zentrum für Feldfor-	that's the wrong	*hier*: das ist die
Centre	schung	way round	falsche Sicht der
council	Rat, Gremium		Dinge
charity	*hier*: wohltätige	tremendous	enorm, gewaltig
	Organisation	in effect	im Grunde genommen
be involved in	*hier*: sich befassen mit,	be tuned in	empfänglich sein für
	sich engagieren in	experience	erfahren, durchmachen
environmental	Umwelt-	admire	bewundern
run	*hier*: durchführen	recognize	*hier*: anerkennen
be based around	*hier*: in erster Linie zu	be way	„meilenweit" entfernt
	tun haben mit	outside sth	von etw. sein
the arts	die schönen Künste	avant-garde	avantgardistisch
change hands	den Besitzer wechseln		(= „vorkämpferisch")
come up	frei werden (*Arbeits-*	benefit	Vorteil, Nutzen
	stelle)	hindsight	späte Einsicht
adapt	*hier*: umbauen	with the benefit	mit dem Vorteil, das
dull	stumpfsinnig, trübe	of hindsight	Ganze rückblickend
appreciate	(wert)schätzen		betrachten zu
explore	erkunden, erforschen		können
be aware of	sich bewusst sein	issue	Problem, Frage
be wrapped up	*hier*: eingebunden sein	encourage	ermutigen
respond to	antworten auf, *hier*:	empathy	Einfühlungsvermögen
	reagieren auf	cherish	hegen, umsorgen

UNIT 17C

Jonathan Carter is the *Artistic Director* of the *Arts Festival*. And Eileen Williams is the *Administrator*. Who are the people who come to the Festival events? Old or young? From the town or from the school?

Jonathan: "Ideally it is for the community because the school is part of the community. And
5 the school has a privileged position in this community. And it does in many ways *disrupt* this community, and because of the privilege and because of the necessary disruption, we put on the Festival for the town. We have the facilities, we have the *venues*, the school is in the town, the Festival is part of the town's *calendar of events*."

Jonathan's special interest is the theatre. He directed the production of "Equus", but he also had to
10 choose the programme for the whole Festival. How does he decide what to *put in*?

Jonathan: "The Festival is *aimed at* quite a wide audience. If I have a classical piece of music, my next decision is to find a modern piece of music. If I have a serious piece of drama, my next *policy decision* would be to take a funny piece of drama. So one word is *variety* because my audience is varied."

15 Most festivals find money through sponsorship. Companies give *donations* in cash, or, as they say, *in kind*. Finding sponsors is part of Eileen's job.

Eileen: "Our main sponsor is a company called 'Swiss Life', who are an *insurance* company, and they support us in kind, rather than cash, which means they print the booking brochure and they print the *programme covers* for us, *free of charge*. Publicity for the Festival is extremely important. There
20 is no point in putting on a festival if no one knows it's happening. The Festival is really *operated* by two people, the director and the administrator. But it would not take place if it wasn't for all the *volunteer help* that we get from Sevenoaks School. The staff and pupils here *give their time free*, purely to help with the Festival."

And who are the performers at the Festival? Are they amateurs or professionals?

25 Jonathan: "The talent comes from the professional world. We want to bring in the professional world, simply, I think, because the amateurs in the community can *participate in* a festival with professionals. It's not simply an amateur event. We have an ex-student, in 'Equus'. He was here three years ago, he's now gone on to Manchester University, studying Drama there. *Undoubtedly*, he will go on into the profession. And we have immense talent, young talent. We have a girl called
30 Rebecca Rule, a violinist of huge potential, she has been here two years. Rebecca is one of our most *accomplished* musicians. We have a lot of good musicians, but Rebecca *stands out*."

So much work throughout the year for ten short, but brilliant days.

Jonathan: "If we as a Festival can get the young interested in live theatre, they will come back to see more and more. And to sit there and watch row upon row, all these young children staring at the
35 show, their eyes wide open with excitement and enjoyment, it is a magical moment. Because they are *captivated*. For me it is one of the great *highlights* of any festival to see a young audience enjoying themselves so much."

artistic director	künstlerische(r) Leiter(in)	in kind	in Form von Sach-leistungen, „Naturalien"
arts festival	Kulturfestival	insurance	Versicherung(s-)
administrator	*hier*: organisato-rische(r) Leiter(in)	programme cover	Umschlag des Veran-staltungsprogrammes
disrupt	*hier*: aus der üblichen Ruhe „aufrütteln"	free of charge	kostenlos, -frei
		operate	*hier*: veranstalten
venue	Veranstaltungsort	volunteer help	freiwillige Hilfe
calendar of events	Veranstaltungs-kalender	give one's time free	seine Zeit opfern
put in	*hier*: in den Spielplan aufnehmen	participate in	teilnehmen an
		undoubtedly	zweifellos
aim at	zielen auf	accomplished	vollendet, ausgezeichnet
policy decision	*hier*: taktische Entscheidung	stand out	herausragen
		captivate	faszinieren, fesseln
variety	Vielfalt	highlight	Glanz-, Höhepunkt
donation	Spende		

UNIT 18C

The weather plays an important part in the life of a lifeboat man. William Richardson is the *coxswain*, that means he is the person in charge of a lifeboat and of the people on board, the crew.

"My job as a ... as a coxswain is to *man* the boat and to keep a crew together. The crew come from various *walks of life* and ... and different jobs around the village. They're *on call* all the time. We
5 have a system where there's eighteen crew members, but only six of us go, so we always have enough to man the boat. It's usually the first six at the station go, so it does create a bit of competition and enables us to *launch* very quickly."

The lifeboat station at Dungeness stands on the *tip* of the Kent coast, looking across the *bay* to Dover, and out across the English Channel to the coast of France. This is the busiest *shipping lane* in the
10 world with some of the most difficult and changeable weather. The Royal National Lifeboat Institution, the RNLI, is financed entirely by *voluntary* donations.

"The British Isles *is* very *fortunate* with its *rescue service* as it's the only place in the world where it's absolutely free. The RNLI doesn't *charge* anybody *for* rescues or assisting them. We have an exercise once a *fortnight*, which they get paid about £5 each for two hours' work. So nobody does
15 it for the money. They do it because they like doing it."

In this part of the exercise they are *setting up* the *breeches buoy*. It is used to carry *survivors* from ship to lifeboat, or from ship to land.

"The breeches buoy is a system for getting people aboard the lifeboat or to land, where it's not practical to go *alongside* in the boat itself. We could fire a *rocket line* to the *casualty*, and we'd then
20 pull a rope across and *attach* a *running block* on the end of it, and you can then *ferry* your casualty *back* to the lifeboat."

Another part of the exercise is *dropping the anchor*.

"The lifeboat *is fitted with* a 51-kilo fisherman's anchor which is designed to *grip* in all types of *sea bed*. It's always a lifeboat man's *nightmare* to have an *engine failure* or breakdown on an *onshore*
25 *wind*. So we exercise regularly with the anchor, so they can get it over and make sure it goes clear very quickly."

Today all this is just an exercise. But it is the weather that decides the time and place of a real *emergency*.

"We collect all the weather information we can. We collect the *shipping forecasts* on Radio 4. We
30 also look at the *weather charts* on the televisions and make up our mind to what we're going to get. It's ... it's a lovely day today, isn't it? The wind's about *force* 2 to 3, which is 15 to 20 miles an hour, good for *bathers* providing they stay *inshore*. The wind is *off the land* so you could get blown out to sea."

And that is what has happened to one unlucky swimmer. The *coastguard* at Dover puts out a call.
35 The lifeboat *navigator* takes the call from Dover coastguard. The Dungeness lifeboat can go at speeds of up to 17 *knots*, that's about 31 kilometres per hour. It is fully equipped with radar, *Decca navigator* and *global positioning system* that works by navigation satellites. Below decks there is equipment for giving first aid to survivors. A small but powerful *inflatable craft* comes to join the exercise from the nearby harbour of Rye.

40 "We had a *launch* a little while ago for two *dinghies* that were launched from St Mary's Bay, which is about ten miles to the north of us. At the time they launched and at the time they were last seen it was high water time and by the coastguard's predictions from the *Admiralty charts* and the *almanacs*, it should have driven the dinghies in the northerly direction. So the coastguards asked us to launch to the north of the station, but with our local knowledge we knew that the tide and the
45 weather and the *prevailing* wind were setting everything to the south, and we were fortunate enough to pick them up south of the station."

Today's rescue was in fact part of the exercise. When a real emergency *occurs*, other ships may go to the rescue. As well as saving lives, some of them are interested in the sums of money, called *salvage*, that they can receive from a ship's owners.

50 "When a ship does get into trouble, it's normal a *tug* comes along and pulls it off and they *claim* salvage off the owners of the ships, or its insurers. The RNLI doesn't claim salvage. We're not in the business of claiming salvage, we're in the business of saving lives."

coxswain	Bootsführer	emergency	Notfall
man	bemannen	shipping	Vorhersage des
walk of life	Berufssparte	forecast	Schiff(fahrt)s-
be on call	Bereitschaftsdienst haben		aufkommens
launch	*hier*: Boot ins Wasser	weather chart	Wetterkarte
	lassen, ausfahren	force	*hier*: (*Wind-*)Stärke
tip	Spitze	bather	Badende(r)
bay	Bucht	inshore	nahe der Küste, in
shipping lane	Schifffahrtsweg, -linie		Küstennähe
voluntary	freiwillig	off the land	ablandig
be fortunate	Glück haben, *hier*: sich	coastguard	Küstenwache
	glücklich schätzen können	navigator	Navigator (*für Kurs-*
rescue service	Rettungsdienst		*und Ortsbestimmung*
charge sb	*hier*: jmdm. etw.		*verantwortlicher*
for sth	berechnen, in Rechnung		*Schiffsoffizier*)
	stellen	knot	*hier*: Knoten
fortnight	zwei Wochen, vierzehn		(*Seemeile je Stunde*)
	Tage	Decca	*Navigationssystem*
set up	*hier*: aussetzen, auslassen	global	*Navigationssystem zur*
breeches buoy	„Hosenboje"	positioning	*Positionsbestimmung*
	(*Seerettungsgerät*)	system	*in den Weltmeeren*
survivor	Überlebende(r)	inflatable	aufblasbar
alongside	neben	craft	*hier*: Boot, Schiff
rocket line	*Rettungsleine, die zu den*	launch	Stapellauf, *hier*: Einsatz
	Verunglückten abgefeuert	dinghy	(*aufblasbares*)
	wird		Schlauchboot;
casualty	*hier*: Verunglückte(r)		kleines Segel- oder
attach	befestigen		Ruderboot
running block	*hier*: Seilwinde	Admiralty	*Seekarten der*
ferry back	*hier*: (ins Boot) herüber-	charts	*britischen Marine*
	holen	almanac	Almanach, Jahrbuch
drop (the)	(den) Anker werfen	prevailing	vorherrschend
anchor		occur	sich ereignen,
be fitted with	*hier*: ausgestattet,		geschehen
	ausgerüstet sein mit	salvage	Bergung, *hier*:
grip	greifen		Bergungsprämie
sea bed	Meeresboden	tug	Schlepper
nightmare	Alptraum	claim	*hier*: beanspruchen,
engine failure	Maschinenschaden		verlangen
onshore wind	auflandiger Seewind		

UNIT 19C

Jackie Hails is the *Sports Development Officer* for disabled people in her area.

Jackie: "This facility has been the centre of a project that we've started to enable disabled people to *access* a sports centre *with ease*. And access doesn't just mean to equipment and buildings and *changing-rooms* and activities, but it also means being an accepted part of what's already going on
5   here with *able-bodied people*. With ... dealing with people with disabilities *ranging from* physical, *sensory*, learning disability, and people with a combination of all three, which we would call *profound* and *multiple*-disabled people. People with a learning disability perhaps have problems *relating to* other people and taking part in teams and *sharing* and *interacting* with other people. But people with a physical disability, their problems are more obvious, that they may move slower or
10 differently."

Mike Bishop is a top class basketball player. How did he come to take up wheelchair basketball?

Mike: "The wheelchair basketball started for me when I was in *Stoke Mandeville Hospital*, which is the *spinal unit* in this country, when I was 19, having had a motorcycle accident. At that point sport is primarily a physiotherapy *pursuit*, but having left hospital, I realized that basketball was
15 something that I would enjoy. Wheelchair basketball particularly is a fast physical game. It gives you good exercise, it keeps you fit and gets the blood *flowing*. It stops you from getting too fat, which is a *potential* problem for many of our wheelchair athletes. And also it gives you the ... the element of playing the game with other people, considering other people, being part of a team. And it gives you those ... those important moments of just absolute magic when it all comes together."

20 The swimming pool is very popular with many disabled people. Jackie Hails explains why.

Jackie: "People with a physical disability *get* a bit of *a release from their everyday environment*, if it's a chair or if they use sticks to help them walk. I mean, they're free of those, they can *chuck* them *away* at the side of the pool and get in the water and they're free. They're not necessarily *relying on* anybody else to help them, either, which is part of, perhaps, if they have a profound
25 disability, it's part of their everyday life to be constantly relying on other people. So that I think freedom is ... is the big thing. The *hoist* is needed now in swimming pools because of the new European regulations on lifting and handling and there was an argument several years ago where disabled people said we don't wish to get into a pool using a hoist, we don't wish to *be man-handled* in, or be helped, by other people. Having a hoist, disabled people sometimes feel ... actually
30 sets them apart from the rest of the community, but new regulations mean that ... that no lifting or handling can take place as it used to. The hoist allows disabled people to actually get into the *jacuzzi*, upstairs in the *house suite*, as well as into the pool. And it's ... again it's an activity, it's a ... it's a *leisure*-related activity, which, perhaps, some people would feel, hadn't been an appropriate activity for disabled people."

35 Tanni Grey is one of Britain's most successful disabled athletes. She has won gold medals at the *Paralympic Games* and every year she trains hard for the London Marathon.

Mike: "Disabled people are as serious about their sport as non-disabled people are, right up to top international level."

But Mike Bishop thinks that disabled athletics still has second-class status.

40   Mike: "You've got all the sports in this country, you've got things like the London Marathon, which unfortunately is still, I think, considered a little bit of a ... a second-class race within the whole *set-up* of the London Marathon, *bearing in mind* things like no prize money for the wheelchair athletes."

Top class or elite disabled athletes give encouragement and inspiration to others who are just
45   starting to enjoy sports.

Mike: "It's a long, slow *haul* to get the same *recognition* for disabled athletes as has already been around for the non-disabled athletes. But for disabled people, it's also important to have their own *role models* who are themselves disabled people."

Sports Development Officer	*Beauftragte(r) zur Förderung des Sports*	flow potential	fließen möglich, potenziell
access	Zugang haben zu	release	Befreiung
with ease	ohne Mühe, mühelos	get a release from	*im Sinne von:*
changing-room	Umkleideraum, -kabine	one's everyday environment	*dem Alltag entkommen*
able-bodied people	Gesunde, Nicht-behinderte	chuck away (*coll*) rely on	wegschmeißen sich verlassen auf
ranging from ... (to)	reichen von ... (bis)	hoist	Hebevorrichtung
sensory	Sinnes-, sensorisch	be manhandled	*hier:* von
profound	*hier:* schwer (behindert)		Menschen an-gefasst werden
multiple	mehrfach	jacuzzi	Whirlpool
relate to	Kontakt herstellen zu	house suite	*hier:* „exklusive-rer" Teil des
share	*hier:* gemeinsam etw. erleben		*Schwimmbades*
interact	sich austauschen	leisure	Freizeit
Stoke Mandeville Hospital	*Krankenhaus in der Nähe von London, das sich auf Patien-ten mit Lähmungen spezialisiert hat*	Paralympic Games set-up	Paralympische Spiele (*Behinder-tenolympiade*) Organisation, Drum und Dran
spinal unit	*etwa:* Behandlungs-zentrum für Wirbel-säulenerkrankungen	bearing in mind ... haul	wenn man bedenkt, ... *hier:* Kraftakt
pursuit	*hier:* Zweck, Vorhaben	recognition role model	Anerkennung (Rollen)Vorbild

UNIT 20C

Josh Gifford is one of England's most famous trainers of race horses. At his *stables* in Sussex he trains up to sixty *thoroughbred* horses for the national *hunt* season. That's the autumn and winter sport, when horses race over *fences*, and it can be a very dangerous sport.

Josh: "Well, I think most sports ... there is danger and I don't think a jockey would enjoy it as much
5   if that's the right way of saying it *'cause* most jockeys when they *set off*, you know, they ... they would do it for nothing, hoping to, 'cause they enjoy it, they can't wait to get out there, it's the *challenge*. And it's something that's *bred in* you."

Josh Gifford knows all about the dangers of jumping over fences. He was the champion jockey four times and he suffered many injuries in his great career.

10 Josh: "The worst was when I broke my neck. I suppose I was very lucky then. I broke my *femur* twice, ankle, numerous *collarbones* and *ribs*. But it was all in a day's work."

Like most of the *stable lads* and girls, Mandy Madden always wanted to be a jockey.

Mandy: "I started with horses when ... when I was really young and I just watched racing on the *telly* one ... one day when I was about eight years old and I just wanted to be a jockey from then on. I just
15 had this ... this thing about speed, I wanted to go as fast as I could and horses seemed to be the best thing, and I just love *'em*. I couldn't be a jockey because my weight went against me to start with, I'm not light enough, so I'm always going to be *battling* with my weight and the lads are lighter anyway. Generally speaking the lads are stronger and better riders, they just ... they just get on a horse and ride it and if it falls, so what, they get back up. The lads have no fear."

20 This is like a first class hotel for horses. They get the best of everything. But for the people who work here, it is a *tough* life.

Mandy: "It is hard in the winter, it gets very, very cold, especially up on *the Downs* here it's ... the weather's very bitter, it's dark and depressing. But on the ... on the good points, when the horses run well, you know, it gives you a *boost* and you think, you know, you ... you're really pleased that
25 you've done such a good job looking after them and that they've run well and when they ... when you do get a big winner, then the whole *yard*, it just seems to *lift* the whole yard."

Training horses to win races is Josh Gifford's business and he has trained hundreds of winners. But this horse was special. It returned from serious injury to win Britain's most famous *race for jumpers*: the Grand National.

30 Josh: "Every win is exciting, whether it's a *selling race* or the Grand National. But obviously if you made me pick one out it is the Grand National, you know, that Aldaniti won, and, I mean it really was a *fairy story* with him and Bob Champion. I mean they both were very sick people. I mean Bob was very, very ill, I mean, I didn't think he ... he would be with us very long."

When Bob Champion, the jockey, was close to death with *cancer*, he still dreamed of riding Aldaniti
35 in the big race.

Josh: "And then Nick Embericos, the owner of Aldaniti, went to see him, and ... and rang me up that evening and said we've got to put the old horse back in training, which we did do. I said he ... I told him he *was* completely *crackers*, you know, a: Bob will never ride again and b: Aldaniti will never see a *race course* again. He said, 'never mind, for Bob's sake we will', and he actually won it which
40 was absolute fairy story. One of those fairy stories that couldn't happen, but did."

Obviously Josh knows a lot about winners. But does he gamble on the horses?

Josh: "I don't gamble myself on horses. I'm a gambler by nature, because I think you wouldn't *be in the game* otherwise. You know *if* you went to *the greyhounds*, something I know nothing about, I probably would want to have a bet in every race, or *a pack of cards came out*. But racing is my
45 business. Number 1, I don't think I'd be able to make it pay. Number 2 is we get a percent of all prize money that we win, i.e. first, second and third. I say ... we; it *goes into the kitty*, it goes into the yard. So I don't see any point in ... in losing it to the *bookmakers*. I mean it is a business, and that is the main reason that I don't gamble on horses."

Horse racing may be a business but it is also a passion for everyone who takes part because they all
50 love horses.

Mandy: "For me horses are everything in my life. I couldn't be sat in an office from 9 till 5, I have to be outside, in the open, and with horses. I love 'em dearly, it's like ... once they get into your blood, it's like a disease, you just never get rid of it, and I just have to be with 'em, and race horses are ideal because I love going fast and to feel the power in that ... in the horse underneath you when
55 you're doing a ... a piece of *canter* work is just amazing."

stable	Stall(ung)	race for jumpers	Hindernisrennen
thoroughbred	Vollblut-, reinrassig	selling race	„Verkaufsrennen“
hunt	Jagd		(*Pferderennen vor*
fence	Zaun		*einem Publikum,*
'cause (= because)			*das hauptsächlich*
set off	*hier*: losreiten		*aus potenziellen*
challenge	Herausforderung		*Käufern besteht*)
breed (bred, bred)	züchten	fairy story/tale	Märchen
be bred in	im Blut liegen,	cancer	Krebs
	angeboren sein	be crackers (*coll*)	verrückt, überge-
femur	Oberschenkelknochen		schnappt sein
collarbone	Schlüsselbein	race course	Rennbahn
rib	Rippe	be in the game	*hier*: in diesem
stable lad	Stalljunge		Geschäft sein
telly (= television, *coll*)	Fernsehen	the greyhounds	*hier*: Windhund-rennen
'em (= them)		... if a pack of	... wenn sich ein
battle	kämpfen	cards came out.	Kartenspiel
tough	rau, hart, zäh		ergäbe.
the Downs	*Hügellandschaft im Süden Englands*	go into the kitty	in die Gemein-schaftskasse
boost	Auftrieb		gehen
yard	Hof, *hier*: Gestüt	bookmaker	Buchmacher(in)
lift	*hier*: die allgemeine Stimmung heben	canter	Handgalopp, Kanter

UNIT 21C

Police Constable Jonathan Dyer is *patrolling* the streets of Farnham in Surrey, a typical British bobby on his *beat*.

Jonathan: "A bobby on the beat is as natural as seeing a post office, a pub or a telephone kiosk. People want to see us walking the beat, talking to them and letting them know that we're providing
5 a safe place and we're there to help them if there's a problem where they do need to speak to the police."

Whether they are using traditional methods or the latest technology, the Surrey police employ highly trained officers, men and women.

Julia Buchan: "Today there are no departments within the Surrey police that aren't open to male and
10 female officers *alike*. I don't think that there are any roles left which are specific *gender orientated*, *other than* in specific cases of perhaps searching prisoners, or dealing with specific cases, say of *rape* or serious sexual *assault*, where the *victim requests* or *requires* a female officer."

Jonathan: "My fellow police officers, the female ones, *are* just as *capable of* dealing with violent situations as I am. We're trained to an extremely high standard. I am glad to say that ... that we don't
15 carry firearms, as a norm, on the street and in all the potentially conflict situations I've been in female police officers have been as able as ... as any man."

Julia: "*Initially* your two years are spent doing beat work or *crewing a car* so that you get ... just to *reinforce* your basic policing skills, and after that I went on to the *search team*. We're very aware of terrorist *threats* in Surrey and in other parts of the country, and we were used on *defensive*
20 *searches* for, if we had, say, *army bands* or other *dignitaries* coming to Surrey, we would *clear an area* and ensure that it was safe, using the search team and *explosive dogs* from the dog unit as well."

After her duties with the search team Julia discovered that she was expecting a baby.

Julia: "As soon as you declare *pregnancy* you're taken off from ordinary patrol, so I worked in the control room, the divisional control room, for the *duration* of my pregnancy and then I returned to
25 beat work, patrol work, but *applied for* my initial firearms course, which I attended three years ago, and since then I've been an *authorized firearms officer*."

Although British police officers do not usually carry guns, they do have equipment for their protection.

Jonathan: "Included in what we carry for ... for our safety, our members of the public is what we call
30 the quick *cuff*, or the *rigid* cuff, or the speed cuffs. I'*m loath to* use them, however, for my personal safety, and for safety of members of the public, including the person I might be arresting, they are a good tool."

Julia: "Moving round this way, this is our *asp* which replaced the traditional police *truncheon* that we *were issued with* for many years, which was just a *lump of wood*. As you can see, it's quite
35 compact and holds nicely into the hand, and can, if you're going into a potentially conflict situation, be quite tidily *tucked up* into the *sleeve* so it's not obvious to people that you are, in fact, carrying your asp. It extends in a number of ways, and is obviously a *fairly* useful piece of equipment to use should the need *arise*."

Jonathan: "There's an old saying that in heaven all the policemen would be British, and I'd like to
40 think that's quite true."

patrol	patrouillieren, auf Streife sein	duration	Dauer
beat	*hier*: Runde, Rundgang	apply for	sich bewerben um, für
alike	gleich(ermaßen)	authorized	zum Schuss-
gender orientated	geschlechtsspezifisch, geschlechtsorientiert	firearms officer	waffengebrauch berechtigte(r) Polizei-
other than	außer		beamtin/-er
rape	Vergewaltigung		
assault	*hier*: tätlicher Angriff	cuffs	*hier*:
victim	Opfer	(= handcuffs)	Handschellen
request	bitten um, ersuchen	rigid	starr, steif
require	benötigen, bedürfen	be loath to do sth	etw. ungern tun
be capable of	fähig, in der Lage sein zu	asp	*Eigenname für Schlagstock der*
initially	am Anfang		*englischen Polizei*
crew a car	*hier*: Streife fahren		*(abgeleitet aus den*
reinforce	verstärken, *hier*: verbessern		*Anfangsbuchsta- ben der Hersteller-*
search team	Fahndungstruppe		*firma)*
threat	Bedrohung	truncheon	Schlagstock
defensive search	Sicherungsfahndung *(zur Vorbeugung einer Straftat)*	be issued with	ausgerüstet sein mit
		lump (of wood)	Stück (Holz)
army band	Militärkapelle	tuck up	weg-, hochstecken
dignitary	Würdenträger(in)	sleeve	Ärmel
clear an area	ein Gelände räumen	fairly	ziemlich
explosive dog	Polizeihund zum Auf- spüren von Sprengstoff	arise (arose, arisen)	sich ergeben
pregnancy	Schwangerschaft		

UNIT 22C

Roger Perkins is the *editor* of a local newspaper with offices in the centre of the town.

What is the busiest part of his week?

Roger: "The most hectic part of our week has to be Monday, Tuesday and then Wednesday morning. Monday morning we come in, after one hour of my reporters getting together, things that
5 have happened over the weekend, we have an *editorial meeting*. Already we will be talking about what will make our front page *lead story*, and what might make lead stories for other pages. And a lead story is the main story on the page, so the front page lead is the biggest story of the week. This is an example of a good lead story. (Holding up a front page:) *This is yet to go to print*, but this will be tomorrow's newspaper. This is a story which everybody will be talking about. We had a very
10 *courageous* reader write to us and explain that their life is a living nightmare. They live next door to a *gipsy site* in one of our villages, and some of the gipsies there, not all, but some of the gipsies, are firing stones from *catapults* at their houses, and these people really cannot tolerate it."

One event which took place in the area will always remain in Roger's memory.

Roger: "The biggest story that's ever happened, not only to our newspaper, but obviously to
15 Sevenoaks, had to be the hurricane in 1987 and this was just incredible. It was October 17, and *gale-force winds swept in* across the Channel, *lashed* our countryside and we lost a million trees in this *fiery*, fiery night. Well, in fact, what had happened was we had lost six of our oak trees, and of course we are Sevenoaks, and we became known across the world as 'Oneoak', and there were even prayers said for us in Jerusalem that weekend."

20 Andrew Cruickshank is the newspaper's chief reporter.

Andrew: "The stories which interest our readers most tend to be the human interest ones, I find. It's really about the things that *affect* everyday people, and whether it hits their pockets, or whether it's about their *pets* or their health. Today's story is about two people who set up their own business. They've been going for about three years, but ... because of a ... because of a *council decision*, their
25 *livelihoods* could be ruined. I mean, they ... they run a burger bar on a ... on a site next to a road, which is really a car park, but they've been told to move, because it's *regarded as* a ... as a turning point for lorries and is actually part of the road."

Andrew (talking to the owners of the burger bar): "I'm Andrew Cruickshank from the 'Chronicle', I think we both spoke on the phone."
30 Man: "Right."
Andrew: "*The crux of the matter*, *apparently*, is your customers, they claim, are blocking the road."
Man: "Yeah, well me, actually, they're actually saying that I'm ..."
Andrew: "They claim you are blocking the road."
Man: "I'm blocking the highway, yeah."
35 Andrew: "The actual complaints, do you know where they've come from?"
Woman: "They wouldn't tell us exactly where."
Andrew: "Right."

Andrew (back in the office): "Unfortunately we don't have time always to meet subjects face to face when we do a story. It's just simply pressure of time, and within ... within a working day I could be
40 writing up to fifteen, even twenty, stories. So, *alas*, much of it has to be done over the telephone."

Roger: "One of my tasks is to write *the leader*, this is *jargon* for a *leading article* and I write this myself each week in the newspaper. Journalists have to be very careful not to let their own views colour an article. They cannot let their opinion get into the stories that they write. They must be *unbiased*. Now what is so great about the leader is that it does entirely the *reverse*. It is pure opinion,
45 and I see the leader as a chance to *engender debate on* an important issue. One way in which I have *stamped my mark on* this newspaper is to turn it into more of a *campaigning* newspaper. If there is an issue which I believe the people of Sevenoaks care very strongly about, then I will follow it through. Our stories will still be entirely unbiased, but we will *bring* this issue *to the forefront*, and again, I can use my *leader column* to *highlight* the issue."

editor	*hier*: Chefredakteur	the crux of the	der springende
editorial meeting	Redaktionsbesprechung	matter	Punkt
lead story	Aufmacher, Titel-	apparently	anscheinend
	geschichte	alas	leider
This is yet to go	Dies muss erst noch	the leader,	Leitartikel
to print.	zum Druck gehen.	leading article	
courageous	mutig	jargon	Fachsprache
gipsy site	Zigeunerlager	unbiased	unvoreingenom-
catapult	Schleuder		men, unparteiisch
gale-force winds	orkanartige Winde	reverse	Gegenteil
sweep in	hereinfegen	engender debate	eine Debatte
(swept, swept)		on	hervorrufen über
lash	peitschen (gegen)	stamp one's mark	seinen Stempel
fiery	*hier*: schaurig	on	aufdrücken, prägen
affect	(be)treffen, berühren	campaigning	kämpferisch
pet	Haustier	bring to the fore-	*hier*: zu einem
council decision	Gemeinde-, Stadtrats-	front	Thema machen
	beschluss	leader column	Leitartikel,
livelihood	Lebensunterhalt		Kolumne
regard as	betrachten, ansehen als	highlight	hervorheben

UNIT 23C

Go to London, particularly the West End, from Soho, Carnaby Street to Knightsbridge, outside Harrod's, you will see really *street cred*. You'll see maxis, minis, anything goes.

Joan Barrell is a fashion and a beauty writer who has spent many years working with magazines whose names are familiar to us all. "Cosmopolitan", or "Cosmo" as it is often called, "Company",
5   "She", and "Good Housekeeping".

"I'm often asked: what is fashion? To my mind, fashion is clothes, it's style, it's how you wear it. And today, anything goes, be it maxi, mini or indeed knee length. You can wear it in your own way, in your own style.

'Vogue' magazine has a long history of being known as the bible of the fashion world. It is a
10   leader amongst the world on the trends of fashion, and in it, it shows very, very clearly how you can wear the mini and the maxi, *right the way through*, whatever age group. It's all about style and *accessorizing*, or as *Jean Patou* used to say, little nothings, little *accessories*, which go a long way to make the outfit look perfect.

'She' magazine is another magazine which is a magazine for mothers and young children, but
15   nevertheless it's like an older sister for the great 'Cosmopolitan' and therefore it is very trendy and very fashionable. And it actually shows some really good fashion details. One big fashion editor once said to me: 'Joan, always buy a very expensive suit, a classic suit, and then wear it till it *drops off* that season, but have lots and lots of accessories so you can look different for any hour of the day.' You always feel good in a good suit. (Pointing to some pages in a magazine:) And here again
20   we can demonstrate how a long coat with a short shirt, or a long coat with trousers, how smart it looks for the older woman. So again you're not *restricted* by ideas because of your age. It works extremely well, it's charming and *sophisticated* on these older models. So don't give up, don't *despair*, whatever size or *shape* you are, be happy with your individuality and your own style and take the basic trends of what is known as fashion, or as I said earlier, clothes. Anything goes."

cred (short for "credibility")	Glaubwürdigkeit	Jean Patou	*Gründer eines bekannten*
street cred	*feststehender Begriff: etwas, das breite Zu-stimmung unter jungen Leuten findet (= „im Trend liegen")*		*Haute-Couture-Modehauses*
		drop off	*hier:* aus der Mode kommen
		restrict	einschränken
right the way through	*etwa: durch alle Altersstufen*	sophisticated	*hier:* kultiviert
		despair	verzweifeln
accessory	Accessoire, modisches Zubehör	shape	Form, *hier:* Figur
accessorize	*hier:* die richtigen, passenden Accessoires auswählen		

UNIT 24C

Duncan Brown is a *horticulturalist* and *environmentalist*. Duncan uses plants to find an answer to some of the problems of modern living.

Duncan: "Well, I ... I started off working in ... in our own family business. I was third generation actually. We had our ... our own horticultural shops so we're used to dealing with a broad range of
5   horticultural products. One of our solutions is *willow wall* to *sound-barrier* noise. I mean, I live very close to a very busy road here on the A25 which has in fact increased with ... with traffic flow ever since the M25 was ... was opened, and we found that by using a willow wall barrier, we found that it's not only *dampened* the noise, but it's also improved the *ecological* situation, birdlife population etc."

10 Another innovation from Duncan is a type of grass that grows very quickly. It's called "fast grass".

Duncan: "Fast grass is a treatment to grass *seed*, and virtually any grass seed, where we can take it through the *germination* process and arrest it, and stop it. So that when it actually is *sown*, it's ready to ... to go straight away. The *radicle* is ready to ... to move, we get very rapid *establishment*. We can get in the UK, we can get four inches of growth in seven days which will go on for about five
15 weeks. The other advantages, of course, with ... with fast grass is with agricultural *forage crops*, and it was that ... that lead me when I took, in fact, the ... the fast grass samples to India, that in fact we were getting such tremendous results.
An inch and a half's growth with Blue Panicum, which is a forage grass in India, in twenty-four hours. An inch and a half in twenty-four hours from seed. Now that ... that meant that we could get
20 cows *grazing* in three to four weeks. And when you're ... when you're looking at India, and you're looking at Bombay with all of that *dense* population of 15 million plus, if you can in fact *arrest* that situation of bringing people into the *urban* areas and ... and developing the *rural* areas, it suddenly *occurred to* me that our ... our product could in fact seriously *contribute to* helping the government in India to deal with that problem."

25 But Duncan has used his innovative talents to help find an answer to the Third World's most *pressing* problem - the need for *basic housing*. The idea of fast built houses came to him during his visit to India in 1993.

Duncan: "And it was then that I started working with ... with the ... the need to provide housing in a very, very fast way, in a ... in a very easy way of erection so that, in fact, villages of a hundred to
30 two hundred houses to five hundred houses could be put up very quickly, and that's what led me on to Environ when we came back to the UK."

Environ is a cheap product that Duncan makes from re-cycled material. Houses like these are easy to make and easy to build. Duncan believes that with village houses like these, more people can stay in their own place instead of moving in to the cities.

35 Duncan: "The land is particularly personal to them, and that ... I think that's quite a general ... a general feel that you'll find with the poor in most countries of the world. They love the areas where they live, they don't really want to be moved away from them."

Such simple houses are a long way from the house designed and built for his own use by British architect, Michael Winter. Michael lives in a "green" house.

40 Michael: "The building's a green building because it ... it works with the environment, rather than against it. Therefore, you ... you're trying to use the bonuses of the environment, the sun to heat up, trying to protect it from the ... the elements of the wind and the cold, trying to keep the heat in. There are lots of trees on the site, and we really didn't want to take any trees out at all, so the building is very much a ... an organic shape which actually steps around the trees, and again we've developed
45 that further, and we've actually put the *foundations* on *piles*, or on *pads*, instead of having a *strip foundation* which could cut off the tree *roots*, of the ... of the trees, and kill them."

Wood is the main building material that Michael has chosen for his house.

Michael: "Well, I ... I'm a keen fan of *contemporary* architecture and particularly high tech. High tech, you tend to show the function of the structure, and very often you have the structure on the
50 outside. And that to me had quite a ... a nice feel because we've got trees, I wanted to *build in timber* because it's environmentally friendly material. So you have the *columns* on the outside which really *mimic* the trees. If you keep timber dry and well *ventilated* it should last for years and years and years. In fact, many old houses have timber that isn't *preserved*, and it's just as good now as it was then, and that's hundreds of years ago. We've tried to keep that, and ... and the material is very
55 natural. For instance, the floor, it's a hardwood floor, but we've managed to get that from a ... an old school, they were going to *knock* it *down* and we managed to save it before it was knocked down and cleaned it up, put it onto the floor, and it ... it works very well."

The north side of Michael's house is next to a noisy railway line. To keep out the noise and to conserve energy there are only a few small windows here. The south side of the house receives all
60 the sun's rays. Large *triple-glazed* windows allow the natural heat through. This is one of the four *sources* of heating.

Michael: "The second source really is ... there's a wood burning stove in the *living space*, which gives heat to the living space. The third source is a mechanical ventilation system, which has a heat pump with it. The heat pump really *works like a ... a fridge in reverse*, where it concentrates the heat
65 and the ... *coefficient* of ... of working of that heat pump, it's usually about one to three. So you're putting 1 kilowatt of energy to get 3 kilowatts out. It's very good. The last source of heat really is just to the bathroom spaces, and that's electric."

There are many other "green" *features* about this house. Rain water off the roof is re-cycled and *solar panels* provide hot water. But, does Michael believe it is the answer to future living?

70 Michael: "I don't think it's ... it's a complete answer, but it's certainly a long way towards that. It's trying to work with the environment rather than against it, so you're trying to *minimize* the amount of energy you use. And yes, it goes a long way towards that."

horticulturalist	Fachmann/-frau für Gartenbau	pad	Block
environmentalist	Umweltschützer(in)	strip foundation	Streifen-fundament
willow wall	Weidenbaumhecke	root	Wurzel
sound-barrier	einen Schallschutz errichten gegen	contemporary	zeitgenössisch
dampen	dämpfen	build in timber	in, mit Holz bauen
ecological	ökologisch	column	Säule, *hier*: Querbalken
seed	Samen	mimic	imitieren,
germination	Keimung		nachmachen
sow (sowed, sown)	säen	ventilate	belüften
radicle	Keimwurzel	preserve	schützen (*hier*:
establishment	*hier im Sinne von*: Verwurzelung		*durch die Behand-lung mit Holz-*
forage	Viehfutter		*schutzmitteln*)
crop	Ertrag	knock down	abreißen
graze	weiden	triple-glazed	dreifach verglast
dense	dicht	source	Quelle
arrest	*hier*: unter Kontrolle bringen	living space	Wohnbereich
		... works like a	... funktioniert
urban	städtisch	fridge in reverse ...	genau umgekehrt
rural	ländlich		wie ein Kühl-
occur to sb	jmdm. in den Sinn kommen, einfallen	coefficient	schrank ... Koeffizient,
contribute to	beitragen zu		Faktor
pressing	drängend (*Problem*)	feature	Merkmal,
basic housing	*einfach und ohne großen Kostenauf-wand zu errichtende Häuser*	solar panel minimize	Kennzeichen Sonnenkollektor minimieren, möglichst niedrig
foundation	Fundament		halten
pile	*hier*: Pfahl		

UNIT 25C

David Fitzpatrick is a *consultant engineer* who can get to work in less than a minute. He just walks from his house to his garage.

"The office here is a garage that's been converted and it is virtually *adjacent to* the house, it's not *attached*, but it is adjacent and within a matter of minutes I can come from the house into this office.
5 It's ideal because it is separate, there is no noise, either from me *transmitted* to the house, or from the house transmitted to me. And it's an ideal working space. The disadvantages are, it is small, and it is limited in space. But for one person working it is ideal."

Although his office is small, David works on *large scale* engineering projects. Some of them are near to home, and some of them are on the other side of the world.

10 "The type of work we do is ... is a variety of work, it ranges from *domestic housing*, industrial buildings, office blocks, *high-rise structures*, such as *jobs* in Malaysia. One project that we've completed a few years back was Crown Products, they ... that factory was one of the largest *spans, portable sheds* in the South-east, and it was the request of the client, who are furniture manufac-turers, that he has a clear *span* of at least sixty metres. And another project was Beverly Farm House
15 which was an old *listed building*, which was *deteriorating under loading* and age, and we had to go in there, with an architect and a *sensitive contractor* and complete the *restoration*, and this *entailed* taking out floors, replacing beams, and doing similar construction that was done many, many years ago. Another project that we've recently completed was under contract for Southern Projects, the end user was Southern Water, and this was to carry out the *civil design works* for a water/*sewage*
20 *treatment plant* which dealt with the sewage before *discharging* it into the ... into the sea. That is complete and I think it's due to *go on stream* shortly."

David's office is equipped with all the modern machines that we expect to see nowadays in an up-to-date office.

"This is the only computer I have and it's a dual computer. It runs my Apple programs for *draft-*
25 *ing* and word processing, and it also, as you can see on the screen, it will also do the analytical side of the business, and that's run on a DOS program. *At the rear* there, there's the modem, and that is used for downloading to a London-based server and that can be sent and transmitted to other offices throughout England or to *overseas*."

Although David can fax information through his PC, his personal computer, he prefers to send it by
30 his fax machine.

"I can fax from that machine, through the modem, but I choose sometimes to, most of the time I should say, to fax through the telephone system. I receive faxes on the machine, it's there, and I send faxes on the machine."

For David the fax *facility* is very important. As an engineer he has to fax drawings to clients around
35 the world.

"The current project I'm working on is an *air rights* building together with some high-rise towers at either side and *straddling* a railway track in Malaysia. I think it's one of the largest projects that's currently under construction."

David has been to Malaysia to discuss the project with his client. Now he thinks that he must set up
40 an e-mail facility to link his computer to his client's computer.

"I am now going back to Malaysia at the end of the month and I shall be taking with me my own software, hardware/software in form of a laptop. I will need to get organized when I get there to get my e-mail *site sorted out* so that I can have connections through either CompuServe or Internet to my office."

45 David believes that working at home has its advantages and its disadvantages.

"The advantages of working at home being that you ... you can, when you wish, have total peace and quiet, you're not interrupted, you can switch the phone off, you can have one total day to yourself where you can say, right, that's it, I'm going to get on with a specific project and I'm not having any interruptions. That is the biggest advantage. The disadvantages of working at home are that you are
50 very much alone, on your own, you've got to be a person that's self motivated ... you tend ... if you're a person that requires the *presence of* others around you, then it's very, very difficult because you can have a very lonely life. "

consultant engineer	beratender Ingenieur	civil design	öffentliche Planungs-
adjacent (to)	anliegend,	works	arbeiten
	angrenzend (an)	sewage	Kläranlage
attached	*hier*: angebaut	treatment plant	
transmit	übertragen, durch-	discharge	ablassen, ablaufen
	dringen		lassen
large scale	groß angelegt	go on stream	*hier im Sinne von*: in
domestic housing	Wohnhäuser		Betrieb genommen
high-rise structures	Hochbauten		werden
job	*hier*: Aufgabe	draft	entwerfen
span	*hier*: lang gestreckte	at the rear	hinten
	(Lager-)Halle	overseas	nach, in Übersee
portable	transportabel	facility	*hier*: (*technisches*)
shed	Schuppen, (kleinere)		Gerät
	Halle	air rights	das Recht,
span	Spannweite		„in der Luft" über
listed building	unter Denkmalschutz		dem Grundbesitz
	stehendes Gebäude		eines anderen zu
deteriorate	verfallen, verkommen		bauen *(hier z.B. ein*
under loading	*hier:* unter seinem		*Gebäude, das sich*
	eigenen Gewicht		*über eine Eisenbahn-*
sensitive	*hier:* erfahren in der		*linie erstreckt)*
	Restaurierung von	straddle	*hier*: sich erstrecken
	denkmalgeschützten		über
	Gebäuden	site	*hier*: Anschluss
contractor	Baumeister	sort out	*hier*: (funktionstüch-
restoration	Restaurierung		tig) installieren lassen
entail	mit sich bringen,	presence (of)	Anwesenheit (von)
	erforderlich machen		

UNIT 26C

Margaret McIntyre has had to fight against *misfortune* in her life. The story starts with her experiences at school.

Margaret: "I was born into a middle class family. I was the fourth child attending school and we had an examination at the age of eleven to *determine* what school we would attend after that.
5 Unfortunately I failed this exam and I was sent to what in those days was classed as a second class school."

When she grew up, Margaret married, but it was an unhappy marriage and Margaret separated from her husband. She had two children and no money.

Margaret: "Fifteen years ago I was in a position that I was homeless with two children, and we
10 acquired a house, but with no contents, no furniture, nothing. They went to school, I worked, and I would say they were very, very happy years. There was no *pressure* because I told them what happened to me, and when they were eleven they had the choice whether to take an exam. Both decided they would not and they went to a comprehensive school where there was no pressure at all put on them, and they both did exceptionally well, and were happy to do it, for themselves, not for
15 me, or the family, just for themselves. Well, my son, Martin, he left school after his A levels and he went to Maidstone College for one year, to do a *B Tech Art Foundation course*, and a week ago he started at Brighton University to do his *BA* in Art. And my daughter left school and went to Nottingham University to do *Genetics*. She left in June, with a First, and she's now at Oxford, Keble College, to do her *PhD*."

20 Margaret was delighted with the success of her two children. This was one of the reasons why she decided to return to education for a second chance. She had been working in a hospital, and she decided to do a *course in caring for elderly people*.

Margaret: "I wanted to learn more about the elderly. And by saying it, through them, and through seeing something in the paper about an opening at the college, I was encouraged to go along and
25 have a look. I found the *initial* start very hard because you had to concentrate and I was a little bit older than some of them in the classroom and I felt it difficult to come home, *retain* the knowledge, and then do an *assignment*, fitting in with the children and going to work at the same time."

Margaret had three *tutors* on her course. One of them was Angela Sparke, Tutor in Adult Health and Social Care.

30 Angela: "Many of the students on this course do return to college for further study, either to widen their *scope of knowledge* of older people or indeed to deepen their educational background. My memory is that Margaret had quite a difficult start and, after a few weeks, became *enthusiastic*, gained confidence in herself and began to demonstrate very different attitudes to study and much, much more confidence."

35 The course helped Margaret in many ways. Improving her *self esteem*, her image of herself, was an important part of it.

Margaret: "I ended up having a ... a higher self image and I felt I had more *worthiness* than I had before I started the course."

This was a new start for Margaret. When her course finished, she started a voluntary group. She
40 called it Community Link, a group which cares for *carers*. Carers are people who spend much of
their time looking after *the* elderly and *infirm* in their own homes.

One of the elderly people she regularly cares for is Reg. Reg's wife usually cares for him, but
Margaret takes over for a few hours each week to give Reg's wife a break.

Margaret: "Well, we provide a service that gives carers time off, and we take over the role of the
45 carer. Reg is quite a funny man because he was a champion *chess* player. And although he's
supposedly *grown frailer* and frailer, I'm not up to his standard with chess. I think if you've been a
champion at chess, then *draughts* is a little bit an *inferior* game, and he certainly can beat me. We
are there not to *intrude*, because we have to respect it is Reg's home, not ours, but we're there to
help him with whatever he wants to do."

50 The office of Community Link is at the local hospital. Here Margaret interviews new volunteers,
people who want to give up some of their free time to help carers. Margaret has forty volunteers on
her books, and Community Link is getting stronger all the time. Margaret has come a long way from
that unhappy child who failed her examination at the age of eleven.

Angela: "People who find the courage to come back to education as *mature* adults, many of them
55 are ... gain self confidence, begin to believe in themselves, are able to *wipe out* bad memories of
learning from childhood and to become fresh new people. It's very exciting, working with ... with
adults who return to learning and ... and very *rewarding* work."

Margaret: "I think it doesn't matter who the individual person is, they deserve a second chance in
life."

misfortune	Unglück, Pech	tutor	Tutor, Dozent(in)
determine	festlegen, bestimmen	scope of	Bandbreite des Wissens,
pressure	Zwang, Druck	knowledge	der Kenntnisse
B Tech Art	*etwa: Grundstudium*	enthusiastic	begeistert, wissbegierig
Foundation	*im Fach Kunst*	self esteem	Selbstachtung
course		worthiness	Wert
BA	*erster akademischer Grad*	carer	*hier:* Altenpfleger(in)
(Bachelor	*an angelsächsischen*	the infirm	die Schwachen,
of Arts)	*Universitäten*		Gebrechlichen
genetics	Genetik, Vererbungslehre	chess	Schach
PhD	Doktorgrad	grow frail	gebrechlich werden
course in	Kurs in	draughts	Dame(spiel)
caring for	Altenpflege	inferior	geringwertiger, *hier:* von
elderly			geringerem (geistigem)
people			Anspruch
initial	Anfangs-, anfänglich	intrude	eindringen
retain	im Gedächtnis behalten,	mature	reif *(geistig)*
	sich merken	wipe out	auslöschen, tilgen
assignment	*hier:* wissenschaftliche	rewarding	lohnend
	Hausarbeit		
	(college, Universität)		

KEY TO EXERCISES

UNIT 14

14A

Text

1. b) (lines 5–6) – **2.** b) (lines 15–16) – **3.** a) (lines 19–21) – **4.** c) (line 42) – **5.** a) (lines 49–50) – **6.** Yes, I think he was pleased with Mr and Mrs Richards' visit because they enjoyed looking around the brewery and tasting the beers. The Richards will probably order Shepherd Neame beers for their pub. – **7.** b) – **8.** c) – **9.** a), b) and d) – **10.** a), c) and d) – **11.** *Example*: English pubs are not like German *Gaststätten*. In an English pub, for example, there are usually two main rooms: a bar and a lounge. The lounge is more comfortable than the bar and the drinks are often more expensive. English pubs and German *Gaststätten* do not have the same opening hours. Many pubs, for instance, are closed in the afternoon. In the evening they open from six o'clock until eleven o'clock. – **12.** *Example*: English people use first names (Christian names) much more than German people do, even in business. However, if you call somebody by their first name in English this is not the same as using *du* in German.

Exercises

   I. 1. b) – 2. b) – 3. a) – 4. a) – 5. a)

  II. ... have been living (have lived) ... moved ... sold (had sold) ... drove ... was ... have never regretted ... have made ... can't imagine living ...

 III. **1.** ... first ... – **2.** ... answer ...

  IV. **1.** How do you do. – Fine, thank you. – Oh, that would be lovely. – **2.** Great, thanks. – It was OK. – Yeah, lovely.

   V. formal: d/c/h/g – informal: e/f/b/a

  VI. **1.** False (They close at eleven o'clock at night.) – **2.** True – **3.** False – **4.** True – **5.** True – **6.** True (The pronunciation is / paɪnt /.) – **7.** True – **8.** False. Crisps are „Chips" in German. Chips are „Pommes frites" in German. – **9.** True – **10.** False (It is the pub which you go to regularly.)

14B

Text

1. grist (line 4) – **2.** water (line 5) – **3.** wort (line 6) – **4.** the hops (line 8) – **5.** boiled (line 9) – **6.** fermenting (line 10) – **7.** yeast (line 10) – **8.** pumped (line 12) – **9.** *Example*: I don't like it. It is warm and sweet. – **10.** *Example*: I drink beer and wine quite often but I never drink spirits. I like to drink beer in the summer when I'm sitting outside with friends.

Exercises

  I. **1.** ... was built before ... – **2.** ... are wanted on ... – **3.** ... am being picked up at ... – **4.** ... must not be taken out of ... – **5.** ... computers were made in ... – **6.** ... will be told what to do ...

 II. State: 1/4/6 – Process: 2/3/5 – Translation: **1.** Das Geschäft war geschlossen, als sie ankamen. – **2.** Werden Ihre (deine) Taschen jedes Mal geöffnet (ausgepackt), wenn Sie (du) durch den Zoll gehen (gehst)? – **3.** Die Landschaft wird von Menschen „verschandelt" (ruiniert), die ihren Müll (Unrat) (einfach) fallen lassen. – **4.** Die Koffer sind gepackt. Sollen wir aufbrechen? – **5.** Das Geschäft wurde geschlossen, nachdem der letzte Kunde gegangen war. – **6.** Schauen Sie sich (Schau dir) meine Jacke an! Sie ist ruiniert!

III. 1. Twenty people were badly injured in a car crash. – **2.** 10 million pounds were stolen from a London bank. – **3.** A dog, three cats and a parrot were rescued from a burning house. – **4.** A rock star was caught drinking and driving.

IV. 1. Visitors are not allowed to feed the bears. – **2.** Lunch is served from 12.00 till 2.00. – **3.** Customers are asked not to touch the furniture. – **4.** Tickets can be bought here.

V. ... are roasted ... are ground ... is passed ... is pumped ... is left ... is poured ... is collected and (is) put ... .

14C

I. 1. c) (see page 216, lines 16–17 and 23–24) – **2.** a) (lines 15–16) – **3.** a) (lines 44–47)

II. 1. landlord ... landlady (line 1) – **2.** locals (line 6) – **3.** appointment (line 26) – **4.** real ale (line 29) – **5.** barrels (line 30) – **6.** temperature ... clarity (line 34) – **7.** menu (line 38) – **8.** Produce (line 40)

III. 1. b) – **2.** c) – **3.** a)
1. Niemand hat (jemals zuvor) so etwas wie das (je) gebaut, daher müssen wir ganz von vorne anfangen. – **2.** Sein Englisch ist gut, aber seine Mathematikkenntnisse sind kaum der Rede wert. – **3.** Der Artikel, den du geschrieben hast, war interessant, aber er „kratzte" eigentlich nur die Oberfläche an. (..., aber er berührte das Thema eigentlich nur an der Oberfläche.)

14D

I. b)

II. 1. While Meterman is out of the room she mixes him a very strong cocktail. – **2.** She doesn't want him to drink alcohol and drive.

III. 1. ... keep ... – **2.** ... alcohol – **3.** stopping (pausing)

UNIT 15

15A

Text

1. ... would like to buy a house of their own (line 2). – **2.** ... see a larger one (line 13). – **3.** ... have (need) to get some financial advice (line 21). – **4.** b) – **5.** b) – **6.** b) – **7.** to pay rent (line 2) – **8.** If it's convenient? (line 10) – **9.** master bedroom (line 14) – **10.** 3m by 2m (line 15)
11. *Example*: Houses are generally much cheaper in England than in Germany and many more people in England buy houses when they are young. **12.** *Example*: I would like to live in a city because it is easier to find a job. Also there is more to do in a city. I can go to the theatre, cinema or an exhibition, for example.

Exercises

I. 1. DC is the cheapest. – **2.** P is the most modern. – **3.** P is the most spacious. – **4.** DC has got the fewest bedrooms. – **5.** DC is the least convenient for the shops. – **6.** ... less ... than ... more ... . – **7.** modern ... 60 ... . – **8.** ... spacious ... bedrooms ... . – **9.** nearer ... double ... . – **10.** ... a larger ... closer/nearer ... . – **11.** How much does it cost? – **12.** When was it built? – **13.** How many bedrooms has it got? – **14.** Has it got a garage? – **15.** How far is it from the nearest town?

II. 1. Yesterday we went for a ten-mile walk. – **2.** She lives in a two-room flat. – **3.** It is a tiring eight-hour flight to the USA. – **4.** They had a lovely five-course meal in an exclusive restaurant. – **5.** He gave a boring one-hour talk to the group. – **6.** She wrote a funny three-word postcard.

III. *Some examples*: This is paradise. See you soon. Weather is great. Bed is hard.

15B

Text

1. True (line 2) – **2.** Doesn't say – **3.** False (lines 14–15) – **4.** She means she could lose her job or become seriously ill or she could have a baby. (lines 10–12) – **5.** He can tell them how much money they can borrow from the bank and how much they will have to repay every month. (lines 6–8) – **6.** He cannot tell them if they should buy the house or not. That is their decision. (line 17) – **7.** to fill in a form (lines 3–4) – **8.** salary (line 8) – **9.** monthly repayment (line 8) – **10.** insurance (line 13) – **11.** *Example*: I think they should buy. If they cannot afford the mortgage they can sell the house. If they have children one day then perhaps someone in their family can help them financially. **12.** *Example*: I don't think so. In Germany most houses are not as cheap as they are in England so first-time buyers need a lot of capital if they are going to finance a house by themselves.

Exercises

I. 1. d) – 2. e) – 3. a) – 4. c) – 5. b)

II. 1. b) – 2. d) – 3. e) – 4. a) – 5. c)

III. **1.** formula – **2.** form – **3.** borrow – **4.** lend – **5.** still – **6.** already – **7.** injure – **8.** insure
    1. Es gibt keine Zauberformel für das Erlernen einer Fremdsprache. – **2.** Bevor du (Sie) eine Hypothek beantragen kannst (können), musst du (müssen Sie) dieses Formular ausfüllen. – **3.** Wieviel kostet es (Wie teuer ist es), ein Buch aus der Bibliothek auszuleihen? – **4.** Banken verleihen Geld (an andere), weil es ein gutes Geschäft für sie ist. – **5.** Bist du (Sind Sie) immer noch hier? Ich dachte, du seist (Sie seien) vor fünf Minuten weggegangen. – **6.** Bist du (Sind Sie) schon da? Du bist (Sie sind) doch erst vor fünf Minuten weggegangen. – **7.** Hast du dich (Haben Sie sich) verletzt, als du (Sie) vom Fahrrad fielst (fielen)? – **8.** Hast du dein (Haben Sie Ihr) Gepäck versichert, bevor du (Sie) in Urlaub fuhrst (fuhren)?

IV. **1.** took out ... would have to pay back – **2.** fell ill ... was (were) ... would cover – **3.** would also pay ... had – **4.** would David's salary be ... had ... stopped – **5.** started ... would she be able – **6.** Would David be able to earn ... changed – **7.** got ... would Janet's parents help – **8.** knew ... would be able to make ...

V. **1.** would the burglar do ... knew – **2.** Would he run away? – **3.** were ... would you do? – **4.** Would you phone ...? – **5.** were ... would you shout – **6.** would you wait ... came – **7.** didn't come ... were not able ... would you follow ...? – **8.** were not ... would be ...

VI. **1.** bedroom – **2.** kitchen – **3.** attic – **4.** garden – **5.** kitchen – **6.** bathroom – **7.** in a bedroom – **8.** in a kitchen – **9.** in a lounge – **10.** in a bathroom

15C

I. **1.** c) (see page 218, lines 5–6) – **2.** b) (lines 8–9) – **3.** c) (lines 23–24)

II. **1.** contract (lease) (line 26) – **2.** tenant (line 34) – **3.** estate agent (line 37)

III. 1. c) – 2. b) – 3. d) – 4. a)
    5. have a roof over her head – **6.** got on like a house on fire – **7.** brought the house down – **8.** on the house

IV. *Example*: I think that German people are not as mobile as English people. Many stay in the area where they were born and settle there. Also there are a lot of German people who build their own houses and expect to stay there for the rest of their lives. In England, on the other hand, it would not be unusual to buy and sell ten houses during your lifetime.

15D

  I. 1. e) – **2.** f) – **3.** a) – **4.** b) – **5.** d) – **6.** c)

  II. 1. elevenses – **2.** a bank holiday – **3.** to interrupt – **4.** straightforward

UNIT 16

16A

Text

1. b) (lines 2–3) – **2.** b) (lines 5 and 17–18) – **3.** a) (lines 14–15 and 21) – **4.** They get lost and cannot find their map. (line 6) – **5.** It seems as if they are going for longer because they have got paints and canvasses with them. (line 16) – **6.** b) – **7.** c) – **8.** to cycle (line 2) – **9.** to be in a hurry (line 10) – **10.** responsibility (line 13) – **11.** The county of Suffolk is in East Anglia. The main city in Suffolk is Ipswich (see map on page 8). – **12.** Other famous English painters are William Hogarth (1697–1764), Thomas Gainsborough (1727–1788) and Joseph Turner (1775–1851). An example of a well-known contemporary British painter is David Hockney (b. 1937).

Exercises

  I. 1. ... which we saw on TV last weekend? – **2.** ... which you recommended to us. – **3.** ... which I gave you this morning? – **4.** ... which I used to wear at school. – **5.** ... which they were talking about.

  II. 1. ... which was hanging here yesterday? – **2.** ... which explains the meanings of words. – **3.** ... which begins with the sentence ...? – **4.** ... which designs computer software. – **5.** ... which used to belong to my grandfather.

  III. 1. ... where you bought it. – **2.** ... where we can get something quick to eat? – **3.** ... where they serve German beer. – **4.** ... where I can send a fax? – **5.** ... where we used to lie.

  IV. 1. This is the town where I grew up. – **2.** Where are the pictures which I showed you (to you) yesterday? – **3.** This is the place where I had a car accident. – **4.** What's the name of the programme which we watched yesterday? – **5.** I didn't get the job which I wanted.

  V. 1. *Example*: ... there are no cars. – **2.** *Example*: ... I enjoy getting up to do.

  VI. c) anger

  VII. 1. reminds/of/had – **2.** prize/getting/mark – **3.** to me – **4.** When/lived/country – **5.** ride/to/ getting – **6.** well/taught – **7.** are/they/easily

16B

Text

1. False (lines 4–5) – **2.** Doesn't say – **3.** True (line 13) – **4.** True (lines 20–22) – **5.** People needed water to operate the mill. If the water level got too high there was a danger of flooding. (lines 6–8) – **6.** It told people when they were going to start milling and it warned them when the water level was high so that they had enough time to look after their animals. (lines 6–10) – **7.** The number of people who have visited the Mill has doubled in the last ten years. (lines 21–22) – **8.** flooding (line 8) – **9.** to grind, to mill (lines 5 and 8) – **10.** to double (line 21) – **11.** *Example*: Yes, I could. I like being outside in the countryside and I'm interested in finding out more about painting. **12.** *Example*: I don't think so. The Industrial Revolution brought great changes to everyday life in Britain. People moved into the towns and cities to work in the factories. Working conditions were very bad and the pay was terrible. People had to work very hard and many died when they were young.

Exercises

I. 1. did you go – went – **2.** Was it – were – **3.** were you – stayed – **4.** Did you have – had – **5.** Did you enjoy – learnt – made – **6.** Did you come – flew – did – **7.** did you think – thought

II. 1. did they use to grow – **2.** did they use to bring – **3.** did they use to ring – **4.** Did it not use to warn – used to tell – **5.** Did Constable use to work – used to help (to) grind

III. 1. would be (would play) – **2.** would come – **3.** would have – would go – **4.** would play – **5.** would often think

IV. 1. has lost – **2.** has gone – **3.** have run out – **4.** have spent – **5.** has broken – **6.** has lost – **7.** have painted – **8.** have just had

V. 1. told ... has not spoken – **2.** Did you manage to save – **3.** bought ... gave (has given) – **4.** has not been – **5.** Was Mike ... did not see – **6.** did not feel ... went – **7.** did not have ... were (had been) – **8.** has had ... has not heard ... has been

VI. 1. b) – 2. a) – 3. a) – 4. b) – 5. b) – 6. a) – 7. b) – 8. a)

VII. 1. b), c), e) – 2. a), d), f)

16C

I. 1. True (see page 220, lines 5–6) – **2.** False (lines 3–5) – **3.** False (lines 1 and 9–12) – **4.** True (lines 26–27) – **5.** True (lines 27–28)

II. 1. c) (line 33) – **2.** a) (lines 41–43) – **3.** b) (line 46)

III. b)

16D

I. d) – a) – f) – c) – e) – g) – b)

II. 1. d) – **2.** c) – **3.** a) – **4.** e) – **5.** b)
1. Rom wurde auch nicht an einem Tage erbaut. – **2.** Einem geschenkten Gaul schaut man nicht ins Maul. – **4.** Man soll das Fell des Bären nicht verkaufen, ehe man ihn hat.

III. The word "struck" has two meanings in this sentence. First, it means "hit" (*getroffen, geschlagen*). Second, it means "impressed" (*beeindruckt*).

UNIT 17

17A

Text

1. rehearsing (line 4) – **2.** praising (lines 20–21) – **3.** practising (lines 22–23) – **4.** encouraging (lines 24–25) – **5.** director – **6.** conductor – **7.** the arts – **8.** art – **9.** play (line 4) – **10.** woodwind and brass (instruments) (line 26) – **11.** *Example*: No, I don't. Being a director for example must be very demanding. You must know the play you are directing very well and you must know what to expect from your actors and actresses. And when something goes wrong during rehearsals you must be confident that everything will be all right on the first night. **12.** *Example*: I am interested in films but I have not been to the cinema for over a year now. The reason is that I don't have much time to go out. I work all day and have a family.

Exercises

I. 1. taught us to speak – **2.** encouraged us to think – **3.** wanted us to give – **4.** advised me to practise – **5.** expect the audience to understand

II. 1. advised us to ring for a doctor – **2.** persuaded me to go out with her – **3.** invited Helen to have dinner with him – **4.** reminded Alex not to forget the shopping – **5.** would like Daryl to come to the party

III. 1. I want (would like) you to marry me. – **2.** He wanted her to win the game. – **3.** They asked us to be on time. – **4.** She didn't expect it to snow. – **5.** We told him to call (ring) later.

IV. 1. falling off my bike and breaking a tooth – **2.** spraying perfume in my eyes and having to go to hospital – **3.** falling into the pond while feeding the ducks – **4.** driving my mother's car to the shops

V. 1. seeing – **2.** to ring – **3.** to put – **4.** going

VI. 1. Er unterbrach (z.B. seine Arbeit), um zu rauchen./Er blieb stehen, um zu rauchen. – **2.** Er hörte mit dem Rauchen auf.

17B

Text

1. False (lines 6–9) – **2.** True (line 18) – **3.** Doesn't say – **4.** No. One boy said he felt nervous. (line 14) – **5.** They all liked his work. (lines 20–25) – **6.** Yes. The first and second women both found the performance shocking. (lines 30–31) – **7.** exhibition (line 16) – **8.** performance (line 27) – **9.** interval (line 26) – **10.** except (line 34) – **11.** *Example*: I would like to go to a theatre performance. A puppet show is more suitable for children and I don't understand much about painting. **12.** *Example*: It depends. I don't think it is good to always show your feelings to everybody you know. In some situations it may be better to control your feelings rather than say something that you might later regret. On the other hand, if you never express your feelings nobody will know what you really think and that would also not be right.

Exercises

I. 1. d) – **2.** e) – **3.** f) – **4.** a) – **5.** b) – **6.** c) (Other combinations are possible.)

II. 1. didn't let me read the letter – **2.** never let me stay out late – **3.** doesn't let us use dictionaries – **4.** let me drive his car yesterday

III. 1. She likes acting very much. – **2.** Were you at the party on Saturday night? – **3.** He plays the piano well. – **4.** (Every morning) She walks to work (every morning). – **5.** Does he rehearse all day? – **6.** Have you (recently) been to the theatre (recently)?

IV. 1. excited – **2.** exciting – **3.** shocking – **4.** shocked – **5.** convinced – **6.** convincing – **7.** interesting – **8.** interested

V. 1. costumes – **2.** cast – **3.** set – **4.** direction – **5.** review – **6.** performance

VI. They are talking about Alan Strang, who blinded six horses in one night (see page 59).

17C

I. 1. town community (see page 222, line 4) – **2.** wide variety (lines 13–14) – **3.** very (line 19) – **4.** professional (line 25) – **5.** young (lines 36–37)

II. 1. venue (line 7) – **2.** donation (line 15) – **3.** classical (line 11) – **4.** volunteer (line 22) – **5.** staff (line 22) – **6.** drama (line 28) – **7.** violinist (line 30) – **8.** row (line 34)

17D

I. 1. He eats a sandwich. – **2.** It begins to rain. – **3.** Perhaps all the tickets have been sold. – **4.** It's nearly time for lunch. The guitar was a present from his uncle. – **5.** The church bells ring. – **6.** A bird flies past his head.

II. 1. a row (sixth paragraph, line 6) – **2.** note (first paragraph, line 3) – **3.** bonnet (second paragraph, line 2)
Yes: **2.** / nəʊt / – **3.** / ˈbɒnɪt / – No: **1.** argument = row / raʊ /; number of people in a line = row / rəʊ /

III. 1. control – **2.** check – **3.** work – **4.** job – **5.** notice – **6.** note – **7.** Perhaps – **8.** eventually
1. Es ist nicht einfach (leicht), ein Fahrrad unter Kontrolle zu halten, wenn man über eine Eisfläche fährt. – **2.** Können Sie bitte, bevor Sie das Flugzeug verlassen, nachsehen (kontrollieren), ob Sie alles mitgenommen haben. – **3.** Ich habe im Augenblick eine Menge Arbeit und kann daher am Wochenende nicht ausgehen (weggehen). – **4.** Ich habe eine interessante Stelle, aber sie wird nicht gut bezahlt. – **5.** Hast du (Haben Sie) das Hinweisschild an diesem Schaufenster gesehen? Darauf stand: „Bitte kommen Sie herein und stöbern Sie herum." – **6.** Kann ich mir deine (Ihre) Telefonnummer notieren? – **7.** In der Bibliothek brennt kein Licht. Vielleicht ist sie heute geschlossen. – **8.** Nach einer langen Fahrt durch die Nacht kamen sie endlich in England an.

UNIT 18

18A

Text

1. b) (lines 4–5) – **2.** a) (eg lines 20–21 and 25) – **3.** c) (lines 16–18) – **4.** b) – **5.** a) – **6.** We know the children "won" the argument because at the end of the TV scene the parents put on their shirts. – **7.** deck chair (line 3) – **8.** ozone layer (line 23) – **9.** ridiculous (line 25) – **10.** harmful (line 22) – **11.** *Example*: No, I don't like to have a suntan. Lying in the sun is bad for your skin and very boring and by the end of the summer the tan will have disappeared anyway. **12.** *Example*: There is not really a hole in the ozone layer. The layer of ozone is getting thinner and thinner in certain parts because the ozone is being destroyed by certain substances such as CFCs (= chlorofluorocarbons). Where there is little ozone the sun's rays can pass through and harm us.

Exercises

I. 1. rose – **2.** raised – **3.** rises – **4.** raises – **5.** rise – **6.** raise
1. Sie erhoben sich vom Tisch und verließen den Raum. – **2.** Sie erhob ihr Glas und sagte „Prost". – **3.** Mögen Sie (Magst du) es, wenn die Temperatur über 30° C steigt? – **4.** Wenn er ärgerlich wird, erhebt er seine Stimme. – **5.** Wir standen gewöhnlich mit der Sonne auf und gingen mit der Dämmerung (sobald es dämmerte) schlafen. – **6.** Früher pflegten die Männer ihren Hut zu lüften, wenn sie auf der Straße an einer Frau vorbeigingen.

II. 1. Lay – **2.** lie – **3.** lay – **4.** laid – **5.** has lain – **6.** has laid

III. 1. The castle lies in the centre of the town (town centre). – **2.** She raised her hand to answer the question. – **3.** The sun rises in the east. – **4.** He laid his bag on the table. – **5.** The number of accidents has risen. – **6.** The dog lay down on the floor.

IV. 1. b) – 2. d) – 3. a) – 4. c) – 5.+3. – 6.+2. – 7.+4. – 8.+1.

V. 1. What is she like? – **2.** Do you like Germany? – **3.** What does he look like? – **4.** What would you like?

VI. 1. London – **2.** Folkestone – **3.** Birmingham, Buxton and Scarborough – **4.** No, it was dull in Belfast but there was drizzle in Glasgow. – **5.** Buxton – **6.** Yes, it was cold and foggy in both cities.

18B

Text

1. stop the risk of flooding (line 7) – **2.** they rest unseen on the riverbed (lines 4–5) – **3.** predict when they have to close the Barrier (line 19) – **4.** they have to close it (it has to be closed) four times a year on average (lines 26–27) – **5.** No, it was built in 1982. (lines 14–15) – **6.** Yes, it does seem effective because there are regular surge tides but no risk of flooding. (lines 2-3 and 15–16) – **7.** ... it varies (line 27) – **8.** How long does it take to close the Thames Barrier? (line 23) – **9.** on average (line 27) – **10.** four times a year (line 27) – **11.** *Example*: Strong winds or hurricanes, earthquakes and volcanic eruptions are all types of natural disasters which can affect cities. – **12.** *Example*: I have been to Ireland. Two years ago I flew to Dublin and had a camping holiday. We went all around the country and met a lot of very friendly people. Ireland is a beautiful place and I would like to go back there again soon.

Exercises

I. 1. have you been living – **2.** has been working – **3.** have you been doing – **4.** have been walking – **5.** have been reading – **6.** has he been ringing

II. 1. have been driving – **2.** have crashed – **3.** have you been doing – **4.** have lost

III. 1. How long have you been waiting for my call? – **2.** When I was 16 I went to school in Scotland for one year. – **3.** We have never been to Britain. – **4.** When did you last go to the cinema (go to see a film)?

IV. 1. What's your name? – **2.** What is she like? – **3.** How long does the flight take? – **4.** What does „Lineal" mean in English? – **5.** What does he look like? – **6.** What's the time? (What time is it?) – **7.** How old is she? – **8.** How do I get to the airport?

V. 1. starvation – **2.** hurricanes – **3.** flooding – **4.** air pollution – **5.** waste disposal – **6.** over-population

VI. *Example*: I think overpopulation is the most serious environmental problem in the world. In parts of Africa, South America and South-East Asia, for example, the population is exploding. Young people in these parts of the world are in an impossible situation. They grow up in terrible conditions, have little food and receive no education. They, like their parents, marry young and have lots of children. It is a vicious circle (*Teufelskreis*).

18C

I. 1. b) (see page 224, lines 1–2) – **2.** a) (lines 4–6) – **3.** c) (lines 12–13) – **4.** a) (lines 29–33) – **5.** b) (lines 51–52)

II. 1. It is financed wholly by donations. (lines 10–11) – **2.** When he talks about a "nightmare" he talks about a situation when the lifeboat engine breaks down during a rescue operation and the anchor has to be used to make sure the boat does not drift away. (lines 24–26) – **3.** Salvage is the money someone receives for helping to save a ship in danger. (lines 48–51)

III. station – tip – bay – Channel – lane – changeable

IV. 1. / 'kɒksən / – **2.** / bɔɪ / – **3.** / 'sælvɪdʒ / – **4.** / nɒts / – **5.** / 'dɪŋgɪ /

18D

I. beach – sky – bucket – lotion – argument – replies – competitive – fetch – water – carries – dreaming – foot

II. 1. a) – **2.** c) – **3.** d) – **4.** b)

UNIT 19

19A

Text

1. True (line 3) – **2.** True (lines 11–12) – **3.** Doesn't say – **4.** He wants to show his visitors some of the sights in and around Gravesend. – **5.** Gravesend is on the coast (the Thames Estuary) and near London so there is a lot of traffic passing by. – **6.** home town (line 3) – **7.** view (line 6) – **8.** port (line 11) – **9.** sights (line 7) – **10.** ferry (line 14) – **11.** *Example*: As people in wheelchairs have difficulty getting into places there are many things which they cannot do very easily such as finding a job or going on holiday. I suppose one of the main problems they face, however, is being accepted by non-disabled people. – **12.** *Example*: I would show them some famous buildings in the town where I live, give them a tour of the surrounding countryside (including a boat trip on a lake) and then invite them out to dinner at a restaurant which serves local specialities.

Exercises

I. into ... up to ... along ... At ... opposite ... on ... on ... next to

II. *Example*: Leave Gravesend station and turn right into Clive Road. Walk up to the roundabout and cross Windmill Street. Go straight ahead into Manor Road. At the end of Manor Road turn right into Parrock Street. As you walk along Parrock Street you will see the tourist information office on your right.

III. **1.** on – **2.** in – **3.** in – **4.** at – **5.** on – **6.** at ... on – **7.** in – **8.** on

IV. **1.** in ... in – **2.** at – **3.** at – **4.** on – **5.** on – **6.** at (on, *AE*) – **7.** in – **8.** on ... at

V. **1.** from – **2.** against – **3.** by – **4.** about – **5.** in – **6.** at – **7.** on – **8.** for (on)

VI. **1.** a cyclist – **2.** a river – **3.** a ship – **4.** a tree – **5.** a driver – **6.** a train

19B

Text

1. ... is more aware of disabled people's needs. (lines 2–3) – **2.** ... the crossing places have dots and the traffic lights give acoustic signals. (lines 8–9) – **3.** ... (they) have special requirements. (line 12) – **4.** There are pavements with slopes, toilets for disabled people, shops with automatic doors, a pedestrianized town centre and special crossing places. (lines 2–9) – **5.** Paul needs lots of room (space) to get in and out of his car. (lines 12–15) – **6.** pavement (line 3) – **7.** access (line 4) – **8.** to apologize (line 16) – **9.** car park (line 13) – **10.** sticker (line 15) – **11.** *Example*: No, I don't think so. If you are not disabled yourself or do not have a member of the family or a close friend who is disabled then I think it is difficult to imagine (appreciate) what it is like to have a disability. How, for example, can a person who can see understand what it must be like to be blind? – **12.** *Example*: No, I don't think so. There are of course pedestrianized town centres in many parts of Germany and shops with automatic doors but Gravesend seems to have a lot more facilities than the average German town or city.

Exercises

I. **1.** anybody – **2.** anything – **3.** something – **4.** Somebody – **5.** any – **6.** some – **7.** somewhere – **8.** anybody

II. **1.** much – **2.** many – **3.** much – **4.** A lot of (Lots of) – **5.** many – **6.** much – **7.** much – **8.** a lot of (lots of)

III. **1.** a) – **2.** b) – **3.** a) – **4.** b) – **5.** a) – **6.** a)

IV. 1. every – **2.** Each – **3.** several – **4.** every – **5.** several – **6.** each

  V. 1. inside a shop: b) – **2.** at an airport: d) – **3.** in a car park: a) – **4.** in a park: e) – **5.** on a packet of cigarettes: f) – **6.** on a shop window: c)

VI. 1. clink – **2.** crackle – **3.** creak – **4.** clip-clop – **5.** clang

19C

  I. I think it is Jackie Hails because Mike Bishop talks a lot about the problems disabled athletes have to face. (see page 228, lines 39–48)

II. 1. She means that disabled people should not only have the possibility to go into a sports centre and use the facilities there. She also means that disabled people should be treated in exactly the same way as non-disabled people are in sports centres. (lines 1–5) – **2.** In water they are able to move about easily and without assistance. (lines 21–26)

III. 1. It keeps him fit and it's good fun. (lines 11–19) – **2.** He thinks disabled athletes are still second-class athletes. (lines 39–43)

  IV. 1. c) – 2. d) – 3. e) – 4. a) – 5. b)

  V. A "physicist" (*Physiker/in*) is a scientist, i.e. somebody who studies physics or does research work in physics.
A "physician" (*Arzt, Ärztin*) is a doctor, i.e. somebody who tries to help sick people. (The word "physician" is used mainly in American English.)

19D

  I. b)

  II. 1. d) – 2. c) – 3. b) – 4. a)

III. 1. the blind leading the blind – **2.** does not take a blind bit of notice of me – **3.** turns (turned) a blind eye
(The expression "not to take a blind bit of notice" is informal.)

UNIT 20

20A

Text

1. b) – **2.** a) – **3.** c) – **4.** Not really. Both men think gambling is acceptable. – **5.** Not really. Neither of them thinks that gambling is wrong. The third man, however, cannot afford it. – **6.** salary (line 11) – **7.** mortgage (line 12) – **8.** single (line 10) – **9.** wife (line 12) – **10.** to spend (line 11) – **11.** *Examples*: Some people gamble because they are addicted (*süchtig*) to it. Others gamble because they think it could be a quick way of paying off their debts (*Schulden*). – **12.** *Example*: I don't gamble because I think the odds (*Chancen, Aussicht*) are that you will lose your money. On the other hand, the principle behind gambling is that you can win money, which in itself is an attractive idea. The key to being a successful gambler is knowing when to stop. That's not my problem.

Exercises

  I. 1. contains – **2.** does the return fare to Birmingham cost? – **3.** looks – **4.** wants – **5.** do you come – **6.** don't understand

II. 1. Have you had your computer for (a) long (time)? – **2.** I've always wanted a dog. – **3.** How long have we known each other? – **4.** I've hated getting up early since my childhood (since I was a child).

III. 1. are you looking – **2.** looks – **3.** do you think – **4.** are you thinking – **5.** are seeing – **6.** (can) see – **7.** (can) feel – **8.** am feeling
1. Was ist los? Was schaust du dir da an? – **2.** Dein Auto sieht neu aus. Ist es neu? – **3.** Dies ist mein neuestes Gedicht. Was hältst du davon? – **4.** Du bist (so) still. Worüber denkst du nach? – **5.** Wir sind heute Abend nicht zu Hause. Wir treffen ein paar Freunde (von uns). – **6.** Ich sehe das Schild (die Mitteilung), aber ich kann die Schrift (Handschrift) nicht lesen. (Ich kann ... sehen, ...) – **7.** Ich fühle (spüre) etwas in meinem Schuh. – **8.** Ich bin müde. Ich muss ins Bett.

IV. 1. of telling – **2.** at cooking ... at doing – **3.** about going – **4.** of cycling – **5.** in travelling – **6.** about staying – **7.** of getting – **8.** for making

V. 1. intention of making – **2.** prospect of working – **3.** way of finding – **4.** job of clearing – **5.** wish to live – **6.** reason for behaving – **7.** point in waiting – **8.** opportunity of studying

VI. 1. for ringing – **2.** in giving up – **3.** of starting – **4.** on paying – **5.** for being – **6.** to seeing – **7.** about emigrating – **8.** to waiting

VII. *Examples*: **2.** I would drop my pen on the floor (or make some other noise) and signal to the other student that it is not fair to cheat in exams. – **4.** I would politely refuse his (or her) very generous offer.

20B

Text

1. False (lines 27, 30) – **2.** True (lines 21, 28) – **3.** False (line 30) – **4.** False (line 29) – **5.** It is an outsider so if it wins Tessa knows she will win a lot of money. (lines 18–21) – **6.** The odds were 7 : 1 because he bet £4 and won £28. (line 27) – **7.** cautious (line 4) – **8.** mad (line 21) – **9.** Have you made up your mind? / Have you decided? (lines 9 and 12) – **10.** to take sb out to dinner (line 24) – **11.** *Example*: No, I wouldn't. I know nothing about horses and have not got the money to lose on a bet. – **12.** *Example*: I would go on holiday and put the rest of the money in the bank.

Exercises

I. 1. past – **2.** present – **3.** future – **4.** present – **5.** future – **6.** past

II. 1. offer – **2.** possibility – **3.** ability – **4.** necessity – **5.** prohibition – **6.** permission – **7.** suggestion – **8.** advice

III. 1. permission – **2.** possibility – **3.** permission – **4.** possibility

IV. 1. It might be warm enough to go swimming. – **2.** She might be right. – **3.** I might come to the party. – **4.** We might go away over Christmas this year.

V. 1. c) – 2. d) – 3. a) – 4. b)

VI. 1. will miss ... don't hurry – **2.** grows ... rains – **3.** don't put ... goes – **4.** won't go ... is – **5.** barks ... comes – **6.** works ... will do

20C

I. 1. (see page 229, lines 3–11) – **3.** (lines 27–40) – **5.** (lines 41–48)

II. 3. (lines 51–55)

III. 1. He means the occasion when he trained a sick horse and a sick jockey to win Britain's most famous horse race, the Grand National. (lines 30–40) – **2.** She means horses are in her blood and she can't imagine a life without them. (lines 53–55)

IV. 1. fence (line 3) – **2.** lad (line 12) – **3.** weight (line 16) – **4.** collarbone (line 11) – **5.** cancer (line 34) – **6.** bookmaker (line 47) – **7.** passion (line 49)

20D

   I. 2.

   II. a), c), d) and f)

UNIT 21

21A

Text

1. The man who drove over red lights did something wrong. (line 3) – **2.** The woman whose house was burgled. (lines 7–9) – **3.** We do not know what happened in the disco. What happened to the man who was arrested? (line 14) And we do not know what happened to the two girls. Did they find the bag? (lines 16–20) – **4.** He had driven over some red lights. (line 3) – **5.** Someone had broken into her house. (line 7) – **6.** They had received some information about drugs being used there. (lines 12–13) – **7.** One of them had lost her bag. (lines 16-17) – **8.** to phone (line 9) – **9.** immediately (line 9) – **10.** to realize (line 17) – **11.** *Example*: They are interested in televisions, video recorders and hi-fi equipment because they can sell these sorts of goods easily. **12.** *Example*: No, I don't think so. I think I would have to pay a fine (*Strafe*) and take some lessons at a driving school if I drove over red lights in Germany.

Exercises

   I. 1. I had never given a speech before. – **2.** I had never ridden a motorbike before. – **3.** I had never told a joke in public before. – **4.** I had never cooked for twenty people before. – **5.** I had never flown before. – **6.** I had never won a prize before.

   II. 1. He had seen the film before. – **2.** She hadn't eaten anything at home. – **3.** He had fallen in love with her the day before. – **4.** She hadn't told her parents that she was out with friends.

   III. 1. had been dancing – **2.** had been running – **3.** had been dreaming – **4.** had been working

   IV. 1. The group had been playing for half an hour when the lead singer felt ill. – **2.** We had been living in our new house for six months when the heating stopped working. – **3.** She had been travelling for fifteen minutes when she saw that she was on the wrong train. – **4.** He had been smoking for 40 years when he decided to give it up. – **5.** They had been living in Spain for six months when they got very homesick and came back to Germany. – **6.** She had been sitting in front of her computer for five minutes when she realized that it was an hour later than she thought.

   Also possible: **1.** After the group had been playing for half an hour, the lead singer felt ill. (*etc*)

   V. 1. was waiting – **2.** had been waiting – **3.** had eaten – **4.** were eating

21B

Text

1. b) (lines 2–3) – **2.** a) (lines 9–10) – **3.** b) (lines 14–15) – **4.** a) (lines 20–21) – **5.** b) (lines 23–25) – **6.** c) – **7.** hard (line 15) – **8.** small (line 19) – **9.** dark (line 20) – **10.** last (line 23) – **11.** *Example*: I think people steal cars because they can sell them again and make money. People also steal cars for fun. They race the cars for a few hours and then abandon them. **12.** *Example*: Yes, I think so. Of course he would not say anything about milk. In Germany we do not have milkmen who bring milk to your door every morning.

Exercises

I. 1. c) – 2. d) – 3. g) – 4. f) – 5. a) – 6. e) – 7. h) – 8. b) (Other combinations are possible.)

II. **2.** applauded enthusiastically. – **3.** is working there temporarily. – **4.** smiled happily. – **5.** laughed loudly. – **6.** arrived unexpectedly. – **7.** was raining heavily. – **8.** ran slowly.

III. **1.** true – **2.** true – **3.** true – **4.** not true (the verb is irregular) – **5.** robbed – **6.** stolen – **7.** robbed – **8.** stole

IV. **1.** burglary – **2.** shoplifting – **3.** assault – **4.** arson – **5.** bribery – **6.** forgery
1. Einbruch – **2.** Ladendiebstahl – **3.** tätlicher Angriff – **4.** Brandstiftung – **5.** Bestechung – **6.** Fälschung

V. **1.** Gericht – **2.** Prozess – **3.** carried out – **4.** do not

21C

I. **2.** (see page 231, lines 7–16)

II. **1.** b) (line 3) – **2.** a) (lines 13–16) – **3.** c) (lines 22–23) – **4.** b) (lines 33–36)

III. *Example*: I think he means that the British policemen are the best anybody could imagine. They are friendly, helpful and efficient – and they do not carry weapons.

21D

I. She must put the lights on in her house so that the tourists can see the rooms. – He does not want the thief to escape. – He was not. He arrested the real vicar, not the man who was disguised as a vicar.

II. **3.** (see Module 22D, page 152)

III. 1. c) – 2. f) – 3. e) – 4. b) – 5. d) – 6. a)

UNIT 22

22A

Text

1. True (lines 2–4) – **2.** Doesn't say – **3.** False (line 9) – **4.** False (lines 20–21) – **5.** True (line 22) – **6.** She is very upset about the burglary and thinks it will affect her for many months. (lines 20–21) – **7.** not easy – **8.** loud noise – **9.** returned – **10.** an awful – **11.** *Example*: I think it is a terrible experience because you know somebody has been inside your house or flat and looked through all your personal possessions in order to find money, jewellery or electrical equipment. A burglary is an invasion of your privacy. – **12.** *Example*: She has to find out as much as she can about the burglary without upsetting the victim more than is necessary.

Exercises

I. **1.** He told me that/He said that he had been on holiday (the month before) and that he had flown to Spain. – **2.** ... his sister had had a baby and (that) it had been born on June 20. – **3.** ... he was not enjoying his job and (that he) was looking for another one. – **4.** ... he had bought a second-hand car the previous weekend. – **5.** ... his girlfriend had fallen in love with someone else. – **6.** ... his father had been in hospital for a week.
(Note that when you put sentences into reported speech you also have to change the time expressions, for example "last month" becomes "the month before".)

II. **1.** told – **2.** said – **3.** said – **4.** told

III. 1. She asked me when I got up. – **2.** ... where I worked. – **3.** ... if I drove to work. – **4.** ... what time I finished work. – **5.** ... if I spent my evenings at home. – **6.** ... if I was (were) the sort of person who stayed up late.

IV. 1. She told me to read all the local papers. – **2.** ... to apply for as many jobs as possible. – **3.** ... to be polite on the phone. – **4.** She advised me to arrive for the interview on time. – **5.** ... to smile at the interviewer. – **6.** ... not to worry if I was (were) not successful the first time.

V. 1. Have a good holiday. – **2.** Oh, that's a shame. – **3.** Oh, we'd love to. – **4.** Good luck! I hope it goes well.

VI. 1. Are you going to the concert? – **2.** I've got the job I've always wanted. – **3.** She has had to go to hospital. – **4.** We're driving to Italy for a week's holiday. (Other sentences are possible.)

22B

Text

1. small firms in Britain – **2.** hard – **3.** hand – **4.** their work – **5.** orders – **6.** It is a small metal container. The people who buy the rocking horse can put something in it – for example a newspaper – so that one day the child can see what was happening in the world when she or he was smaller. – **7.** They have won many awards. (lines 33–34) – **8.** Mind the step. (line 19) – **9.** We have been incredibly lucky. (line 32) – **10.** You'd better get your order in right away. (line 37) – **11.** *Example*: Yes, I would like to have my own company because I think it must be rewarding to work for yourself (to be self-employed). – **12.** *Example*: Yes, I do. I think many parents today are prepared to spend money on wooden toys that look good and last for many years.

Exercises

I. 1. he should accept the job – **2.** to accept the job – **3.** he should accept the job – **4.** to accept the job

II. 1. (that) he would ring her the following day – **2.** her that he would ring her the following day – **3.** to her that he would ring the following day – **4.** to ring her the following day

III. 1. him to get up earlier – **2.** him to get up earlier – **3.** him to get up earlier – **4.** he should get up earlier

IV. 1. that her son never rang her – **2.** (that) he had broken the tea pot (breaking the tea pot) – **3.** for being late – **4.** having a game of cards ((that) they should have ...) – **5.** to give her the money – **6.** her son to ring Tom

V. 1. reasonably (surprisingly) cheap – **2.** bitterly disappointed – **3.** completely different – **4.** incredibly lucky – **5.** seriously ill – **6.** surprisingly (reasonably) easy

VI. *Example*: I have had a number of jobs. When I was at school, for example, I did a paper round. I delivered papers to the houses in our neighbourhood. I was only fourteen at the time. It was good fun and I earned a bit of money. One summer I spent three months working as a painter. I helped a friend of mine, who is a qualified painter and decorator. We painted the outside of houses. It was nice to work outside in the warm weather and I learnt a lot about painting but I wouldn't like to do this sort of job for the rest of my life. At the moment I am working as an electrician. I work for a small firm in the town where I live. I like the job but I would like to get more qualifications so that I can do something else in the future.

22C

    I. a) (see page 233, lines 8–12), c) (lines 14–19), e) (lines 21–37) and g) (lines 41–49)

    II. 1. A hurricane swept over southern England blowing down buildings and houses. Sevenoaks lost six of its famous oak trees. (lines 14–19) – **2.** Because it is a local newspaper the readers are most interested in stories which affect their everyday lives. (lines 21–23) – **3.** He likes writing the leader because it gives him the chance to express his opinion about an important issue. (lines 44–49)

    III. 1. advertisements – **2.** obituary / əˈbɪtʃʊərɪ / – **3.** horoscope – **4.** letters page – **5.** gossip column – **6.** weather forecast – **7.** review – **8.** crossword

22D

    I. hostage – pounds – freedom – valuables – keys – ladder – handle – story

    II. *Example*: I don't like it. It is a bit silly. I don't think someone can be knocked out by a rake.

    III. 1. d) – 2. f) – 3. b) – 4. c) – 5. a) – 6. e)

UNIT 23

23A

Text

1. b) (line 4) – **2.** c) (lines 21 and 25) – **3.** b) (line 35) – **4.** I think she means something for a wedding, a special party or a dance. – **5.** She thought the assistant did well – except for when she stuck a pin into the "customer". (lines 30–31) – **6.** b) – **7.** b) – **8.** b) – **9.** I sometimes take an 18. (line 10) – **10.** Can I try these dresses on? (line 13) – **11.** *Example*: No, I wouldn't. It must be a very tiring job and not very well paid. – **12.** *Example*: Yes, I do. I think it is important to learn how to handle customers, particularly in difficult situations. I also think it is necessary to learn how to make customers come back again and again to your shop.

Exercises

    I. 1. recovering from – **2.** manage – **3.** arrive – **4.** spent

    II. 1. come off – **2.** come round – **3.** came across – **4.** came up

    III. 1. c) – 2. d) – 3. a) – 4. b)
        1. Wir haben eine Autopanne? Ich fürchte/Leider, ja. – **2.** Wie viele Leute kamen gestern Abend? Etwa 50. – **3.** Kannst du dir vorstellen, wen ich gestern zufällig getroffen habe? Nein, wen? – **4.** Sollen wir sie zum Flughafen begleiten? Wann geht das Flugzeug?

    IV. 1. break down, turn up – **2.** run into sb, see sb off – **3.** see sb off – **4.** run into sb

    V. *Example*: 3 and 5. I would not complain about shoes which are too small. If I went to a shoe shop, tried on some new shoes and decided to buy them then it is my fault, and not the shop assistant's, if they do not fit me. Similarly, if I buy a jacket which costs twice as much as the same jacket a friend of mine has bought, then it is purely bad luck. Next time I will have to shop around more before I buy anything.

23B

Text

1. True – **2.** False – **3.** False – **4.** True – **5.** No, they are not. They are students so they are making the clothes as part of their course. – **6.** The sixth student seems to have a special role in the team. She is not involved in designing or making the clothes. She only has to wear them. – **7. – 10.** (These words are difficult to pronounce above all "clothes", which is quite a common word.) – **11.** *Example*: No, I'm not. I think it is important to wear clothes which suit me and look good on me but I don't go shopping for the latest trends. – **12.** *Example*: No, I don't. I think many young people would like to be fashion designers so competition for jobs is probably very tough (hard). I can also imagine that you have to work very hard to get a reputation as a fashion designer.

Exercises

   I. 1. c) – 2. a) – 3. d) – 4. b)

  II. 1. ... is a person who doesn't eat meat. – **2.** ... is a person who breaks into houses and steals things. – **3.** ... is a person who presents new fashions. – **4.** ... is a person who studies a subject at a high level.

 III. 1. ... who served us was very impolite. – **2.** ... which came out of the shop bit my leg. – **3.** ... who bought ten dresses was a film star. – **4.** ... which has closed sold lovely bread and cakes.

 IV. 1. The fish (which) we had for breakfast was delicious. – **2.** We stayed in a hotel (which) you recommended. – **3.** I liked the dress (which) you were wearing yesterday. – **4.** Where is the book (which) you gave me this morning?

  V. 1. The bed (which) I slept in was very hard. – **2.** The party (which) they went to last night was really boring. – **3.** The ferry (which) we wanted to travel on was booked up. – **4.** The job (which) she had applied for was not very well paid.

 VI. 1. sunglasses – **2.** youth hostels – **3.** alarm clock – **4.** credit card – **5.** mother tongue – **6.** traffic lights

23C

   I. a) (see page 235, lines 9–22) and e) (lines 6–8 and 22–24)

  II. 1. She thinks that accessories can make your outfit look very different. (lines 12–13 and 18–19) – **2.** She says you should develop your own style. (lines 22–23)

 III. 1. suit – **2.** suite – **3.** cloth – **4.** clothes – **5.** shirt – **6.** skirt – **7.** story – **8.** history

 IV. *Example*: The words "street cred" (short for "street credibility") express to what extent something you wear is generally accepted by young people. As fashion is constantly changing, what is street cred today might not be street cred tomorrow. For the fashion industry I think it must be important to design clothes and encourage styles which young people find interesting and acceptable. In other words, the fashion business influences what is street cred, and not the other way round.

23D

   I. d. – b. – e. – a. – c. – f.

  II. 1. consumption – **2.** explanation – **3.** rehearsal – **4.** complaint – **5.** announcement – **6.** reply – **7.** description – **8.** organization

 III. 1. secure – **2.** safe – **3.** secure – **4.** safe

UNIT 24

24A

Text

1. b) (line 4) – **2.** c) (lines 8–9) – **3.** a) (line 12) – **4.** She thinks car fumes (exhaust fumes) affect our health. (lines 2–3) – **5.** The motorway at the bottom of her garden has got busier. (lines 8–9) – **6.** He's happy about the traffic calming system but disappointed that it took so long to introduce it. (lines 12–14) – **7.** exhaust fumes (line 2) – **8.** speed limit (line 12) – **9.** They should have done it before. (line 6) – **10.** We have (got) to put up with it. (line 10) – **11.** *Example*: I think driving too fast is the most serious problem of the three. If you drive too fast there is a greater chance (that) you will have an accident and hurt innocent people. – **12.** *Example*: Yes, I think cars are a danger to the environment. However, more and more is being done to make cars consume less petrol (the 3-litre car, for example) or for cars to be powered by alternative energy sources (batteries, for instance).

Exercises

I. 1. I wish people wouldn't drive so fast. – **2.** I wish somebody would offer me a job. – **3.** I wish spring would come. – **4.** I wish the person in the flat next to me wouldn't play his music so loudly.

II. 1. I wish I was (were) fit. – **2.** I wish I had enough money for a holiday. – **3.** I wish my friend was (were) here. – **4.** I wish I could give up eating chocolate. – **5.** I wish I knew how to type properly. – **6.** I wish I didn't live in a small flat.

III. 1. I wish I hadn't talked to my friend about my new boss. – **2.** I wish I hadn't forgotten to take my camera. – **3.** I wish we hadn't stayed in that hotel. – **4.** I wish I had visited him in hospital. – **5.** I wish I hadn't visited my parents last weekend. – **6.** I wish I had stayed at school longer.

IV. 1. You could have flown. – **2.** You could have left it on the bus. – **3.** You could have gone to the cinema with me. – **4.** You could have spent the night with my uncle and aunt.

V. 1. She must have gone away. – **2.** I must have been listening to some music on my headphones. – **3.** Someone must have told him. – **4.** She must have worked hard.

VI. 1. I should have reserved a seat. – **2.** I should have gone to the party. – **3.** It should have opened half an hour ago. – **4.** I should not have drunk so much wine last night.

24B

Text

1. False (lines 5 and 9) – **2.** False (lines 14 and 19–21) – **3.** True – **4.** He is less happy about the fact that it took so long to decide to build the by-pass. (line 16) – **5.** If they had built a railway near his house, he would have moved to Scotland so we can see that he likes peace and quiet. (lines 19–22) – **6.** No, the first young person does not mention technology at all. – **7.** busy – **8.** pleased – **9.** progressing – **10.** a solution – **11.** *Example*: I use the train to get to work. I buy as much as I can in recyclable bottles and have a compost heap at the bottom of my garden. – **12.** *Example*: I think we will have electric cars in twenty years' time because electric cars exist today. The only real problem at the moment is that these cars are too expensive. In the future I think the car industry will have found a way of making electric cars cheaper than petrol-driven ones. As soon as this happens, people will buy them.

Exercises

I. 1. c) – 2. a) – 3. d) – 4. b)

II. 1. If I had missed the train, I would have missed the bus ... . – **2.** We wouldn't have gone to that restaurant if you hadn't recommended ... . – **3.** If you had given me your address, I would have sent you ... . – **4.** If she had reminded him about her birthday, he would have bought her ... .

III. 1. If my father hadn't lent me the money, I wouldn't have bought a motorbike. – **2.** If I hadn't gone to bed late, I wouldn't have been tired yesterday. – **3.** If you had said we needed some bread, I would have bought some. – **4.** If somebody had told me the lesson began at 9.00, I wouldn't have come late.

IV. 1. ... she wouldn't have got wet. – **2.** ... her credit cards wouldn't have been stolen. – **3.** ... the train wouldn't have been an hour late. – **4.** ... her son wouldn't have been waiting for her outside the front door.

V. 1. ... will have already started. – **2.** ... will have used up all our money. – **3.** ... will have lived here for exactly a year. – **4.** ... will have been married for 25 years.

VI. 1. ... will have been living ... . – **2.** ... will have been using ... . – **3.** ... will have had ... . – **4.** ... will have been doing ... . **5.** ... will have been running ... .

VII. *Example*: In the year 2020 people in some countries on Earth will be driving electric cars. They will be working from home and they will be communicating with each other by computer and video phones. They will be working shorter weeks and they will be having longer holidays. By the year 2020 people in some parts of the world will have fought long wars with each other. Many people will have died from starvation or AIDS. People will have made the ozone hole larger and cut down billions of trees in the process. By the year 2020 people will not have learnt from the mistakes of the past.

24C

I. a) (see page 236, lines 5–8), d) (lines 10–24) and f) (lines 26–37)

II. 1. One of the problems which India has is her rapid growth in population. More and more people are moving from the country into the cities. Fast grass gives people from the country a chance to raise cattle and grow crops and look after themselves. In other words, having fast grass stops people moving into the cities where there is no future for them. (lines 15–24) – **2.** Many people in India do not have a roof over their heads. They need simple, effective and cheap housing as soon as possible. (lines 25–31)

III. d) [a) = line 47, b) = line 68, c) = line 60, e) = line 69, f) = line 64]

IV. 1. He wanted to have a "green" house because it makes use of what the environment can offer, such as heat, light and trees. – **2.** No, he doesn't think it is "the" answer. He thinks he has designed a house which minimizes the amount of energy we use on a day-to-day basis. (lines 70–72)

V. 1. horticulturalist (line 1) – **2.** innovation (line 10) – **3.** timber (line 51) – **4.** floor (line 55) – **5.** fridge (line 64)

24D

I. wood – easy – stops – should – fish – polluting – box – measures – powerful – disappears

II. a wish. The German equivalents are „retten", „sparen", „halten".

UNIT 25

25A

Text

1. a) (line 2) – **2.** b) (lines 8–9) – **3.** c) (lines 28–30) – **4.** She is pleased Jane rang because she now knows that the new tenants for a cottage have arrived. (lines 5–7) – **5.** It is annoying because Rose Farm Cottage is one of the cottages she rents. If there is a problem with a radiator, then Maggie will not be able to rent it. – **6.** He wants to pick up the key for Rose Farm Cottage. (line 33) – **7.** tenant (line 6) – **8.** radiator (line 20) – **9.** plumber (line 21) – **10.** mobile (phone) (line 26) – **11.** *Example*: Yes, I can. I suppose Britain is a popular tourist attraction, even for British people, and many families would like to spend some time in a cottage or flat near the sea. – **12.** *Example*: No, I wouldn't. I am not a very disciplined person so I think I would not be able to work very well from home. I would always find something else to do instead of my work.

Exercises

    I. 1. promise (*Versprechen*) – **2.** threat (*Drohung*) – **3.** offer (*Angebot*) – **4.** request (*Bitte*) – **5.** refusal (*Weigerung*) – **6.** intention (*Absicht*)

    II. 1. "I'll answer it." – **2.** "I'll go!" – **3.** "I'll take you." – **4.** "I'll get some water." – **5.** "I'll call you back." – **6.** "I'll open a window."

    III. 1. "... I'll scream!" – **2.** "... I'll open ... ." – **3.** " ... I'll see you ... ." – **4.** " ... It won't start." – **5.** "... I'll fetch ... ." – **6.** "... and I'll have a beer."

    IV. 1. I'll do ... . – **2.** I'm going to buy ... . – **3.** ... are you going to paint it? – **4.** I'll show you. – **5.** I'll see you ... . – **6.** ... I'm going to be sick.

    V. 1. Have the new brochures arrived? I think so. – **2.** Has the plumber called? I don't think so. – **3.** Has the post arrived? I suppose so. – **4.** Have you lost the key? I hope not.

    VI. f. – b. – c. – e. – g. – d. – a. – h.

    VII. 1. a) – 2. b) – 3. b) – 4. b) – 5. a) – 6. a) – 7. a) – 8. a) – 9. a) – 10. a) – 11. d) – 12. a) – 13. e) – 14. b) – 15. c)

25B

Text

1. False (lines 6 and 17) – **2.** True (line 10) – **3.** Doesn't say – **4.** True (line 17) – **5.** If you send a fax at night it costs less than if you send it during the day. – **6.** It means to see if somebody has sent you an e-mail message. – **7.** brochure (line 9) – **8.** property (line 14) – **9.** b) – **10.** c) – **11.** *Example*: With a visual display you have all the information you need together in one place. On a computer it is not so simple: you have to move from one page to another to see all the information. – **12.** *Example*: No, I couldn't. If I worked together with my brother or my sister, there would be too many arguments and this would not be good for business. I'd rather work with people who are not part of my family.

Exercises

    I. 1. raised – **2.** destroy – **3.** re-introduce – **4.** lowering

    II. 1. set aside some money (set some money aside) – **2.** set out – **3.** set up a business (set a business up) – **4.** set off

    III. 1. boot it up – **2.** set it aside – **3.** set it up – **4.** click it on

    IV. 1. catch – **2.** buy – **3.** understand – **4.** arrived at – **5.** annoy – **6.** receive – **7.** growing ... growing – **8.** prepare

V. 1. a – 2. d – 3. g – 4. f – 5. c – 6. i – 7. j – 8. h – 9. b – 10. k – 11. l – 12. e

VI. **1.** Would you ...? – **2.** Do you ...? – **3.** Did you ...? – **4.** Are you ...? – **5.** Have you ...? – **6.** Did you ...?

25C

I. **1.** b) (see page 239, line 1) – **2.** a) (line 3) – **3.** c) (lines 22–44)

II. **1.** He needs a computer, a modem, a fax, a telephone, a laptop and e-mail. – **2.** The advantage is that you can concentrate on your work and not be interrupted. The disadvantage is that you are alone and have to be self-motivated. (lines 45-52)

III. **1.** adjacent (line 3) – **2.** ideal (line 5) – **3.** transmit (line 5) – **4.** client (line 13) – **5.** currently (line 38) – **6.** interrupt (line 47)

25D

I. b)

II.

1. praktisch	–	handy	Handy	–	mobile (phone)
2. Stockwerk	–	floor	Flur	–	hall
3. Arbeitszimmer	–	study	Studium	–	(course of) studies
4. persönlich	–	personal	Personal	–	personnel
5. übrig haben	–	spare	sparen	–	save
6. regeln, steuern	–	control	kontrollieren	–	check
7. mitfühlend, verständnisvoll	–	sympathetic	sympathisch	–	nice/likeable

III. 1. d) – 2. f) – 3. e) – 4. a) – 5. b) – 6. c)
7. You will get into hot water – **8.** left me cold – **9.** got cold feet – **10.** is blowing hot and cold

UNIT 26

26A

Text

1. This is false because the text says she enjoyed working with children. (lines 6–8) – **2.** This is true because the text says she had been helping out in a classroom for several years. (lines 5–6) – **3.** This is true because the text says she is a parent. (line 5) – **4.** This is false because the text says he left school with no qualifications. (lines 12–13) – **5.** This is true because the text says he ran his own shop. (line 15) – **6.** This is false because the text says he is going to study law. (line 10) – **7.** to return to (line 4) – **8.** I'm afraid that (line 12) – **9.** several (line 15) – **10.** to find (line 15) – **11.** *Example*: I would prefer to be a lawyer. I think being a teacher must be very tiring, especially if you teach small children. A lawyer has a more varied job. – **12.** *Example*: I think they are very important in Germany. Without certain qualifications it is impossible to get the job you want.

Exercises

I. **1.** were you going – **2.** Are you still living – **3.** had been (were) driving – **4.** have you been waiting – **5.** I was trying ... were you talking to – **6.** I'm lying

II. **1.** Who did you meet on the train yesterday? – **2.** Where does she live? – **3.** When did the performance finish? – **4.** How long does the course last? – **5.** How does he come to work? – **6.** What did they see as they were driving to France?

III. **1.** have you had – **2.** had already closed – **3.** will have been living – **4.** has been – **5.** Had anybody known – **6.** will have done

IV. 1. a) – 2. b) – 3. a) – 4. a) – 5. b) – 6. a)

V. 1. could – **2.** May – **3.** will – **4.** shouldn't – **5.** Shall – **6.** mustn't

VI. 1. to ring – **2.** being – **3.** working – **4.** to get – **5.** going – **6.** to reach

26B

Text

1. b) (lines 5–6) – **2.** a) (lines 6–10) – **3.** a) (line 26) – **4.** b) (lines 27–28) – **5.** b) (lines 34–35) – **6.** b) (line 44) – **7.** They all enjoy doing the course they have chosen. (lines 16–17, 32 and 44) – **8.** chance – **9.** intending – **10.** finish – **11.** *Example*: They have other commitments like a family or a job so this makes it difficult for them to concentrate on their studies. – **12.** *Example*: I think it will become more important in the future because people will not be offered jobs for life. Jobs in the future will be short-term contracts so people will have to be more flexible and more mobile in their approach to finding employment.

Exercises

I. 1. but – **2.** Although – **3.** When – **4.** in order to

II. 1. because – **2.** so as to – **3.** If – **4.** While

III 1. although – **2.** as if – **3.** so – **4.** As (Other answers are possible.)

IV. 1. be on time – **2.** during the week she doesn't have the time – **3.** I decided to go back to school and get some more qualifications – **4.** he didn't do very well (Other answers are possible.)

V. 1. Member of Parliament – **2.** United Kingdom – **3.** Compact Disk – **4.** United States of America – **5.** Very Important Person – **6.** Unidentified Flying Object – **7.** Compact Disk Read Only Memory – **8.** Value Added Tax

VI. *Example*: I went to school in a small town near Heidelberg. I was good at Maths and Physics but not very good at German and English. I left school at sixteen and did an apprenticeship in a bank. I completed my training when I was 19. After that I did military service for a year. I have been working at the bank where I trained for the last four years. I like my job but I am thinking about going back to college to get better qualifications so that I can study something like Business Management at college or university.

26C

I. b) (see page 241, lines 35-38)

II. b) (lines 1–6) – d) (line 7) – a) (lines 7–9) – e) (lines 12–14) – i) (lines 20–24) – c) (lines 25–26) – g) (line 32) – h) (line 39) – f) (lines 35–36)

III. 1. It looks after people who care for the elderly. (It cares for the carers.) (lines 39–41) – **2.** *Example*: She means people should be given another chance to do something they did not do well the first time. I agree with her. Some people develop an interest or skill in something much later in life.

IV. d) – c) – e) – a) – b)

26D

I. drives – is – doesn't seem – don't take – lives – were – saw – knew – left – became – took – goes – carefully – will be – does that mean

II. 1. measures – **2.** furniture – **3.** vehicles – **4.** tools – **5.** pork – **6.** wind – **7.** autumn – **8.** press

III. 1. sauce – **2.** blue – **3.** way – **4.** role – **5.** war – **6.** sail – **7.** cheque – **8.** peace

IV. *Example*: Perhaps he will do a course in Drama and become an actor.

ENGLISH SOUNDS

In der Lautschrift wird jeder Laut durch ein bestimmtes Zeichen dargestellt. Da es mehr Laute gibt als Buchstaben, hat man eine Reihe von zusätzlichen Lautschriftzeichen erfunden.

Vokale (vowels)

ɪ	it, is, him, six
e	yes, red, many, ten
æ	black, at, stamp, hat
ɒ	not, shop, what, song
ʌ	but, number, London, one
ʊ	good, look, put, woman
ə	letter, father, another, sister
i:	he, she, teacher, three
ɑ:	class, ask, past, car
ɔ:	sport, door, wall, four
u:	you, school, blue, two
ɜ:	girl, church, word, first
eɪ	great, name, today, eight
aɪ	my, nice, nine, five
əʊ	no, so, hello, envelope
aʊ	how, now, house, out
ɔɪ	boy, coin, toy, Lloyd's
ɪə	here, dear, beer, near
eə	where, there, chair, pair
ʊə	tour, poor, sure, your

Konsonanten (consonants)

p	pet, stamp, top, up
b	boy, black, bye, Bob
t	ten, water, want, eight
d	day, and, bad, good
k	car, king, ask, desk
g	good, big, great, English
f	four, fifteen, floor, left
v	five, seven, eleven, twelve
s	six, seven, it's, what's
z	is, boys, girls, classes
ʃ	she, English, sure, sugar
ʒ	television, pleasure
tʃ	chair, church, teacher, "h"
dʒ	German, garage, geography
θ	three, thank you, thirteen
ð	they, with, without, weather
w	well, window, where, whether
l	well, wall, hall, also
r	right, wrong, three, true
ŋ	sing, song, English, single

WORDLIST

The numbers refer to the Modules in which the word or expression occur for the first time. The words and expressions in Module C are listed after the corresponding tapescripts (see page 216 ff).

A
A levels ("A" short for Advanced)
ˈeɪlevəlz 26A
abide by əˈbaɪd 14C
able-bodied people ˈeɪbəl ˈbɒdɪd ˈpiːpəl 19C
access ˈækses 19C/25D
accessorize əkˈsesəraɪz 23C
accessory əkˈsesərɪ 23C
accomplished əˈkɒmplɪʃt 17C
acquire əˈkwaɪə 25B
acrylic paints əˈkrɪlɪk ˈpeɪnts 16D
adapt əˈdæpt 16C
adjacent (to) əˈdʒeɪsənt 25C

adjust əˈdʒʌst 23B
administer ədˈmɪnɪstə 18D
administrator ədˈmɪnɪstreɪtə 17C
Admiralty charts ˈædmərəltɪ ˈtʃɑːts 18C
admire ədˈmaɪə 16C
advent ˈædvənt 14C
advertise ˈædvətaɪz 25B
affect əˈfekt 22C
age eɪdʒ 14A
aim at eɪm 17C
air rights ˈeə ˈraɪts 25C
alas əˈlæs 22C
ales eɪlz 14B

alien ˈeɪlɪən 17B
alike əˈlaɪk 21C
allow əˈlaʊ 25D
almanac ˈɔːlmənæk 18C
alongside əˈlɒŋˈsaɪd 18C
alteration ɔːltəˈreɪʃən 16B
answerphone ˈɑːnsəˈfəʊn 25A
appalling əˈpɔːlɪŋ 24A
apparently əˈpærəntlɪ 22C
apply for əˈplaɪ 21C
appointment əˈpɔɪntmənt 14C
appreciate əˈpriːʃɪeɪt 16C
argument ˈɑːgjʊmənt 16A
arise (arose, arisen) əˈraɪz
   [əˈrəʊz, əˈrɪzən] 21C
army band ˈɑːmɪ ˈbænd 21C
arrest əˈrest 21A/24C
artistic director ɑːˈtɪstɪk dɪˈrektə 17C
arts ɑːts 16C
arts festival ˈɑːts ˈfestəvəl 17C
asking price ˈɑːskɪŋ ˈpraɪs 15B
asp æsp 21C
assault əˈsɔːlt 21C
assignment əˈsaɪnmənt 26C
associated with əˈsəʊʃɪeɪtɪd 14C
at last ət ˈlɑːst 25A
at the rear ət ðə ˈrɪə 25C
attach əˈtætʃ 18C
attached əˈtætʃt 25C
authorized firearms officer ˈɔːθəraɪzd
   ˈfaɪərɑːmz ˈɒfɪsə 21C
avant-garde ævã ˈgɑːd 16C
award əˈwɔːd 22B

B
Bachelor of Arts (BA) ˈbætʃelə əv ˈɑːts
   [biː ˈeɪ] 26C
back sth/sb bæk 20B
bank bæŋk 24D
bank holiday ˈbæŋk ˈhɒlɪdeɪ 15D
bar bɑː 17A
bark bɑːk 21B
barley ˈbɑːlɪ 14B
barrel ˈbærəl 14B
basic housing ˈbeɪsɪk ˈhaʊzɪŋ 24C
bat bæt 19D
bather ˈbeɪðə 18C
baton ˈbætɒn 17D
battle ˈbætəl 20C
bay beɪ 18C

be aware ˈbiː əˈweə 19B
be based around beɪst 16C
be bred in bred 20C
be capable of ˈkeɪpəbəl 21C
be covered by ˈkʌvəd 15C
be crackers ˈkrækəz 20C
be fitted with ˈfɪtɪd 18C
be fortunate ˈfɔːtʃənət 18C
be in store for sb stɔː 23D
be involved in ˈɪnvɒlvd 16C
be issued with ˈɪʃjuːd 21C
be loath to do sth ləʊθ 21C
be lost lɒst 16A
be manhandled ˈmænhændəld 19C
be on about sth 24D
be on call ɒn ˈkɔːl 18C
be run off into rʌn 14B
be tuned in tjuːnd 16C
be up to scratch skrætʃ 14C
be upset ʌpˈset 22A
be way outside sth ˈweɪ aʊtˈsaɪd 16C
be wrapped up ræpt 16C
beachcomber ˈbiːtʃkəʊmə 14D
bearing in mind ... ˈbeərɪŋ ɪn ˈmaɪnd 19C
beat biːt 17A/21C
bedazzle bɪˈdæzəl 23D
beech biːtʃ 22B
beeping noise ˈbiːpɪŋ ˈnɔɪz 19B
benefit ˈbenɪfɪt 16C
bet bet 20B
bet on 20A
bin bɪn 24D
bless bles 14C
blind blaɪnd 17A/19D
bonfire ˈbɒnfaɪə 24D
bookmaker ˈbʊkmeɪkə 20C
boost buːst 20C
boot up buːt 25B
bottom ˈbɒtəm 24A
branch brɑːntʃ 19D
brass (instrument) ˈbrɑːs ˈɪnstrʊmənt 17A
breeches buoy ˈbrɪtʃɪs ˈbɔɪ 18C
breed (bred, bred) briːd [bred] 20C
brewery ˈbrʊərɪ 14A
bric-a-brac ˈbrɪkəbræk 22D
brick brɪk 24B
burglar ˈbɜːglə 21A
burglary ˈbɜːglərɪ 21A
Business Studies ˈbɪznɪs ˈstʌdɪz 26B
busy ˈbɪzɪ 24A

butt bʌt 16B
buttery ˈbʌtərɪ 16B
by-pass ˈbaɪpɑːs 24B

C

calendar of events ˈkælɪndə əv ɪˈvents 17C
calico ˈkælɪkəʊ 23B
campaigning ˈkæmpeɪnɪŋ 22C
cancer ˈkænsə 20C
canter ˈkæntə 20C
canvas ˈkænvəs 16A
capsule ˈkæpsjuːl 22B
captivate ˈkæptɪveɪt 17C
carer ˈkeərə 26C
carving shop ˈkɑːvɪŋ ˈʃɒp 22B
cask kɑːsk 14B
casualty ˈkæʒjʊəltɪ 18C
catapult ˈkætəpʌlt 22C
catwalk ˈkætwɔːk 23D
cautious ˈkɔːʃəs 20B
challenge ˈtʃælɪndʒ 20C
change hands ˈtʃeɪndʒ ˈhændz 16C
changing-room ˈtʃeɪndʒɪŋ ˈruːm 19C
charge sb for sth ˈtʃɑːdʒ 18C
charity ˈtʃærɪtɪ 16C/23D
cheerful ˈ ˈtʃɪəfəl 15D
cherish ˈtʃerɪʃ 16C
chess tʃes 26C
choir ˈkwaɪə 17D
chuck away ˈtʃʌk əˈweɪ 19C
circumstances ˈsɜːkəmstənsɪz 15B
claim kleɪm 18C/20D
classroom assistant ˈklɑːsrʊm əˈsɪstənt 26A
coastguard ˈkəʊstgɑːd 18C
coefficient kəʊɪˈfɪʃənt 24C
collarbone ˈkɒləbəʊn 20C
column ˈkɒləm 24C
come off kʌm 18A
come up 16C
compere ˈkɒmpeə 23D
composer kəmˈpəʊzə 17D
computing skills kəmˈpjuːtɪŋ ˈskɪlz 26B
conductor kənˈdʌktə 17A
confidence trickster ˈkɒnfɪdəns ˈtrɪkstə 15D
considerable kənˈsɪdərəbəl 18B
consultant engineer kənˈsʌltənt
    endʒɪˈnɪə 25C
contemporary kənˈtempərərɪ 24C
contractor kənˈtræktə 25C
contribute to kənˈtrɪbjuːt 24C

convenient kənˈviːnjənt 15A
convincing kənˈvɪnsɪŋ 17B
copper ˈkɒpə 14B
council ˈkaʊnsəl 16C
county ˈkaʊntɪ 19A
courageous kəˈreɪdʒəs 22C
coxswain ˈkɒksən 18C
craft krɑːft 18C
craftsman ˈkrɑːftsmən 22B
crash kræʃ 22A
credibility ˈkredɪbɪlətɪ 23C
crew a car ˈkruː ə ˈkɑː 21C
crop krɒp 24C
crush krʌʃ 14B
crux of the matter ˈkrʌks əv ðə ˈmætə 22C
cuffs kʌfs 21C
custom ˈkʌstəm 14C

D

dampen ˈdæmpən 24C
dare deə 16D
dazzle ˈdæzəl 23D
deaf def 19D
deal with diːl 23A
dear dɪə 22A
Decca ˈdekə 18C
deceitful dɪˈsiːtfəl 15D
defensive search dɪˈfensɪv ˈsɜːtʃ 21C
degree dɪˈgriː 15C/23B
dense dens 24C
density of ˈdensətɪ 15C
desire dɪˈzaɪə 23D
despair dɪˈspeə 23C
deter dɪˈtɜː 21B
deteriorate dɪˈtɪərɪəreɪt 25C
determine dɪˈtɜːmɪn 26C
development dɪˈveləpmənt 15A/24B
device dɪˈvaɪs 24D
dignitary ˈdɪgnɪtərɪ 21C
dinghy ˈdɪŋgɪ 18C
dinosaur ˈdaɪnəsɔː 26D
director daɪˈrektə 17A
disability awareness dɪsəˈbɪlətɪ
    əˈweənɪs 19B
disabled people dɪsˈeɪbəld ˈpiːpəl 19B
discharge dɪsˈtʃɑːdʒ 25C
disgusting dɪsˈgʌstɪŋ 24A
disrupt dɪsˈrʌpt 17C
disturbing dɪˈstɜːbɪŋ 17B
domestic housing dəʊˈmestɪk ˈhaʊzɪŋ 25C

donation dəʊˈneɪʃən 17C
dot dɒt 19B
double as ˈdʌbəl 25B
draft drɑːft 25C
drain off dreɪn 14B
drape dreɪp 23A
draughts drɑːfts 26C
driveway ˈdraɪvweɪ 21B
driving licence ˈdraɪvɪŋ ˈlaɪsəns 21A
drop off drɒp 23C
drown draʊn 18D
dull dʌl 16C
dummy ˈdʌmɪ 23A
duration djʊˈreɪʃən 21C

E

easel ˈiːzəl 16D
ecological iːkəˈlɒdʒɪkəl 24C
editor ˈedɪtə 22C
editorial meeting edɪˈtɔːrɪəl ˈmiːtɪŋ 22C
elderflower cordial ˈeldəˈflaʊə ˈkɔːdjəl 14D
elevenses ɪˈlevənzɪz 15D
emergency ɪˈmɜːdʒənsɪ 18C
empathy ˈempəθɪ 16C
encourage ɪnˈkʌrɪdʒ 16C
engender ɪnˈdʒendə 22C
engine failure ˈendʒɪn ˈfeɪljə 18C
enquiry ɪnˈkwaɪərɪ 25A
enrol ɪnˈrəʊl 26D
entail ɪnˈteɪl 25C
enthusiastic ɪnθjuːzɪˈæstɪk 26C
environmental ɪnvaɪərənˈmentəl 16C
environmentalist ɪnvaɪərənˈmentəlɪst 24C
eraser ɪˈreɪzə 23B
especially ɪˈspeʃlɪ 20A
establishment ɪˈstæblɪʃmənt 24C
estate agent ɪˈsteɪt ˈeɪdʒənt 15C
evening wear ˈiːvnɪŋ ˈweə 23B
exhaust fumes ɪgˈzɔːst ˈfjuːmz 24A
expenses ɪkˈspensɪz 20A
experience ɪkˈspɪərɪəns 16C
explore ɪkˈsplɔː 16C
explosive dog ɪkˈspləʊsɪv ˈdɒg 21C
extinct ɪkˈstɪŋkt 26D

F

fabrics ˈfæbrɪks 23B
facility fəˈsɪlətɪ 25C
fairly ˈfeəlɪ 21C
feature ˈfiːtʃə 24C

feel upset ˈfiːl ʌpˈset 22A
felted woollens ˈfeltɪd ˈwʊlənz 23B
femur ˈfiːmə 20C
fence fens 20C
ferment fəˈment 14B
fermenting vessel fəˈmentɪŋ ˈvesəl 14B
ferry back ˈferɪ ˈbæk 18C
fiery ˈfaɪərɪ 22C
first thing in the morning ˈfɜːst ˈθɪŋ ɪn ðə ˈmɔːnɪŋ 25B
fit sth/sb in fɪt 25A
fitting room ˈfɪtɪŋ ˈruːm 23A
flavour ˈfleɪvə 14B
flood flʌd 16B
flow fləʊ 19C
fly up (flew, flown) flaɪ [fluː, fləʊn] 22D
fonts fɒnts 25B
forage ˈfɒrɪdʒ 24C
force fɔːs 18C
fortnight ˈfɔːtnaɪt 18C
foundation faʊnˈdeɪʃən 24C
frankly ˈfræŋklɪ 20D
free of charge ˈfriː əv ˈtʃɑːdʒ 17C
fruit machine ˈfruːt məˈʃiːn 20D
furtive ˈfɜːtɪv 21B
fuse box ˈfjuːz bɒks 17D

G

gale-force winds ˈgeɪl fɔːs ˈwɪndz 22C
gamble ˈgæmbəl 20A
garment ˈgɑːmənt 23B
gather information ˈgæðə ɪnfəˈmeɪʃən 22B
GCSE dʒiː siː es ˈiː 26A
gender orientated ˈdʒendə ˈɔːrɪenteɪtɪd 21C
genetics dʒɪˈnetɪks 26C
germination dʒɜːmɪˈneɪʃən 24C
get around get 19A
get one's order in ˈɔːdə 22B
get over sth 22A
get rid of rɪd 15C
get round to 15C
get sb 25A
get on 14C
gigantic dʒaɪˈgæntɪk 17B
giggle ˈgɪgəl 17B
gipsy site ˈdʒɪpsɪ ˈsaɪt 22C
give one's time free ˈgɪv wʌnz ˈtaɪm ˈfriː 17C
glasspaper ˈglɑːspeɪpə 15D

global positioning system ˈgləʊbəl
  pəˈzɪʃənɪŋ ˈsɪstəm 18C
gravel ˈgrævəl 21B
graze greɪz 24C
grind (corn) (ground, ground) graɪnd
  [graʊnd] 16B
grip grɪp 18C
grist grɪst 14B
grow (grew, grown) frail ˈgrəʊ [gruː, grəʊn]
  freɪl 26C
grow up 26D
guess ges 14C
guide dog ˈgaɪd ˈdɒg 19B
guild gɪld 22B

H
habit ˈhæbɪt 15C
handle ˈhændəl 25B
hang (hung, hung) about (around) hæŋ
  [hʌŋ] 21B
hardwood ˈhɑːdwʊd 22B
haul hɔːl 19C
have a bite to eat ˈhæv ə ˈbaɪt tə ˈiːt 25A
have a flutter flʌtə 20A
have a row raʊ 16A
have access to ˈækses 25D
health inspector ˈhelθ ɪnˈspektə 14C
hide (hid, hidden) haɪd [hɪd, hɪdən] 21B
high-rise structures ˈhaɪ ˈraɪz ˈstrʌktʃəz 25C
high-speed railway ˈhaɪ ˈspiːd ˈreɪlweɪ 24B
highlight ˈhaɪlaɪt 17C/22C
hindsight ˈhaɪndsaɪt 16C
hoist hɔɪst 19C
home loan ˈhəʊm ˈləʊn 15B
homely ˈhəʊmlɪ 14C
hops hɒps 14B
hopscotch ˈhɒpskɒtʃ 26D
horrific hɒˈrɪfɪk 17A
horse racing ˈhɔːs ˈreɪsɪŋ 20A
horticulturalist hɔːtɪˈkʌltʃərəlɪst 24C
hostage ˈhɒstɪdʒ 22D
house suite ˈhaʊs ˈswiːt 19C
human mind ˈhjuːmən ˈmaɪnd 15D
hunt hʌnt 20C

I
icon ˈaɪkɒn 25B
immobilize ɪˈməʊbɪlaɪz 24D
in effect ɪn ɪˈfekt 16C
in kind ɪn ˈkaɪnd 17C

inferior ɪnˈfɪərɪə 26C
infirm ɪnˈfɜːm 26C
inflatable ɪnˈfleɪtəbəl 18C
initial ɪˈnɪʃəl 17D/26C
initially ɪˈnɪʃəlɪ 21C
inshore ˈɪnʃɔː 18C
insurance ɪnˈʃʊərəns 17C
interact ɪntəˈrækt 19C
interval ˈɪntəvəl 17B
introduce ɪntrəˈdjuːs 24A
intrude ɪnˈtruːd 26C
intrudor ɪnˈtruːdə 22A
issue ˈɪʃuː 16C

J
jacuzzi dʒəˈkuːzɪ 19C
jar dʒɑ: 14D
jargon ˈdʒɑːgən 22C
job dʒɒb 25C
jug dʒʌg 14D

K
kerb kɜːb 19D
kitty ˈkɪtɪ 20C
knock down ˈnɒk ˈdaʊn 24C
knot nɒt 18C

L
lager ˈlɑːgə 14B
large scale ˈlɑːdʒ ˈskeɪl 25C
lash læʃ 22C
launch lɔːntʃ 18C
lead story ˈliːd ˈstɔːrɪ 22C
leader column ˈliːdə ˈkɒləm 22C
leak liːk 25A
lease liːs 15C
leisure ˈleʒə 19C
lend a hand ˈlend ə ˈhænd 16A
let let 25A
let sth out 23A
lie (lay, lain) laɪ [leɪ, leɪn] 18A
lift lɪft 20C
lighting ˈlaɪtɪŋ 17B
lime cordial ˈlaɪm ˈkɔːdjəl 14D
liquid ˈlɪkwɪd 14B
listed building ˈlɪstɪd ˈbɪldɪŋ 25C
livelihood ˈlaɪvlɪhʊd 22C
living space ˈlɪvɪŋ ˈspeɪs 24C
lobster ˈlɒbstə 18A

lollipop lady/man ˈlɒlɪpɒp ˈleɪdɪ/mæn 26A
lump (of wood) ˈlʌmp [əv ˈwʊd] 21C

M
make up one's mind ˈmeɪk ʌp wʌnz ˈmaɪnd 20B
male meɪl 23D
malted barley ˈmɔːltɪd ˈbɑːlɪ 14B
man mæn 18C
mash mæʃ 14B
mash tun ˈmæʃ ˈtʌn 14B
master bedroom ˈmɑːstə ˈbedruːm 15A
mature məˈtjʊə 24B/26C
meal miːl 14B
Media Studies ˈmiːdjə ˈstʌdɪz 26B
mellow ˈmeləʊ 24B
menu ˈmenjuː 14C
mess mes 15D
metre rule ˈmiːtə ˈruːl 23B
mill mɪl 16A/16B
mimic ˈmɪmɪk 24C
minimize ˈmɪnɪmaɪz 24C
misfortune mɪsˈfɔːtʃən 26C
mortgage adviser ˈmɔːgɪdʒ ədˈvaɪzə 15B
moustache məˈstɑːʃ 25D
multiple ˈmʌltɪpəl 19C

N
navigator ˈnævɪgeɪtə 18C
need niːd 19B
neighbourhood watch ˈneɪbəhʊd ˈwɒtʃ 21B
never mind ˈnevə maɪnd 14D
nightmare ˈnaɪtmeə 18C
nothing but ˈnʌθɪŋ ˈbʌt 24B
notice ˈnəʊtɪs 18B
nurse nɜːs 17A
nursery school ˈnɜːsərɪ ˈskuːl 26A

O
occur əˈkɜː 18C/24C
odds ɒdz 20B
oils ɔɪlz 16D
"Omniometer" ˈɒmnɪəʊmiːtə 24D
on duty ɒn ˈdjuːtɪ 21A
on spec ɒn ˈspek 14C
onshore wind ˈɒnʃɔː ˈwɪnd 18C
operate ˈɒpəreɪt 17C
order book ˈɔːdə bʊk 22B
other than ˈʌðə ðən 21C
overlocker ˈəʊvəlɒkə 23B

overseas əʊvəˈsiːz 25C
overwhelm əʊvəˈwelm 21D
ozone layer ˈəʊzəʊn ˈleɪə 18A

P
pack of cards ˈpæk əv ˈkɑːdz 20C
package ˈpækɪdʒ 25B
pad pæd 24C
pantry ˈpæntrɪ 16B
Paralympic Games pærəˈlɪmpɪk ˈgeɪmz 19C
part-time ˈpɑːt ˈtaɪm 26B
participate in pɑːˈtɪsɪpeɪt 17C
paste peɪst 15D
pastel pæˈstel 16D
path pɑːθ 21B
pathetic pəˈθetɪk 20B
patrol pəˈtrəʊl 21C
pattern ˈpætən 23B
pattern-cutter ˈpætən ˈkʌtə 23B
pattern-master ˈpætən ˈmɑːstə 23B
pedestrianize pɪˈdestrɪənaɪz 19B
pet pet 22C
PhD piː eɪtʃ ˈdiː 26C
philanthropist fɪˈlænθrəpɪst 19D
pile paɪl 24C
pin pɪn 23A
place a bet ˈpleɪs ə ˈbet 20B
plead pliːd 22D
plumber ˈplʌmə 25A
point pɔɪnt 15C
policy decision ˈpɒləsɪ dɪˈsɪʒən 17C
pop round pɒp ˈraʊnd 25A
portable ˈpɔːtəbəl 25C
post pəʊst 19D
potential pəˈtenʃəl 19C
prediction prɪˈdɪkʃən 18B
pregnancy ˈpregnənsɪ 21C
presence (of) ˈprezəns 25C
preserve prɪˈzɜːv 24C
pressing ˈpresɪŋ 24C
pressure ˈpreʃə 26C
prevailing prɪˈveɪlɪŋ 18C
prick up one's ears ˈprɪk ʌp wʌnz ˈɪəz 19D
process ˈprəʊses 14B
produce ˈprɒdjuːs 14C
produce prəˈdjuːs 14D
profound prəˈfaʊnd 19C
property ˈprɒpətɪ 15A
proposal prəˈpəʊzəl 24B
provide entry prəˈvaɪd ˈentrɪ 21B

psychiatrist saɪˈkaɪətrɪst 17A
public address system ˈpʌblɪk əˈdres
ˈsɪstəm 20D
publishing company ˈpʌblɪʃɪŋ
ˈkʌmpənɪ 26B
puppet show ˈpʌpɪt ˈʃəʊ 17B
pursuit pəˈsjuːt 19C
put (put, put) in pʊt [pʊt] 17C
put up with 24A

R
race course ˈreɪs kɔːs 20C
race for jumpers ˈreɪs fə ˈdʒʌmpəz 20C
radiator ˈreɪdɪeɪtə 25A
radicle ˈrædɪkəl 24C
raid reɪd 21A
rake reɪk 22D
ranging from ... (to) ˈreɪndʒɪŋ 19C
ransom (money) ˈrænsəm 22D
rape reɪp 21C
read (read, read) riːd [red, red] 22D
recognition rekəgˈnɪʃən 19C
recognize rekəgˈnaɪz 16C
record ˈrekɔːd 18A
redundancy rɪˈdʌndənsɪ 15B
redundant rɪˈdʌndənt 15B
refuse rɪˈfjuːz 24B
regard as rɪˈgɑːd 22C
regular ˈregjʊlə 14C
rehearsal rɪˈhɜːsəl 17A
reinforce riːɪnˈfɔːs 21C
relate to rɪˈleɪt 19C
release rɪˈliːs 19C
relief rɪˈliːf 25A
rely on rɪˈlaɪ 19C
repayment riːˈpeɪmənt 15B
request rɪˈkwest 21C
require rɪˈkwaɪə 21C
rescue service ˈreskjuː ˈsɜːvɪs 18C
resident ˈrezɪdənt 21B
resources rɪˈsɔːsɪz 24B
respond to rɪˈspɒnd 16C
responsibility rɪspɒnsəˈbɪlətɪ 16A/20A
restoration restəˈreɪʃən 25C
restrict rɪˈstrɪkt 23C
retain rɪˈteɪn 26C
reverse rɪˈvɜːs 22C
revoke rɪˈvəʊk 14C
rewarding rɪˈwɔːdɪŋ 26C
rib rɪb 20C

right away raɪt əˈweɪ 22B
rigid ˈrɪdʒɪd 21C
ritual ˈrɪtʃʊəl 17A
rocket line ˈrɒkɪt ˈlaɪn 18C
rocking horse ˈrɒkɪŋ ˈhɔːs 22B
role model ˈrəʊl ˈmɒdəl 19C
roof ruːf 15C
root ruːt 24C
row raʊ 16A
rubbish ˈrʌbɪʃ 24D
run (ran, run) rʌn [ræn, rʌn] 16C
running block ˈrʌnɪŋ ˈblɒk 18C
rural ˈrʊərəl 24C

S
salary ˈsælərɪ 15B
salvage ˈsælvɪdʒ 18C
sample ˈsɑːmpəl 14A/23B
sample machinist ˈsɑːmpəl məˈʃiːnɪst 23B
savings account ˈseɪvɪŋz əˈkaʊnt 15C
schedule ˈʃedjuːl 14C
scope of knowledge ˈskəʊp əv ˈnɒlɪdʒ 26C
scream skriːm 23A
sea bed ˈsiː bed 18C
search ˈsɜːtʃ 21A/25A
search team ˈsɜːtʃ tiːm 21C
seaweed ˈsiːwiːd 18D
secretive ˈsiːkrətɪv 21B
secure sb sɪˈkjʊə 21D
security sɪˈkjʊərətɪ 21B
see (saw, seen) to sth siː [sɔː, siːn] 25A
seed siːd 24C
self esteem self ɪˈstiːm 26C
selling race ˈselɪŋ reɪs 20C
sensory ˈsensərɪ 19C
set set 17B
set (set, set) off set [set] 20C
set up 18C
set-up ˈsetʌp 19C
sewage treatment plant ˈsjuːɪdʒ ˈtriːtmənt
ˈplɑːnt 25C
shape ʃeɪp 17B/23C
share ʃeə 19C
shed ʃed 25C
sheepish ˈʃiːpɪʃ 15D
shipping forecast ˈʃɪpɪŋ ˈfɔːkɑːst 18C
shipping lane ˈʃɪpɪŋ ˈleɪn 18C
shop assistant ˈʃɒp əˈsɪstənt 23A
short-term ˈʃɔːt ˈtɜːm 15C
show house ˈʃəʊ ˈhaʊs 15A

shut up ʃʌt 16A
sickness ˈsɪknɪs 15B
site saɪt 25C
sketch sketʃ 16D
skint skɪnt 20D
sleeve sliːv 14D/21C
slope sləʊp 19B
smooth smuːð 26D
snooze snuːz 18D
soft drink ˈsɒft ˈdrɪnk 14C
solar panel ˈsəʊlə ˈpænəl 24C
solution səˈluːʃən 15C
sophisticated səˈfɪstɪkeɪtɪd 23C
sort out ˈsɔːt 25C
sound-barrier ˈsaʊnd ˈbærɪə 24C
source sɔːs 24C
sow (sowed, sown) səʊ [səʊd, səʊn] 24C
spacious ˈspeɪʃəs 15A
span spæn 25C
sparkle spɑːkəl 23D
spinal unit ˈspaɪnəl ˈjuːnɪt 19C
spouse spaʊs 23D
spread (spread, spread) spred [spred] 19D
stable ˈsteɪbəl 20C
stable lad ˈsteɪbəl ˈlæd 20C
stamp one's mark on ˈstæmp wʌnz ˈmɑːk ˈɒn 22C
stand (stood, stood) out ˈstænd [stʊd] 17C
steam iron ˈstiːm ˈaɪən 23B
stick to stɪk 19D
stillage ˈstɪlɪdʒ 14C
sting stɪŋ 14D
stocking ˈstɒkɪŋ 22A
store stɔː 14B
straddle ˈstrædəl 25C
straightforward streɪtˈfɔːwəd 15D
street cred ˈstriːt ˈkred 23C
stringent ˈstrɪndʒənt 14C
strip foundation ˈstrɪp faʊnˈdeɪʃən 24C
subsidence səbˈsaɪdəns 15C
suit sjuːt 23B
surge tide ˈsɜːdʒ ˈtaɪd 18B
survive səˈvaɪv 23A
survivor səˈvaɪvə 18C
suspicious səˈspɪʃəs 21B
sustainable forests səˈsteɪnəbəl ˈfɒrɪsts 22B
swap sth for swɒp 24D
sweep in (swept, swept) swiːp [swept] 22C

T
tail teɪl 14D
take (took, taken) on teɪk [tʊk, teɪkən] 18D
take out a mortgage ˈmɔːgɪdʒ 15B
take sth in 23A
tap tæp 14C
teetotal tiːˈtəʊtəl 14D
telly ˈtelɪ 20C
tempting ˈtemtɪŋ 14C
tenant ˈtenənt 25A
theft θeft 21B
thoroughbred ˈθʌrəbred 20C
threat θret 21C
throw (threw, thrown) away on θrəʊ [θruː, θrəʊn] 20B
tidy up ˈtaɪdɪ 14D
tip tɪp 18C
toss a coin ˈtɒs ə ˈkɔɪn 20D
tough tʌf 20C
trade treɪd 14C
traffic calming system ˈtræfɪk ˈkɑːmɪŋ ˈsɪstəm 24A
trainee reporter treɪˈniː rɪˈpɔːtə 22A
transmit trænzˈmɪt 25C
travel industry ˈtrævəl ˈɪndəstrɪ 26A
tremendous trɪˈmendəs 16C
tribe traɪb 18A
triple-glazed ˈtrɪpəl ˈgleɪzd 24C
truncheon ˈtrʌntʃən 21C
tuck up tʌk 21C
tug tʌg 18C
tulip ˈtjuːlɪp 22B
turn down tɜːn 24B
turps (= turpentine) tɜːps [ˈtɜːpəntaɪn] 16A
tutor ˈtjuːtə 26C
twin brother ˈtwɪn ˈbrʌðə 22B

U
unbiased ʌnˈbaɪəsd 22C
understanding ʌndəˈstændɪŋ 21A
undoubtedly ʌnˈdaʊtɪdlɪ 17C
unforgivable ʌnfəˈgɪvəbəl 23A
ungrateful ʌnˈgreɪtfəl 15D
university degree course juːnɪˈvɜːsətɪ dɪˈgriː ˈkɔːs 26B
unpleasant ʌnˈplezənt 22A
urban ˈɜːbən 24C

V
valley ˈvælɪ 24B
vanish ˈvænɪʃ 21D
variety vəˈraɪətɪ 17C
vent vent 14C
ventilate ˈventɪleɪt 24C
venue ˈvenjuː 17C
verbal warning ˈvɜːbəl ˈwɔːnɪŋ 21A
victim ˈvɪktɪm 22A
village hall ˈvɪlɪdʒ ˈhɔːl 17D
visual display ˈvɪzjuəl dɪˈspleɪ 25B
voluntary ˈvɒləntrɪ 18C
volunteer vɒlənˈtɪə 17C/24D

W
waist weɪst 23A
walk of life ˈwɔːk əv ˈlaɪf 18C
walnut ˈwɔːlnʌt 22B

warm to sth wɔːm 20D
warrior ˈwɒrɪə 18A
weather chart ˈweðə ˈtʃɑːt 18C
wheelchair wiːlˈtʃeə 19A
wheelchair user wiːlˈtʃeə ˈjuːzə 19A
willow wall ˈwɪləʊ ˈwɔːl 24C
wipe out waɪp 26C
with ease wɪð ˈiːz 19C
wizard ˈwɪzəd 17B
woodwind (instrument) ˈwʊdwɪnd 17A
work out wɜːk 20B
workshop ˈwɜːkʃɒp 22B
wort wɜːt 14B
worthiness ˈwɜːðɪnɪs 26C

Y
yard jɑːd 20C
yeast jiːst 14B